TOP 10 WINES
FRANCE

TOP 10 WINE
SELECTIONS BY
VINCENT GASNIER

Contents

Left **Bordeaux** *barriques* Right **Château Cos d'Estournel, St-Estèphe**

LONDON, NEW YORK,
MELBOURNE, MUNICH AND DELHI
www.dk.com

Produced by Blue Island Publishing,
Studio 218, 30 Great Guildford Street,
London SE1 0HS

First published in Great Britain in 2006
by Dorling Kindersley Limited
80 Strand, London WC2R 0RL
A Penguin Company

**Based on Wines of the World,
first published by Dorling Kindersley in 2004**

**This compilation © 2006
Dorling Kindersley Limited, London**

A CIP catalogue record is available from the British Library.

ISBN–10: 1-4053-1582-2
ISBN–13: 978-1-4053-1582-1

Within each Top 10 list in this book, no hierarchy of quality or popularity is
implied. All 10 are, in the editor's opinion, of roughly equal merit.

Reproduced by Colourscan, Singapore
Printed and bound in China by Leo

Discover more at www.dk.com

Every effort has been made to ensure that this book is as up-to-date as possible at
the time of going to press. Some details, however, such as telephone numbers,
website addresses, and wine label names are liable to change. The publishers cannot
accept responsibility for any consequences arising from the use of this book, nor
for any material on third party websites, and cannot guarantee that any website
address in this book will be a suitable source of information. Please address any queries to
Dorling Kindersley Ltd at the above address

Left **Château de la Maltroye, Burgundy** Centre **Alfred Gratien label** Right **Paul Jaboulet bottle**

Contents

Hand-selecting grapes at Château Suduiraut, Sauternes

Key to Symbols

▨ soil types
▧ red grape varieties
▨ white grape varieties
▨ wine styles
✆ contact details
▢ open to the public
▪ not open to the public
★ notable wine brands
  or varietals

The World of Wine

Wine is as simple or as complex as you wish: on one level it can be an immediate sensory pleasure, or, at a deeper level, the embodiment of a piece of land and a moment in time. Wine is a pure reflection of its terroir (see box opposite), and no other product expresses its cultural and geographical origins in quite the same way. Each harvest yields wines that are the culmination of different climatic and human processes, so no two wines are ever identical.

Origins and Cultural Significance of Wine

Wine is thought to have originated in the Caucasus mountains of Georgia and it has been part of world culture since historical records began. In ancient Greece and Rome the god Dionysus (or Bacchus) embodied the spirit of celebration with wine.

Bacchus, painted by Caravaggio (c.1593)

Firmly established as part of the Mediterranean way of life, wine subsequently became an important part of the Christian religion. In the Middle Ages European monasteries did much to advance the quality of wine, improving vine cultivation and developing new winemaking techniques in their cellars.

In the 16th century, as Europeans ventured into the New World, their religion and their vines went with them. Being clean and safer to drink than water, wine became as much a part of daily life for slaking thirst as it was an important element of religious tradition. Meanwhile, wine trading in Europe burgeoned (out of the major export centres of Bordeaux, Porto, and Venice), bottle-making techniques were perfected, sparkling winemaking evolved, and the wines of Bordeaux, Burgundy, Germany, and Portugal became increasingly prized. The wine world as we know it began to take shape.

Today, more than ever, wine is a part of everyday life throughout the world, both as a celebratory drink and a versatile partner to food. That it has become so intrinsic to world culture is hardly surprising. Aside from the relaxing effects of alcohol, wine continues to fascinate with its ever-changing character, so inextricably linked to the land, people, and culture that created it.

Vineyards at Monthélie, Côte de Beaune

Wine Regions of the World

At the beginning of the 21st century the world has over 8 million hectares under vine and is producing nearly 300 million hectolitres of wine each year. Vineyards are concentrated between 32° and 51° in the northern hemisphere, and between 28° and 42° in the southern. Wine is now made in virtually all parts of the world that enjoy a suitable climate, from Chile to New Zealand, and from South Africa to China. France is the biggest producer, followed by Italy, Spain, the USA, and Australia.

While winemaking continues to expand into new regions, Mediterranean Europe remains the traditional heartland of viticulture. Vineyards ideally need around 240 hours of sunshine a month, temperatures averaging 17°C in the growing season, an annual rainfall of around 600mm, and a crisp coldness to the winters, which allows the vines a period of dormancy. The classic regions of Bordeaux, Burgundy, and the Rhône Valley in France are among those benefiting from these ideal conditions, and they join Rioja in Spain, Tuscany in Italy, and other Mediterranean areas whose wines and *terroirs* have developed as global benchmarks.

What is Terroir?

In every vineyard, a unique combination of climate, topography, and soil type shapes the character of the vines that grow there. Rich soils can lead to excessive leaf growth and mediocre fruit. Soils of low fertility are therefore better. Soil structure is considered even more important than chemical make-up, with good drainage being essential. The grapes that the vines yield and, in turn, the wine made from these grapes reflect aspects of this distinct place. The French word *terroir*, literally meaning "soil", is used to describe not only the soil, but the entire environment in which the vine grows. Find the right *terroir* and the resulting wines will have the most harmonious composition with acidity, sweetness, fruit flavours, and tannins, all poised to perfection. With the wrong *terroir*, the harvest will all too often fail.

As growers have ventured into viticulturally unexplored areas of Europe and the New World, they have found that the best wines come from vineyards where heat is tempered by the soothing effects of water. When near to a lake, river, or the sea, or with the cooling influence of altitude, grapes can develop more refined flavours.

For more general information about wine, including styles, tasting terminology, and a glossary **See pp136–153**

Old versus New Wines

Today, wine is said to come from the Old World or the New. The classic regions of France, Italy, and Spain are at the core of the Old World. The New World comprises the southern hemisphere and North America. Until recently it was relatively easy to pick up a glass of wine and identify, with a small sniff and a sip, whether it was from the New World or the Old. A New World wine would have all the rich fruit flavours and aromas that reflect warm-climate vineyards. An Old World example would be more subtle with delicate, complex aromas and leaner flavours. Today, however, improved techniques mean that an Old World wine can taste as luscious and ripe as a New World version. Meanwhile, the New World is busy using Old World techniques such as barrel-fermenting, wild yeasts, and lees-stirring to create more complexity.

Estate versus Branded Wines

Techniques in the winery are now so advanced that, with recourse to appropriate grapes, a winemaker has many options. The art of making the mass-production wines is to make each batch and vintage the same so that the brand is reliable and affordable. Estate wines, by contrast, are a true reflection of their land and culture. These are the wines that evoke passionate discussion, genuine loyalty – and a hugely variable price range. They are also the wines that can undergo near-miraculous flavour transformations when laid down to age.

Trends in Wine Consumption

The traditional wine-drinking countries of France, Italy, and Spain have actually seen a slump in consumption over the last 30 years. There are several reasons for this. In the first place, because water quality has improved, wine is no longer needed as a general beverage, and it is perceived as an impediment to work performance. There has also been a decline in café drinking. In an effort to combat the ever-growing European "wine lake", wine is thus produced in smaller quantities and to a higher standard (and price) in these countries. It is no longer regarded as a drink for quaffing, but for sipping and enjoying.

In the English-speaking world, the picture is quite different; wine consumption in the UK for example has risen by over 500 per cent since 1970. The surge in wine's popularity is a direct result of the huge quantities of affordable ripe-fruited New World wines flooding onto the market and the advent of "branded" wines. Wine is no longer the preserve of a wealthy elite.

There is a general belief that wine is part of healthy living. Wine's benefits as a sociable beverage, a health-giver, and an all-round focus of interest suggest it will be part of culture for years to come.

Château Beaucastel, Southern Rhône

Vincent Gasnier

"It always gives me great pleasure when I can pass on what I have learnt from tasting many of the world's finest – and not so fine – wines in a simple, easily-assimilated form. So I was delighted when Dorling Kindersley invited me to provide lists of the Top 10 Wines of France, category by category. Obviously there was not room to include every deserving wine, but the lists have been devised to cover a broad range. They naturally feature many well-known labels from major producers, but they also contain names that may be unfamiliar to many readers, from the fabulous – and, in many cases, fabulously expensive – wines of Bordeaux and Burgundy to the country's best-kept secrets, with remarkably good-value wines from lesser known appellations, produced by talented, up-and-coming winemakers."

Vincent Gasnier
London, May 2006

Selections

No hierarchy of quality is implied by the order in which the wines appear in the Top 10 lists. The 10 selections are of roughly equal merit.

About Vincent Gasnier

A young French sommelier, now working in Britain, Vincent Gasnier has enjoyed a rapid rise to pre-eminence in his profession. In 1994–5, while working at the Restaurant Laurent, on the Champs-Élysées in Paris, he was promoted to Sommelier under Philippe Bourguignon, regarded as one of the best sommeliers in France. In 1997, at the age of 22, he qualified as Master Sommelier: the youngest person in the world to achieve this distinction. After a period as Chef-Sommelier at the Hotel du Vin, Winchester, he set up in business for himself. Since August 2000 he has been Managing Director of Vincent Gasnier Wine Consultant Limited, offering advice on wine purchase, cellar management, VIP wine events, and exclusive wine tours. He shares his expertise with many distinguished individual and corporate clients, including the Houses of Parliament in London. He is a wine judge and has appeared on TV and in magazines.

WINES OF FRANCE

Introducing French Wine

France is still the envy of the wine-producing world, and its global influence is far-reaching. Other nations have made great strides in winemaking but no other has the conditions to produce such a range of great and varied wines. Geographical diversity, noble grape varieties linked to specific sites, and pride in the country's great traditions combine to keep France firmly in the limelight.

The Early Years

The vine was introduced to Mediterranean France by Greek settlers who established colonies along the south coast around 600 BC. The Romans then spread the knowledge of wine further afield. From their early settlement at Narbonne there were two important trading routes: west through Garonne to Bordeaux and north via the Rhône Valley. Viticulture developed along these axes, eventually extending as far north as the Loire Valley and Champagne. With the fall of the Roman Empire in the 5th century AD, the Church became the most important influence in the spread of viticulture in France. Monastic land holdings became extensive, and wine for the sacrament provided a source of revenue.

Illustration from a 15th-century manuscript showing workers in a French vineyard

By the 12th century Benedictine and Cistercian orders owned extensive vineyards in Burgundy, the Loire Valley, and Champagne.

The Wine Trade

Trade in wine also became well established during the late Middle Ages. Bordeaux, under the jurisdiction of the English crown, had a ready market for its wines in the British Isles and developed links with other countries in northern Europe. The Atlantic port of La Rochelle exported wines from the Loire Valley and the neighbouring province of Poitou. In the east, the Dukes of Burgundy, who also ruled over large parts of Flanders, helped advance trade through the Low Countries.

The expansion of French vineyards continued through the 17th to the mid-19th century. The French Revolution at the end of the 18th century had little effect on wine production. The religious orders, however, were stripped of their land, resulting in a significant change of ownership in many regions, especially in Burgundy. Bordeaux entered a period of extraordinary wealth and expansion thanks to lucrative foreign trade, particularly with the French West Indies. This was reflected in the rising reputation of individual wine estates, the construction of many of the prestigious châteaux that can still be seen today, and the establishment of the famous 1855 classification system.

Preceding pages **Château de Corton-André in Aloxe-Corton, Côte de Beaune, Burgundy**

Wine Regions of France

Varied climate and topography suit a wide range of grape varieties and wine styles. Along the Atlantic coast, Bordeaux and the Loire experience maritime influence. Champagne, Alsace, Burgundy, and the Northern Rhône (as well as the Central Loire) have a continental climate, while the south enjoys a Mediterranean climate.

CHAMPAGNE pp126–132

LOIRE VALLEY pp112–123

BURGUNDY pp46–77

ALSACE p133

RHÔNE VALLEY pp80–93

BORDEAUX pp18–43

SOUTH OF FRANCE pp96–109

Modern History

In the mid-19th century France's flourishing wine industry was hit by three deadly viticultural afflictions imported from North America. First the fungal diseases oidium and mildew, then the vine louse phylloxera devastated vineyards throughout the country.

Economic decline in the early 20th century, exacerbated by two world wars, meant that French viticulture fell into a poor state. Quality dropped and Languedoc-Roussillon, in particular, became the source of an unlimited supply of inferior table wine. Standards and authenticity were threatened by cheap imports and imitations. To combat this problem the Appellation d'Origine Contrôlée (AOC) system *(see p14)* was introduced in the 1930s. Renewed investment and the interest of a new generation in the 1970s revived the industry, ushering in the high standards found today.

Theatre of Wine and Food

Wine and food are inextricably linked in France, both forming part of a strong cultural and gastronomic inheritance. Regional wine is traditionally used to partner and complement food from the same region. Having evolved alongside each other over the centuries, local dishes and wines are tailored to suit one another. Classic pairings include the rich, textured cuisine of Bordeaux and its tannic, digestible reds; river fish in a buttery sauce with flavoursome white Burgundy; crisp, tangy Muscadet from the Loire with fresh local seafood; and unctuous sweet Sauternes with the rich flavours of foie gras.

The Wine Industry Today

France vies with Italy for the position of the world's number one wine producer in terms of volume. Production over the past 20 years, however, has fallen from 69 million hectolitres in 1985 to 52 million in 2002. The total vineyard area is around 860,000ha, AOC vineyards accounting for 55 per cent, *vin de pays* 31 per cent, and *vin de table* 14 per cent.

In terms of internal consumption, France again leads the way, consuming 34.5 million hectolitres of wine a year, at an average of 57 litres per person. In export markets around the world, France has been losing ground to the growing competition but remains second to Italy in volume with around 15 million hectolitres per year.

The fabric of the industry is maintained by somewhere in the region of 145,000 grape growers. They either produce and bottle their own wines under the banner of a domaine, château, or estate; deliver their grapes to a co-operative; or sell their grapes or wines to a *négociant*.

Viticulture and Vinification

Recent advances in wine production have been focussed mainly on the vineyards, where the hours of work have multiplied in an attempt to improve standards. Much work is carried out mechanically, but at the top estates labour is much in demand for tasks such as hand-pruning and harvesting. There has also been a general move away from the wholesale use of chemical fertilizers and sprays (as seen in the 1960s and 70s) to a more pragmatic approach. Treatment for disease is linked to local weather reports and adjustments to the soil made after analysis. Those seeking a more comprehensive

Harvesting at Clos de Vougeot in Burgundy

organic approach have gone as far as adopting the biodynamic system of cultivation *(see p66)*. Over the past 20 years, programmes of vine-pulling and replanting have altered the proportions of land allocated to each grape variety. Syrah, Merlot, Cabernet Sauvignon, Chardonnay, and Sauvignon Blanc have shown a strong increase while Carignan and Sémillon, for example, are in decline.

The 1980s saw enormous improvements in technology. Current developments continue to concentrate on improvements in hygiene and safety controls and investment in equipment such as systems of temperature regulation and new oak barrels.

Red Grape Varieties and Wine Styles

In Bordeaux's mild climate, Merlot, Cabernet Sauvignon, and Cabernet Franc are used in a variable blend to produce more top-quality wine than any other region. Styles vary from grassy and fruity to firm, full, and long-ageing. The same three varieties are also vinified individually as varietal *vin de pays*, chiefly in Languedoc-Roussillon. In Provence, Cabernet Sauvignon is used to add complexity and tannic structure to some blends, while

For more on wine styles See pp136–137

cousin Cabernet Franc takes ascendancy in the Loire Valley, where it makes a fresh, fruity, invigorating wine.

Pinot Noir appears in the cooler north as Burgundy's red grape, giving vibrant, perfumed, and potentially long-lived wines. It also produces the only red wine in Alsace and is used as part of the blend in Champagne. The inherent fruitiness of Beaujolais stems from Gamay, which also appears in the Loire Valley.

Syrah holds sway in the Northern Rhône, where the wines are deep coloured with a spicy, dark-fruit intensity. This grape is also increasingly used in blends in the Southern Rhône and Languedoc-Roussillon. The major variety in both these regions, though, is warm, generous Grenache. Mourvèdre is the other noble grape found in southern blends.

White Grape Varieties and Wine Styles

Chardonnay is the most widely planted white variety in France. In Burgundy it reaches its apogee, producing a range of styles from rich, buttery, barrel-aged Meursault to intense, minerally wines in the more extreme climate of Chablis. It is also one of the chief components of Champagne, where it can appear as a single variety *blanc de blancs*. Elsewhere Chardonnay is cultivated in the Loire Valley and has had great success as a fruity varietal *vin de pays* in Languedoc-Roussillon.

Crisp, tangy Sauvignon Blanc is found in the cool to mild climes of the Loire Valley and Bordeaux. In the latter, it is often blended with Sémillon for both dry and sweet wine styles. The Loire's other major white grape is Chenin Blanc, which produces everything from dry to luscious sweet wines.

The distinctive wines of Alsace showcase a range of white grapes, the principal varieties being dry, fragrant Riesling, perfumed Gewürztraminer, and full-bodied Pinot Gris. Further south in the Rhône Valley and the South of France, a host of white varieties are grown. These generally have less acidity as a result of the warmer climate. The most characteristic are the grapey Muscat and the opulently fragrant Viognier of Condrieu.

Château Pichon-Longueville in the Pauillac region of Bordeaux

French Wine Law

France has one of the most extensive and widely imitated systems of wine legislation in the world today. Founded in the 1930s, the Appellation d'Origine Contrôlée (AOC or AC) regulations today provide the model for all the wine industries in the European Union. The boundaries of each AOC region are clearly defined, and within these areas producers must follow strict rules.

The AOC system is founded on the principle that distinct geographical locations (rather than grape varieties in isolation) are responsible for the unique flavour and character of individual French wines. An AOC designation on a label guarantees that a wine originates from the specified region and is produced according to local legislation.

With the exception of wines from Alsace, the name of the grape is rarely found on AOC wine labels, thus placing considerable demands on the knowledge of the drinker. AOC sits at the top of the French classification hierarchy with the virtually extinct VDQS directly beneath it; both apply to so-called quality wine. Beneath these there is *vin de pays* or country wine which comes from a broad region

(and can be high quality) and the distinctly inferior *vin de table* or basic table wine, which can originate from anywhere in France.

Wine Classification

There are four categories of French wine, two for high-quality wines and two lower ratings. The top classification, Appellation d'Origine Contrôlée (AOC or AC), guarantees that a wine has been produced in a designated area in accordance with local laws and regulations. These cover the boundaries of the appellation, permitted grape varieties, the style of wine, vine training, yield, harvest dates, minimum levels of alcohol, and other winemaking specifications.

AOCs are sometimes categorized further by classifying individual estates or vineyards. Bordeaux has the most famous – and most complex – system of classification *(see p19)*. Its prestigious Médoc châteaux on the Left Bank are divided among five levels from *premier* to *cinquième cru*. Across the Gironde Estuary on the Right Bank, St-Émilion has its own hierarchy, with *premier grand cru classé* for the most highly regarded châteaux. In Burgundy, individual vineyards, rather than estates, are classified; *grands crus* are the most

Common Terms on French Labels

blanc white.
cave cellar.
château estate, especially in Bordeaux.
coopérative a collective that makes wine for a number of growers.
côte(s)/coteaux hillside(s).
cru "growth", mainly used to mean vineyard.
cru classé classified vineyard.
demi-sec medium-dry.
domaine estate.
doux sweet.
grand cru great growth.
méthode classique/ traditionnelle sparkling wine made using the same techniques as those used for making Champagne.

mis(e) en bouteille au château/domaine/à la propriété estate bottled.
négociant merchant who buys from growers and then sells wine under its own individual label.
premier cru first growth.
propriétaire the estate or vineyard owner.
récolte vintage or harvest.
rouge red.
sec dry.
supérieur a wine with a higher level of alcohol.
vigneron/viticulteur vinegrower.
vignoble vineyard.
vendange tardive late harvest.
vin wine.

For more wine terms See pp148–153

Reading a French Wine Label

When faced with an unfamiliar French wine label, first consider the appellation or other classification. This will provide an idea of the style of the wine and the main grape varieties used. Terms such as grand cru or grand cru classé may indicate the potential quality, but the *name of the producer tends to be the most important factor. A good producer's basic wine might be superior to another's grand cru. The vintage is also important. The label illustrated here is from Château Margaux, one of Bordeaux's most prestigious first growths.*

Château Margaux is the name of the producer. This could be a château, domaine, maison, or simply a brand name.

Grand vin literally means "great wine", but is generally used to indicate the top wine of the estate.

Mis en bouteille au château indicates the wine was bottled at the estate, generally a sign of a quality-conscious producer.

MIS EN BOUTEILLE AU CHÂTEAU
CHÂTEAU MARGAUX
GRAND VIN
2000
PREMIER GRAND CRU CLASSÉ
12%vol.   75cl
MARGAUX
APPELLATION MARGAUX CONTRÔLÉE
S.C.A. CHATEAU MARGAUX PROPRIÉTAIRE A MARGAUX · FRANCE

2000 indicates the vintage: the year in which the grapes were harvested.

Appellation Margaux Contrôlée confirms that the wine comes from and conforms to the regulations of the AOC Margaux.

Premier Grand Cru Classé indicates that Margaux attained first growth status in the Bordeaux 1855 Classification.

celebrated, followed by *premiers crus*. Champagne villages are also classified with *grand cru* at the top, then *premier cru*. There is no *premier cru* rating in Alsace, but the best vineyards are entitled to the designation *grand cru*.

The second classification, Vin Délimité de Qualité Supérieure (VDQS), is a relatively unimportant category, which is in the process of being phased out. VDQS is in effect a stepping stone for regions hoping to attain AOC status.

The third and fourth categories are *vin de pays* and (VdP) and *vin de table* (VdT). The former, which

means "regional wine", originates from a broad, designated area. Regulations are not as strict as those for AOC and VDQS, and some producers adopt the category in order to make wine from grape varieties prohibited under AOC or VDQS laws. A vintage and one or two grape varieties can be stated on the label. *Vin de table*, humble table wine, can originate from any region in France. This is the least regulated category and the label is not allowed to indicate the vintage, the region, or the grape varieties used.

BORDEAUX

BORDEAUX

ORDEAUX IS MORE THAN *a world-famous wine region, it is an empire, with nearly 120,000ha of vineyards producing 6.5 million hectolitres of wine a year. The region boasts many of the world's most prestigious and expensive wines – Châteaux Margaux, Lafite, Haut-Brion, and Cheval Blanc, to name but a few – and these are just the icing on a very large cake.*

The Romans were probably the first to cultivate the vine in Bordeaux, but it was not until the 12th century that the wine trade really took off. The marriage of Eléanor of Aquitaine to Henry Plantagenet (later Henry II of England) in 1152 effectively ceded the region to the English crown and opened the gateway to trade with Britain. This political tie was severed in 1453, but trading links with Britain remained, and Bordeaux's other overseas markets steadily developed.

Key

■ Bordeaux

The Bordeaux Wine Industry

Today, wine is Bordeaux's lifeblood: there are 57 appellations in the region, with some 12,500 winegrowers, 57 co-operatives, 400 *négociants*, and 130 brokers. The numerous producers consist of grape growers – the majority members of co-ops – and "châteaux", which are individual viticultural estates, not necessarily grand residences. Generic appellation Bordeaux accounts for half the annual production, then there are the *petites appellations* like the Côtes de Bourg, and finally illustrious appellations such as Pomerol and Margaux.

For most oenophiles, Bordeaux is about red wine – and statistically, reds account for 85 per cent of production. These are made from a blend of three principal varieties: Cabernet Sauvignon, Merlot, and Cabernet Franc. Dry and sweet white wines, although dwindling in production, still have an important place on the Bordeaux landscape. Sweet Sauternes is one of the world's great wines, while Bordeaux's crisp, fresh, dry whites have improved immeasurably. Both are blends of Sémillon, Sauvignon Blanc, and occasionally a little Muscadelle.

The people of Bordeaux like to know where they stand – hence the need to rank their wines in a table of merit. However, there is not just one system of classification; several different hierarchies have been introduced at different times over the past two centuries, each with its own history and intricate set of rules.

The 1855 Classification

The most famous Bordeaux classification relates to the red wines of the Médoc peninsula and the sweet white wines of Sauternes. The system was drawn up at the demand of Emperor Napoleon III for the wines that were being exhibited at the Universal Exhibition in Paris in 1855. The Bordeaux Syndicat des Courtiers ranked the wines based on decades of trading statistics. Sixty châteaux from the Médoc and one (Château Haut-Brion)

 Preceding pages **Vineyard at Château Mouton-Rothschild, Pauillac, one of the Médoc's celebrated** *premiers crus*

Château Pichon Longueville in the Pauillac region of Bordeaux

years of the 1930s recession, and there are now 247 châteaux listed. This is basically for estates located in one of the eight appellations in the Médoc that missed out on classification in 1855. Today, the classification is more structured, and implies a level of quality, but is still a promotional vehicle for less well known châteaux. The ranking system has three broad categories: *crus bourgeois exceptionnels* (9), *crus bourgeois supérieurs* (87), and *crus bourgeois* (151).

from Graves were ordered in five different grades (*premier cru* to *cinquième cru* or first to fifth growth) according to commercial value. Likewise 26 châteaux in Sauternes and Barsac were ranked as either first or second growths, with Château d'Yquem singled out as *premier cru supérieur*. The list has changed only once: in 1973, Château Mouton-Rothschild was upgraded from second to first growth. The classification is still a fair indication of quality today, although some châteaux are more deserving of their status than others, and this is generally indicated by the price of the wines.

Médoc Crus Bourgeois
A new classification of the *crus bourgeois* in the Médoc peninsula was announced in 2003, following a review of all the Médoc properties by a committee of experts. The first classification in this category started as a form of promotion in the difficult

Graves Classification
The Graves classification was first compiled by the Institut National des Appellations d'Origine (INAO) in 1953 and updated in 1959. There is only one category, Graves *cru classé*, and châteaux are classified for either red wines or white wines, or both. The 16 châteaux selected are all located in AOC Pessac-Léognan.

Château Mouton-Rothschild

Classifications of St-Émilion
The originality of this classification is that it is revised every 10 years. The first edition was announced in 1955, and the most recent was in 1996. There are two categories, *premier grand cru classé* and *grand cru classé*. Thirteen châteaux are currently ranked as *premier grand cru*. Châteaux Ausone and Cheval Blanc are distinguished further by their "A" status; the others have "B" status. The *grands crus classés* number 55.

For wines of the Médoc, Graves, and Sauternes **See pp22–31**
For St-Émilion and other Right Bank wines **See pp32–39**

Wine Map of Bordeaux

The Garonne and Dordogne rivers carve their way northwest through Bordeaux towards the Atlantic. They divide the region into three segments: west of the Garonne are the Left Bank vineyards of the Médoc, Graves, and Sauternes; east of the Dordogne is the Right Bank area including St-Émilion, Pomerol, and Fronsac. In between is the wedge of land known as Entre-Deux-Mers, literally "between the two seas".

 Producers are listed alphabetically by their common name here. Their full château or domaine names appear in the main listings

Château Palmer in Margaux

Regional Information at a Glance

Latitude 44.5–45.5°N.

Altitude 0–100m.

Topography Land form has little impact on viticulture in this flattish region. Aspect in relation to the thermal warmth of the Gironde Estuary can affect ripening.

Soil Varied; the best, such as St-Émilion's limestone plateau and the gravelly soils of the Médoc and Graves, help regulate the water supply to the vine.

Climate Temperate and maritime. Marked diifferences in temperature and rainfall patterns each year affect the quality of the vintage. Overall, winters are mild and summers are hot.

Temperature July average is 20.5°C.

Rainfall Annual average is 900mm.

Viticultural Hazards Harvest rain; spring frost; water stress; grey rot.

Red wines from Bordeaux

Wine Areas of Médoc & the Left Bank

The Left Bank is the favoured zone for Cabernet Sauvignon, as the gravel soils of St-Estèphe, Pauillac, St-Julien, and Margaux on the Médoc peninsula, and Graves further south, are ideally suited to this late-ripening variety. The wines of the top châteaux have great ageing potential. The Left Bank is also home to Sauternes, one of the world's finest sweet whites.

Médoc

The AOC Médoc is located, confusingly, only in the north of the Médoc peninsula. Formerly known as Bas-Médoc, the area has 5,000ha under vine. The land is flat with marshy areas and pasture, interspersed with the occasional gravelly outcrop. The wines can be earthy, rustic, and even a little lean, but an increase in Merlot plantings has added flesh and finesse. Much of the production is handled by co-operatives, but there are a growing number of good-value wines from individual châteaux.

limestone-and-clay, sand, gravel
Cabernet Sauvignon, Merlot, Cabernet Franc, Petit Verdot red

Haut-Médoc

In the southern half of the Médoc, the 4,500ha of viticultural land not covered by the six communal appellations (St-Estèphe, Pauillac, St-Julien, Listrac, Moulis, Margaux) is designated AOC Haut-Médoc. The mainly gravel soils are ideal for Cabernet Sauvignon. Five estates here – Belgrave, Camensac, Cantemerle, La Lagune, and La Tour Carnet – were included in the 1855 classification, but most producers make the often good-value *crus bourgeois*.

gravel, limestone-and-clay
Cabernet Sauvignon, Merlot, Cabernet Franc, Petit Verdot red

St-Estèphe

The most northerly of the Médoc's four pre-eminent communal appellations, AOC St-Estèphe has a more rural feel than its neighbours, and estates remain primarily family owned. St-Estèphe has gravel soils near the estuary, but there are also outcrops of limestone, known as calcaire de St-Estèphe, with sand and clay to the west and north. Cabernet Sauvignon grown on the cooler limestone soils gives wines a slightly austere character, hence a move to the rounder, fleshier Merlot. In general, the wines are mouth-filling, firm, and long ageing. *Crus bourgeois* account for 54 per cent of production.

gravel, limestone-and-clay, sand
Cabernet Sauvignon, Merlot, Cabernet Franc, Petit Verdot red

Pauillac

For many, Pauillac is the perfect Médoc wine – powerful, concentrated, and long-lived with an aroma of blackcurrants, cedar, and cigar box. Three first growths are located in AOC Pauillac (châteaux Lafite-Rothschild, Latour, and Mouton-Rothschild), as well as 15 other classified estates. Separated by a tiny stream from St-Estèphe to the north, Pauillac's deep, gravelly soils and close proximity to the warmth of the Gironde Estuary provide a terroir ideal for Cabernet Sauvignon, the principal grape variety.

gravel *Cabernet Sauvignon, Merlot, Cabernet Franc, Petit Verdot* red

St-Julien

The compact AOC St-Julien comprises two well-well-drained gravelly plateaux on the Gironde. Eighty per cent of its 900ha is owned by 11 high-profile classified châteaux, five of them second

The Top 10 Bordeaux vintages of the last 60 years are: 1945, 1947, 1949, 1953, 1959, 1961, 1982, 1990, 1995, and 1996

Château Cos d'Estournel in the St-Estèphe region

growths. The dominant grape variety is Cabernet Sauvignon, but unlike the concentrated reds of neighbouring Pauillac, St-Julien's show restraint and "balance", with a more mellow fruit character. They are, however, equally long-lived.
gravel Cabernet Sauvignon, Merlot, Cabernet Franc, Petit Verdot red

Listrac-Médoc
Plantings of Merlot in AOC Listrac-Médoc now exceed those of Cabernet Sauvignon. The cool limestone-and-clay soils and the greater distance from the warming Gironde Estuary make it harder to ripen Cabernet Sauvignon fully. In the past this meant tougher wines, but the use of more Merlot has added flesh and helped to soften tannins. The Listrac co-op is an important producer, but the best wines come from the 20 individual *cru bourgeois* châteaux.
limestone-and-clay, gravel, sand Merlot, Cabernet Sauvignon, Cabernet Franc, Petit Verdot red

Moulis
The smallest of the Médoc's communal appellations, with 590ha, AOC Moulis has a ridge of gravel to the east, where Cabernet Sauvignon ripens fully. A handful of châteaux here produce wines of a quality and style similar to good Haut-Médoc. Inland, on the cooler limestone-and-clay soils, there is a greater percentage of Merlot and the wines are fruitier and less intense. As in Listrac-Médoc, the best wines are the *crus bourgeois*.
gravel, limestone-and-clay Cabernet Sauvignon, Merlot, Cabernet Franc, Petit Verdot red

Margaux
The largest of the Médoc's communal appellations, Margaux has 1,400ha under vine around the villages of Arsac, Labarde, Cantenac, Soussans, and Margaux itself. The gravelly soils are suitable for little other than the vine. Ideal for Cabernet Sauvignon, they result in wines of delicate weight, fragrant aroma, and fine tannic structure. They are often described as "feminine", although modern winemaking techniques produce some more concentrated wines. With 21 classified châteaux (1855), including first growth Château Margaux, standards should be high, but until the mid-1990s producers were complacent. Now, with a younger generation at the helm, this AOC has gained considerably in quality and consistency.
gravel Cabernet Sauvignon, Merlot, Cabernet Franc, Petit Verdot red

 Recent good vintages in Bordeaux were 2000, 2003, and 2005 – fine wines from these years need to be cellared at present 23

Bordeaux – Médoc and the Left Bank

Pessac-Léognan

In 1987 the northern part of Graves became the separate appellation of Pessac-Léognan, taking its name from its two principal communes. Some vineyards lie within the urban sprawl of the city of Bordeaux. With its gravel soils, the region has great potential and has benefited from considerable investment in recent years. It has always been noted for its reds, similar to those of the Médoc, but a little fuller on the palate. These account for 80 per cent of the 1,450ha under vine. The tiny production of dry white is Bordeaux's finest: full, persistent, and with an aroma and flavour of citrus fruits and an ability to age.

gravel *Cabernet Sauvignon, Merlot, Cabernet Franc, Petit Verdot* *Sauvignon Blanc, Sémillon, Muscadelle* *red, white*

Graves

This is a region of small, family-owned estates that lacks the level of investment of Pessac-Léognan. Good-value wines can be found, though, and increasingly so. As the name suggests, gravel soils exist, but there is also limestone-and-clay and sand. Reds from AOC Graves, produced from 2,500ha, have an increasing percentage of Merlot in the blend. These are fruity and should be drunk at four to five years. Dry white Graves, from a further 800ha, comes in two styles: crisp, fresh, aromatic, and bone dry, or rich and barrel-aged. There is also a small amount of sweet Graves Supérieur made from late-harvested grapes.

gravel, limestone-and-clay, sand *Cabernet Sauvignon, Merlot, Cabernet Franc* *Sauvignon Blanc, Sémillon, Muscadelle* *red, white, dessert*

Sauternes

Home to some of the world's most luxurious sweet, aromatic wines, Sauternes lies on the left bank of the Garonne, 40km upstream from the city of Bordeaux. The AOC, for white wines made only from botrytized grapes, totals some 2,200ha in the communes of Bommes, Fargues, Sauternes, Preignac, and Barsac. Producers in Barsac are permitted to label their wines either Sauternes or Barsac – generally a lighter, less powerful wine than Sauternes. The top châteaux were classified in 1855, the most famous being Château d'Yquem. The grapes, mainly Sémillon, ripen naturally at first, but in the autumn, if all goes well, the cool Ciron stream running into the warmer Garonne gives rise to the mists that provoke the onset of botrytis. This reliance on climate means vintages vary considerably, and top châteaux occasionally forego a vintage altogether. The hand-picking may go on into December, and yields are very low, officially no more than 25hl/ha.

gravel, limestone, sand *Sémillon, Sauvignon Blanc, Muscadelle* *white, dessert*

Noble Rot

Noble rot *(pourriture noble)* is caused by a fungal spore, *Botrytis cinerea*, common in Sauternes. Botrytis reduces the water content of the grape, increasing its sugar levels, acidity, viscosity, and flavour to give sweet, unctuous, aromatic wine. The humidity of misty autumn mornings followed by sunshine is ideal for the development of botrytis, enabling it to perforate the fruit's skin but leave the pulp untouched. The rot first appears as a brown spot, which then extends to cover the grape until it eventually shrivels. As the onset of noble rot is always irregular, the grapes are harvested selectively, often with several passages, or *tris*, through the vines. This explains the relatively small quantities of wine and the high production costs.

Appellations of Southwest France

Outside the Bordeaux region, southwest France encompasses some 30 lesser AOCs, dispersed over a wide and varying terrain. The regions of **Bergerac**, **Monbazillac** (known for its sweet white wines), **Buzet**, **Côtes de Duras**, **Cahors**, and **Gaillac** were serious rivals to Bordeaux in the Middle Ages. In these areas today, the co-ops supply a large percentage of the wines. The climate is temperate, with winters a little colder inland. Bordeaux grape varieties are widely cultivated, and the wines, both red and white, are comparable in style to those of Bordeaux. In Cahors, Malbec (known locally as Auxerrois) produces dark, minerally, tannic red wines, while Gaillac has an array of local grape varieties, including the white Mauzac and Len de l'El, resulting

Key

■ Southwest France

in a range of styles. The Négrette grape appears in the AOC **Côtes de Frontonnais**, producing spicy, aromatic reds.

South towards the Spanish border and the Pyrenees are the appellations of **Madiran**, **Jurançon**, and **Irouléguy**. A revival in quality winemaking has taken place here in recent years, led by a number of individual producers. The climate is again maritime, but with the influence of altitude in Jurançon and Irouléguy, where the vine is grown at 300 to 400m. The Tannat grape in Madiran produces firm, tannic reds softened by modern winemaking practices. The same variety blended with Cabernet Franc and Cabernet Sauvignon is found in Irouléguy. Tangy Jurançon comes in sweet and dry white versions made from Petit and Gros Manseng and Petit Courbu.

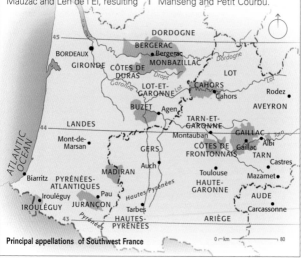

Principal appellations of Southwest France

Left **Cellar at Château Lafite-Rothschild** Right **Ruined château in Sauternes**

Major Producers of the Left Bank

Château Cos d'Estournel
St-Estèphe
Cos d'Estournel was founded in 1811 by Louis Gaspard d'Estournel, whose fascination with Asia led to the construction of the eye-catching pagoda-like cellars that are still in use today. One of two second growths in St-Estèphe, Cos makes a distinctively rich, dense, and finely textured grand vin, with an uncharacteristically high percentage of Merlot in the blend, which adds extra body. The noteworthy second wine, Les Pagodes de Cos, was introduced in 1994. The property is currently owned by a French businessman and managed by Jean-Guillaume Prats – whose family were previous owners. ◈ *St-Estèphe* • *05 56 73 15 50* • *www.cosestournel.com* ◻ *by appt* ▨ *red*

Château Montrose
St-Estèphe
Owned by the Charmolüe family since 1896, St-Estèphe's other second growth has a profile similar to that of Château Latour in Pauillac. Montrose's deep, gravelly vineyard lies in close proximity to the Gironde Estuary with a southeasterly exposure, and the Cabernet Sauvignon-dominated wines are firm, steely, and made for long ageing. In recent vintages, a heightened level of maturity in the wine has helped to soften the sometimes tough exterior. ◈ *St-Estèphe* • *05 56 59 30 12* ◻ *by appt* ▨ *red*

Château Lafite-Rothschild
Pauillac
The history of Château Lafite can be traced back to the 14th century. Its name stems from the Gascon term la hite – meaning "the hillock" – and indeed the 100-ha vineyard is planted on a gravelly knoll facing the Gironde Estuary. The estate was ranked first of the first growths in 1855, and Lafite's wines have always been noted for their elegance and capacity for ageing. Thanks to changes in the selection and in the winemaking processes, vintages since 1995 have been sublime with added weight, volume, and texture. The estate has been owned by the Rothschild family since 1868. Its second label is called Carruades de Lafite, a wine that has also much improved since 1995. ◈ *Pauillac* • *05 56 73 18 18* • *www.lafite.com* ◻ *by appt* ▨ *red*

Château Latour
Pauillac
Château Latour has the classic profile of a Pauillac. Produced mainly from Cabernet Sauvignon grown on deep gravel soils, the wine has a subdued power, cool, steely frame, and scents of blackcurrant and cedar. The heart of the estate is the Enclos vineyard, which surrounds the château and recently renovated cellars (2002); this is the mainstay of the wine, while other parcels of land are used for the excellent second label wine, Les Forts de Latour. Following 30 years of

At tastings held in April 2006 Bordeaux producers hailed the 2005 vintage as superlative, possibly the best in 50 or even 100 years

British ownership, Château Latour was bought by French businessman François Pinault in 1993. ⊗ *Pauillac* • *05 56 73 19 80* • *www.chateau-latour. com* ❏ *by appt* ▦ *red*

Château Lynch-Bages
Pauillac

Château Lynch-Bages has the most distinctive of wine styles. Dominated by Cabernet Sauvignon, opulence and exuberance distinguish the wine here from other more steely and reserved Pauillacs. Its popularity is evident: Lynch-Bages has for a number of years sold well above the price of its fifth growth status. Located on the Bages plateau, the estate was at one time owned by the Lynch family from Galway in Ireland, but is now in the hands of the Cazes. A tiny amount of white wine, Blanc de Lynch-Bages, is also made – from Sémillon, Sauvignon Blanc, and Muscadelle. Something of a rarity for the Médoc, it is similar in style to white Graves. ⊗ *Pauillac* • *05 56 73 19 33* • *www.lynchbages.com* ❏ *by appt* ▦ *red, white*

Château Mouton-Rothschild
Pauillac

Originally known as Château Brane-Mouton, the name was changed in 1853 when Baron Nathaniel de Rothschild bought the property. Classified as a second growth in 1855, Château Mouton-Rothschild was upgraded to first growth status in 1973. This was largely due to the persistence of Baron Philippe de Rothschild, who took over in 1922. Among other things, he initiated the idea of artist-designed labels. Since 1945, every vintage has had a label created by one of a host of illustrious names including Marc Chagall, Salvador Dalí, Joan Miró, and Andy Warhol. Mouton is a

rich, dense, and opulent wine, and there is also a second label, Le Petit Mouton, and a small amount of white, called L'Aile d'Argent. ⊗ *Pauillac* • *05 56 73 20 20* • *www.bphr. com* ❏ *by appt* ▦ *red, white*

Château Pichon-Longueville
Pauillac

In 1850 Baron Joseph de Pichon-Longueville divided the family property equally between his five children. Second growth Château Pichon-Longueville (Baron) was the part inherited by his two sons. Its Cabernet Sauvignon-dominated wine is more classically powerful than the wine from the other division across the road. The estate has been owned since 1987 by insurance company AXA-Millésimes, who restored the château and built a modern winery designed by two international architects. ⊗ *Pauillac* • *05 56 73 17 17* • *www.pichonlongueville.com* ❏ *by appt* ▦ *red*

Château Pichon-Longueville Comtesse de Lalande
Pauillac

This property is made up of the three fifths of the original Pichon-Longueville estate (see above) belonging to Baron de Pichon-Longueville's daughters. As all three parts were managed by one daughter, Virginie, they came to be known by her married name, Comtesse de Lalande. Another indomitable lady, May-Eliane de Lencquesaing has owned and administered the estate since 1978, maintaining its status as a top second growth. The wine, with a slightly higher percentage of Merlot in the blend than is normal in Pauillac, is round and suave, and seductive from an early age. ⊗ *Pauillac* • *05 56 59 19 40* • *www.pichon-lalande.com* ❏ *by appt* ▦ *red*

Bordeaux – Médoc & the Left Bank – Producers

Bordeaux – Médoc & the Left Bank – Producers

Château Ducru-Beaucaillou
St-Julien

This 19th-century château stands close to the Gironde Estuary at the southern end of St-Julien. Set discreetly behind it is a new, hi-tech barrel cellar, built in 1999. The pebbles of quartz, flint, and other rocks, or *beaux cailloux*, which gave the château the second part of its name, are visible in the vineyard. Wood contamination in the old barrel cellars caused problems in the late 1980s, but the estate is now back on top form. The wines of this second growth château are ripe and elegant, but need at least 10 years to develop fully. ✪ *St-Julien Beychevelle* • 05 56 73 16 73 ◖ *by appt* ▨ *red*

Château Gruaud-Larose
St-Julien

Château Gruaud-Larose overlooks a tiny stream to the south of the appellation St-Julien. The well-exposed vineyard is located in a single plot on deep gravel soils

Château Léoville-Barton label

with a high percentage of clay. This partly accounts for the rich, full nature of the wine. The estate has changed hands several times in the last 20 years. In the 1990s it benefited from massive investment under then owners Alcatel-Alstom. The second growth estate is now owned by the Merlaut family. ✪ *St-Julien Beychevelle* • 05 56 73 15 20 ◖ *by appt* ▨ *red*

Château Léoville-Barton
St-Julien

Having bought the château in 1826, the originally Irish Barton family are the longest-standing owners of a classified estate in the Médoc. The present guardian, Anthony Barton, has been managing this second growth property since 1982, maintaining it as one of the most consistent in the Médoc. Traditionally made in wooden vats, the wine is classically long-lived with balance and reserve. Winemaking facilities are shared with third growth Château Langoa-Barton, which is also owned by the Barton family. ✪ *St-Julien Beychevelle* • 05 56 59 06 05 • *www. leoville-barton.com* ◖ *by appt* ▨ *red*

Château Léoville Las Cases
St-Julien

Although situated in St-Julien, the heart of the Léoville Las Cases vineyard – the Grand Enclos – lies close to Château Latour, and not surprisingly the wine has more than a hint of Pauillac steel. A draconian selection system sees only 40 per cent of production destined for the *grand vin*, the rest going to the very good second label, Clos du Marquis, or sold on in bulk to négociants. Although classified as

a second growth, Las Cases now merits comparison with the first growths. ◈ *St-Julien Beychevelle* • 05 56 73 25 26 ☐ *by appt* ▨ *red*

Château Margaux
Margaux
This first growth château, with its imposing colonnaded residence, has hardly put a foot wrong since the Mentzelopoulos family bought it in 1978. The estate has a total of 90ha under production, and the wine, a mainly Cabernet Sauvignon blend with a "seasoning" of Petit Verdot, combines natural power with elegance. The excellent second label is Pavillon Rouge, and there is also a top quality white, Pavillon Blanc, made solely from Sauvignon Blanc and designated, as the appellation rules demand, as a generic Bordeaux. ◈ *Margaux* • 05 57 88 83 83 • *www.chateau-margaux.com* ☐ *by appt* ▨ *red, white*

Château Palmer
Margaux
Established in the 19th century by Major-General Charles Palmer, an officer in Wellington's army, the estate is now owned by a consortium of Dutch, English, and French families. For many years Palmer's reputation has exceeded its third growth ranking, and in the 1960s and 70s the wines were superior even to Château Margaux. A healthy percentage of Merlot contributes to Château Palmer's legendary velvety texture. The second wine, Alter Ego de Palmer, is also excellent. ◈ *Cantenac* • 05 57 88 72 72 • *www.chateau-palmer.com* ☐ *by appt* ▨ *red*

Château Rauzan-Ségla
Margaux
Deemed the appellation's second wine after Château Margaux in the 1855 ranking, Château Rauzan-Ségla had a chequered reputation in the late 20th century. However, since it was bought by the Wertheimer family, owners of Chanel, in 1994, the estate has regained its former glory and consistency. A massive programme of investment has transformed this second growth property, and the wine now has true distinction and elegance. ◈ *Margaux* • 05 57 88 82 10 ☐ *by appt* ▨ *red*

Château Haut-Brion
Pessac-Léognan
Owned by the American Dillon family since 1935, Château Haut-Brion was first established in the 16th century. It was the only estate outside the Médoc to be classified as a first growth in 1855. The 45-ha vineyard is surrounded by Bordeaux's urban sprawl and grapes grown here are some of the earliest in the region to ripen, bringing a reliable maturity. This and a generous helping of Merlot in the blend make Haut-Brion less austere than its Médoc peers. A tiny quantity of lush, rich, dry white is also produced. ◈ *Pessac Cedex* • 05 56 00 29 30 • *www.haut-brion.com* ☐ *by appt* ▨ *red, white*

Château La Mission Haut-Brion
Pessac-Léognan
Château La Mission Haut-Brion was acquired by the Dillon family in 1993 and is now part of the same stable as neighbouring Château Haut-Brion. Despite sharing the same winemaking team and using similar technical facilities, each wine maintains a distinctive style. While Haut-Brion is fine and elegant with a certain subtlety, La Mission is rich and fleshy with a powerful, open character. Haut-Brion is usually the superior wine. ◈ *Pessac Cedex* • 05 56 00 29 30 • *www.haut-brion.com* ☐ *by appt* ▨ *red*

Château Pape Clément
Pessac-Léognan

Pape Clément's history can be traced back to the 14th century, but its modern renaissance began in 1985. A new vinification cellar was built, a second wine, Le Clémentin, introduced, and the vineyards steadily overhauled. A further revolution came in 2001, when 120 people were brought in to destem the grapes by hand. Deeply coloured, rich, and full, Pape Clément has gained even more in concentration and texture since this vintage. A tiny quantity of white Pape Clément is also produced. ◊ *216 ave du Docteur Nancel Pénard, Pessac • 05 57 26 38 38 • www.pape-clement.com* ▢ *by appt* ▣ *red, white*

Château Smith-Haut-Lafitte
Pessac-Léognan

There has been no expense spared to improve this ancient estate since it was purchased by Florence and Daniel Cathiard in 1990. The vineyard has been entirely restructured, yields reduced, and organic methods applied. The cellars have been renovated, new wooden fermenting tanks introduced, and a cooperage, which provides 50 per cent of the barrels, launched. The château's aromatic Sauvignon Blanc was the first to benefit, but since 1994 the red, made from the usual blend of Cabernet Sauvignon, Cabernet Franc, and Merlot, has gained in density, body, and finesse. ◊ *Martillac • 05 57 83 11 22 • www.smith-haut-lafitte.com* ▢ *by appt* ▣ *red, white*

Domaine de Chevalier
Pessac-Léognan

The long-lived, Sauvignon Blanc-based white wine is the star of this property, but quantities are extremely limited. The red, mainly Cabernet Sauvignon, has improved in recent years and is now a classic Graves wine, complex and minerally with balance and great length. Domaine de Chevalier has been immaculately run by Olivier Bernard since 1983. New winemaking facilities have been built, the vineyard revamped, and wind machines introduced to counter the spring frosts. ◊ *102 chemin de Mignoy, Léognan • 05 56 64 16 16 • www.domainedechevalier.com* ▢ *by appt* ▣ *red, white*

Château Climens
Sauternes

First growth Château Climens is the leading estate in Barsac, producing archetypal sweet white wine from this region, rich and concentrated but with a delicate edge of acidity. Usually discreet at first, Climens needs at least 10 years to develop a complex panoply of honeyed aromas, then continues to evolve for a number of years. The property was bought by Lucien Lurton in 1971 and is now owned and run by his daughter Bérénice. ◊ *Barsac • 05 56 27 15 33* ▢ *by appt* ▣ *white, dessert*

VINCENT GASNIER'S
TOP 10 Fabulous Dessert Wines

1. **Château d'Yquem** *opposite*
2. **Château Suduiraut** *opposite*
3. **Château La Tour Blanche** Sauternes *www.tour-blanche.com*
4. **Château de Fesles: Bonnezaux** Anjou-Saumur, Loire *p117*
5. **Château Rieussec** *opposite*
6. **Domaine Rolet: Vin de Paille** Jura *www.rolet-arbois.com*
7. **Deiss: SGN Riesling** Alsace *p133*
8. **Zind Humbrecht: SGN Gewürztraminer** Alsace *p133*
9. **Claude Papin: Quarts de Chaume** Coteaux du Layon, Loire *p117*
10. **Huet: Le Clos du Bourg** Vouvray, Loire *p122*

Harvesting in the vineyard of Château Suduiraut with Château d'Yquem in the distance

Château d'Yquem
Sauternes

Château d'Yquem has been in a league of its own for many years. Classified *premier cru supérieur* in 1855 *(see p19)*, it enjoyed the continuity of single ownership under the Lur-Saluces family from 1785 until its sale to the luxury goods group LVMH in 1996. The grapes, mainly Sémillon with a little Sauvignon Blanc, are harvested selectively in the 100-ha vineyard, sometimes berry by berry. Yields are tiny – the equivalent of a glass of wine per vine. The wine is both fermented and aged in new oak barrels, where it remains for three and a half years. Ⓢ *Sauternes • 05 57 98 07 07 • www.chateau-yquem.fr* 🖾 *white, dessert*

Château Lafaurie-Peyraguey
Sauternes

The magnificent 1983 vintage relaunched the reputation of this first growth château. Since then its sweet white wines have been rich and fragrant with a wonderful concentration of fruit. The property comprises a 13th-century château and a well-exposed vineyard on a hillock in the commune of Bommes. Ⓢ *Bommes • 05 56 76 60 54* ☐ *by appt* 🖾 *white, dessert*

Château Rieussec
Sauternes

If any Sauternes could ever rival Château d'Yquem in its power and concentration, it would have to be neighbouring Château Rieussec. Bought by the Rothschild family of Château Lafite in 1985, this first growth estate has since developed greater continuity and purity of fruit. The selective harvesting is more precise, fermentation takes place in barrel (since 1996), and the period of ageing has been lengthened from 15 months to two and a half years. Ⓢ *Fargues de Langon • 05 57 98 14 14 • www.lafite. com* ☐ *by appt* 🖾 *white, dessert*

Château Suduiraut
Sauternes

Insurance company owners AXA-Millésimes have completely renovated the magnificent 18th-century château of this first growth estate, with its gardens designed by Le Nôtre. The wine, too, has benefited from greater investment both in the 90-ha vineyard and in the cellars. Recent vintages have all produced finely balanced Sauternes with great ageing potential. Ⓢ *Preignac • 05 56 63 61 90 • www.chateausuduiraut.com* ☐ *by appt* 🖾 *white, dessert*

Wine Areas of St-Émilion & the Right Bank

The limestone and clay soils of the Right Bank make earlier ripening Merlot the king in this part of Bordeaux. St-Émilion and Pomerol are the key appellations, producing round, elegant, full-bodied wines. There is also good value from Fronsac and the numerous "Côtes".

Detail of Château Pavie, St-Émilion Grand Cru

St-Émilion & St-Émilion Grand Cru

Vines were cultivated in St-Émilion as far back as Gallo-Roman times. Today, the appellation encompasses exactly the same area that was set out in the original administrative charter of 1289: nine parishes, including the town of St-Émilion. In 1999, the district was declared a World Heritage site by UNESCO. In contrast to the Médoc on the Left Bank, the mainly limestone-and-clay soils are better adapted to Merlot than the later ripening Cabernet Sauvignon. Cabernet Franc, known locally as Bouchet, used to be more widely planted and is an important second element in most blends. St-Émilion wines as a whole offer soft fruit and a cool freshness, the best with a fine tannic structure and the ability to age. Modern styles are darker, riper, and more concentrated. In all, St-Émilion has 5,500ha under production, declared as either AOC St-Émilion or AOC St-Émilion Grand Cru. Both have the same geographical delimitations, but the latter requires a higher minimum alcohol content, lower yields, and the approval of two tasting panels. The superior designation accounts for 65 per cent of production and includes all the classified châteaux. 🞖 limestone-and-clay, gravel, sand 🞖 Merlot, Cabernet Franc, Cabernet Sauvignon 🞖 red

St-Émilion Satellites

The so-called St-Émilion Satellites are the northern extension of the St-Émilion hillslopes, separated from these by the tiny Barbanne stream. Four AOC communes – Lussac, Montagne, Puisseguin, and St-Georges – are authorized to append St-Émilion to their names. The same limestone-and-clay soils can be found as well as silty sand,

VINCENT GASNIER'S Great French Wine Houses

TOP 10

1. **Domaine Jean-Louis Chave**
   Hermitage, Northern Rhône *p91*
2. **Domaine de la Romanée-Conti**
   Côte de Nuits, Burgundy *p59*
3. **Château Latour**
   Pauillac, Bordeaux *p26*
4. **Château Lafite-Rothschild**
   Pauillac, Bordeaux *p26*
5. **Château Pétrus**
   Pomerol, Bordeaux *p39*
6. **Marcel Guigal**
   Côte Rôtie, Northern Rhône *p90*
7. **Château de Beaucastel**
   Châteauneuf-du-Pape, Southern Rhône *p92*
8. **Domaine Dujac**
   Côte de Nuits, Burgundy *p57*
9. **Domaine Armand Rousseau**
   Côte de Nuits, Burgundy *p56*
10. **Domaine François & Jean-Marie Raveneau** Chablis, Burgundy *p52*

Good recent vintages in St-Émilion and Pomerol include 1990, 1995, 1996, 1998, 1999, 2000, 2001, 2003, and 2005

but the ripening cycle is just that bit later, so the autumn weather is critical for the harvest. Merlot is the dominant grape variety, and the wines are similar in style to St-Émilion, although perhaps a touch more rustic. The level of investment is not as high, but this is reflected in the value-for-money prices. There are numerous small producers, but the co-operative Les Producteurs Réunis accounts for 40 per cent of production in AOC Lussac-St-Émilion and 20 per cent in AOC Puisseguin-St-Émilion. All told, there are 3,900ha under production in the area; AOC Montagne-St-Émilion is the largest division. *limestone-and-clay, sand* *Merlot, Cabernet Franc, Cabernet Sauvignon* *red*

Pomerol

At its very best, Pomerol is the ultimate in wine seduction. Rich and unctuous, it has a velvety texture and sumptuous bouquet as well as a firm inner core, which allows it to age well. There are nearly 800ha in production. The average holding is only 6.5ha, so quantities of wine are limited. Accordingly, there is a rarity value and the prices are high. Strangely, these wines were relatively unknown outside of France and the Benelux countries until the 1960s. Unlike neighbouring St-Émilion, there is no limestone in Pomerol, but gravel, sand, and clay make this an early ripening zone in which mainly Merlot (80 per cent) is cultivated with positive results. Located on a gently sloping plateau northeast of the town of Libourne, the richest wines come from the clay and gravel soils of the central plateau. It is here that all the top châteaux, including Pétrus, Lafleur, and Le Pin, can be found. On the lower terraces to the west and south, the soils are sandier and the wines lighter and less powerful in style. AOC Pomerol is the only major wine district in Bordeaux to have no official classification system. *gravel, clay, sand* *Merlot, Cabernet Franc, Cabernet Sauvignon* *red*

Harvest time at the world-famous Château Pétrus in Pomerol

 The grapes at Château Pétrus are picked only in the afternoon when the sun has had time to evaporate any morning dew

Lalande-de-Pomerol

Recent activity in this satellite district has led to new investment, a younger generation coming to the helm, and more interesting wines. Located north of its more prestigious neighbour Pomerol, across the tiny Barbanne stream, AOC Lalande-de-Pomerol has 1,120ha under vine. As in Pomerol, the properties are small, the price of the wines is on the high side (although not in the same league as Pomerol), and Merlot is the dominant variety, with 75 per cent of vineyard space. The soils vary, but there are areas of gravel and clay that have the potential to produce wines similar to Pomerol, if not with the same weight and ability to age. The further west one goes in the appellation, the sandier the soils, and the lighter the wines. ▨ *gravel, clay, sand* 🍇 *Merlot, Cabernet Franc, Cabernet Sauvignon, Malbec* 🍷 *red*

Fronsac & Canon-Fronsac

West of the town of Libourne, AOC Fronsac and the tiny 300-ha enclave of AOC Canon-Fronsac are bounded to the east by the Isle River and to the south by the Dordogne. In the 18th and 19th centuries, wines from this area were as highly regarded as those of St-Émilion. Towards the end of the 19th century, however, phylloxera *(see p11)* destroyed the vineyards, and it was not until the 1970s that a renaissance got under way. The top wines are now back on a par with those of St-Émilion. The soils on this hilly terrain are mostly clay and limestone on a bedrock of loamy-clay known as *fronsadais molasse*. The main grape variety, as in most Right Bank AOCs, is Merlot (78 per cent). The wines have a natural power and concentration, but tend towards astringency and rusticity

---

The Bordeaux Barrique

The famous Bordeaux barrels, or *barriques*, are used all over the world. The classical *barrique* holds 225l of wine. Made of oak staves 20 to 22mm thick, and 95cm in height, it is used for fermenting, maturing, or conditioning wine prior to bottling. Fine wines can spend up to two years in barrel. The slow absorption of tiny amounts of oxygen through the wood helps to soften tannins, stabilize colour, and increase the wine's aromatic complexity. Many top Bordeaux estates use new oak barrels, which are microbiologically more stable than old ones, and give additional aroma and flavour.

---

if not carefully produced. Later harvests and new winemaking equipment have gone some way to eradicating the problem. With its south-facing exposure and higher limestone content, Canon-Fronsac should produce finer wines than Fronsac. This potential, however, is rarely fulfilled, and the quality of the wines is variable. ▨ *limestone-and-clay, sandstone* 🍇 *Merlot, Cabernet Franc, Cabernet Sauvignon, Malbec* 🍷 *red*

Côtes de Castillon & Bordeaux-Côtes de Francs

The AOC Côtes de Castillon has 3,000ha under vine and a similar profile to neighbouring St-Émilion, except that the climate is slightly cooler. The harvest is therefore later, as good fruit ripeness is needed to prevent the wines from becoming too acidic. The limestone plateau and slopes are planted mainly with Merlot, plus some Cabernet Franc, producing full-bodied red wines with a firm, fresh finish. Until recently the area had been held back by limited investment and a lack of technical expertise, but now it is producing some of the most interesting wines on the Right Bank. The AOC Côtes de Castillon takes its name from the town of Castillon-la-Bataille, where in 1453 the French defeated the English, ending 300 years of English rule in Aquitaine *(see p18)*. Northeast of Côtes de Castillon, AOC Bordeaux-Côtes de Francs is a much smaller district producing red and a very limited quantity of white wines. Standards for both tend to be high. Cabernet Sauvignon and Cabernet Franc play a greater role in the reds here, yielding wines that are less aromatic but with a firm presence on the palate and good ageing potential. The whites are full, rich, and fragrant with good acidity. 🏔 *limestone-and-clay, sand, gravel* 🍇 *Merlot, Cabernet Franc, Cabernet Sauvignon* 🍇 *Sémillon, Sauvignon Blanc, Muscadelle* 🍷 *red, white*

Côtes de Bourg

The AOC Côtes de Bourg is known locally as the Gironde's little Switzerland because of the hilly limestone-and-clay terrain. Located at the confluence of the Dordogne and the Gironde Estuary, this area has a slightly warmer climate than other parts of Bordeaux, which helps ward off frost, and low levels of rainfall. The Romans were the first to discover the viticultural potential of this district, and wines have been made here ever since. Merlot is the principal red grape cultivated in the area's 3,900ha, but wines are still very much a blend, occasionally including Malbec, which represents six per cent of the vineyard area. Wines are usually full-bodied and firm with deep colour and earthy fruitiness, which has become more refined in recent years. A small quantity of white is also produced. There are some good individual producers, and the co-operatives are becoming increasingly quality-conscious, in particular the Cave de Bourg-Tauriac. 🏔 *limestone-and-clay* 🍇 *Merlot, Cabernet Franc, Cabernet Sauvignon, Malbec* 🍇 *Sauvignon Blanc, Sémillon, Colombard, Muscadelle* 🍷 *red, white*

Blaye, Côtes de Blaye, & Premières Côtes de Blaye

The district of Blaye surrounds that of Bourg but the vineyards are more spread out and the terrain more varied. Nearly 6,000ha are planted across the region, with mixed agriculture in between. Over 90 per cent of the production is red, labelled AOC Premières Côtes de Blaye. Merlot is the dominant variety, but the wines have less weight and structure than those of the Côtes de Bourg. Since 2000 there has been a superior designation for red wines, AOC Blaye. These are richer, more concentrated wines, requiring lower yields, and verification by a second tasting panel at 18 months. White Premières Côtes de Blaye is Sauvignon Blanc-dominated and often good value. It can be fresh and fruity, as well as generous in style. 🏔 *limestone-and-clay, sand, gravel* 🍇 *Merlot, Cabernet Sauvignon, Cabernet Franc, Malbec* 🍇 *Sauvignon Blanc, Sémillon, Muscadelle* 🍷 *red, white*

Festoons of grape clusters carved on a château in the Premières Côtes de Blaye

Typical Bordeaux *barriques*, the oak barrels used for maturing wine

Major Producers of the Right Bank

Château Angélus
St-Émilion Grand Cru
Château Angélus, a catalyst for improvement in the region since the mid-1980s, was promoted to *premier grand cru classé* in 1996. Better management, skilled cellar techniques, and strict grape selection have been the stamp of owner Hubert de Boüard. The wine, a blend of Merlot and Cabernet Franc, displays a contemporary style of St-Émilion: deep in colour, aromatic, rich, and concentrated, with an overlay of new oak.
⊗ *St-Émilion* • *05 57 24 71 39* • *www. chateau-angelus.com* ☐ *by appt* ▨ *red*

Château Ausone
St-Émilion Grand Cru
One of two A status St-Émilion *premiers grands crus classés*, there is an air of exclusivity about Ausone. Only 2,000 cases are produced per year from the 7-ha vineyard. Those privileged to taste the wines find a freshness and elegance that persists with time. Under owner Alain Vauthier, vintages since 1995 have been exemplary, with great aromatic complexity and a polished texture.
⊗ *St-Émilion* • *05 57 24 24 57* ◐ ▨ *red*

Château Beau-Séjour Bécot
St-Émilion Grand Cru
Château Beau-Séjour Bécot suffered the ignominy of being demoted from *premier grand cru classé* in 1986, but was reinstated 10 years later. Brothers Gérard and Dominique Bécot worked hard to regain the status and now maintain a high-level estate on St-Émilion limestone plateau and *côtes*. The wines have structure and balance for long ageing, complemented by a rich, ripe texture. The Bécots also produce tiny amounts of a garage wine *(see p38)*, La Gomerie.
⊗ *St-Émilion* • *05 57 74 46 87* • *www. beausejour-becot.com* ☐ *by appt* ▨ *red*

Château Belair
St-Émilion Grand Cru
The style of Château Belair's wine is elegant, even delicate, and respectful of its limestone *terroir*. It will never be a hit with those who like big, concentrated wines, but its track record shows that it ages gracefully. Owner and winemaker Pascal Delbeck pursues his own philosophy at this *premier grand cru classé* estate. In 1998, he converted the 12-ha vineyard to the biodynamic system of cultivation *(see p66)*. ⊗ *St-Émilion* • *05 57 24 70 94* • *www.chateaubelair. com* ☐ *by appt* ▨ *red*

Château Cheval Blanc
St-Émilion Grand Cru
An "A status" *premier grand cru classé*, Cheval Blanc is flatteringly alluring when young and also capable of long ageing. There is more than a hint of neighbouring Pomerol, but Merlot is not the main variety at this 37-ha estate. The wine's originality is achieved by 60 per cent Cabernet Franc, which gives aromatic complexity and balance. The second wine, Le Petit Cheval, is also good.
⊗ *St-Émilion* • *05 57 55 55 55* ◐ ▨ *red*

There are more than 1,000 producers within a radius of 10km of the village of St-Émilion

Château de Valandraud
St-Émilion Grand Cru
Jean-Luc Thunevin is the father of the garage movement *(see p38)*, and Château de Valandraud is his *pièce de résistance*. Originally produced in 1991 from three small parcels of vines located mostly on the less favoured Dordogne plain, Valandraud has always been made in a fastidious fashion – low yields, strict selection, only new oak barrels. The wines are big, dark, spicy, and richly concentrated. The prices attained have enabled Thunevin to buy other plots, so the composition of the wine has changed from the early days. ◐ *St-Émilion* • *05 57 55 09 13* • *www.thunevin.com* 🖾 *red*

Château Figeac
St-Émilion Grand Cru
In the 18th century, Figeac comprised 200ha including what is now Château Cheval Blanc. Reduced to 40ha, it is still one of the largest *premiers grands crus classés*. The gravel soils have led to a planting of one third each Cabernet Franc, Merlot, and Cabernet Sauvignon. The wine is fragrant, well structured, and almost Médoc in style, with a deceptive ability to age. ◐ *St-Émilion* • *05 57 24 72 26* • *www.chateau-figeac.com* ☐ *by appt* 🖾 *red*

Château Le Tertre Roteboeuf
St-Émilion Grand Cru
Since taking over this 6-ha estate in 1977, François Mitjavile has propelled it to the top of the appellation. The wines are not classified – a personal choice – but sell at the same price as the *premiers grands crus classés*. They are ripe in style, even exotic, and the warmer vintages have a southern, Mediterranean character. Very ripe grapes and astute barrel-ageing play an

important part in the secret of this estate's success. ◐ *St-Émilion* • *05 57 74 42 11* ⬛ 🖾 *red*

Château Pavie
St-Émilion Grand Cru
This magnificent *premier grand cru classé* situated on St-Émilion's clay-and-limestone *côtes* has been revitalized since its purchase by Gérard Perse in 1998. Yields have been reduced, a replanting programme introduced, and a new winery and barrel cellars built. The wines now have enormous weight, power, and concentration, but are just a little excessive for some. ◐ *St-Émilion* • *05 57 55 43 43* • *www.vignoblesperse.com* ⬛ 🖾 *red*

Château Pavie Macquin
St-Émilion Grand Cru
One of the top *grands crus classés*, Château Pavie Macquin will be a favourite for promotion to *premier grand cru classé* in the next classification. The vineyard is superbly located in a single parcel on St-Émilion's limestone plateau and is astutely managed by Nicolas Thienpont and winemaker Stéphane Derenoncourt. The wines are deep, dark, and firmly structured with a minerally core, and they need at least seven or eight years' bottle age. ◐ *St-Émilion* • *05 57 24 74 23* ☐ *by appt* 🖾 *red*

Clos Fourtet
St-Émilion Grand Cru
Clos Fourtet is the best value of the *premiers grands crus classés*. The wines may be less fashionable than those from other top estates but are well defined, fresh, and structured for ageing. They have also maintained a remarkable consistency in the past 10 years. The property was recently sold to French businessman Philippe Cuvelier. ◐ *St-Émilion* • *05 57 24 70 90* • *www.closfourtet.com* ☐ *by appt* 🖾 *red*

La Mondotte
St-Émilion Grand Cru
La Mondotte was created in 1996 from a 4.5-ha parcel of vines located on St-Émilion's limestone plateau. Owner Stephan von Neipperg's request to have them integrated into his *grand cru classé* Château Canon-la-Gaffelière was refused by the authorities, so he created this garage wine *(see right)*. The Merlot-dominated blend shows expressive, succulent fruit, a density of extract, and powerful tannic structure. Every vintage has been a success from the outset.
✪ *St-Émilion* • *05 57 24 71 33* • *www. neipperg.com* ❑ *by appt* ▨ *red*

Château La Conseillante
Pomerol
The 12-ha vineyard of La Conseillante is situated just opposite that of Château Cheval Blanc on a mix of clay, gravel, and sand soils. As with those of its close neighbour, the wines of this château have a smooth, velvety texture making them appealing when young but belying the fact that they age splendidly. A more rigorous approach in the vineyard and better grape selection would add even greater lustre. ✪ *Pomerol* • *05 57 51 15 32* ▨ ▨ *red*

Château Grand Village
Pomerol
This tiny jewel of a property is located on the Pomerol plateau next to Château Pétrus and Vieux Château Certan. The small vineyard is tended like a garden. The wine, a 50/50 blend of Cabernet Franc and Merlot, is the most elegant in Pomerol, with voluptuous texture, rich fruit, fine tannins, and a mineral complexity. The second wine, Pensées de Lafleur, is also very fine and, given the price of the *grand vin*, excellent value. ✪ *Grand Village, Mouillac* • *05 57 84 44 03* ▨ ▨ *red*

Garage Wines
The so-called garage or cult wines of the Right Bank evolved as a way of bucking Bordeaux's strict historical, hierarchical structure. How could producers make a top quality wine, and have a decent return, when the Bordeaux market was reluctant to register their existence? Technically proficient, handcrafted wines made in tiny quantities from super-ripe grapes provided the formula. The scarcity of the wines and the egos of wealthy collectors around the world have caused prices to rocket. Château Le Pin in Pomerol is often named as the catalyst for the movement, but the real instigator was Jean-Luc Thunevin with Château de Valandraud in St-Émilion. Thunevin made his first vintage, 1991, in his garage, hence the name.

Château Le Pin
Pomerol
This small 2-ha property came to prominence with the 1979 vintage. It has since become one of Pomerol's major sensations, the wines occasionally surpassing Château Pétrus in price and quality. Rich, fragrant, velvety, and with the allure of a top class Burgundy, Château Le Pin has instant appeal but also the structure to age. Production of this Merlot-dominated wine is low – another reason for the high price. Much to the (classically minded) owner's chagrin, Le Pin is also often considered the precursor of the garage movement *(see above)*.
✪ *Pomerol* • *05 57 51 33 99* ▨ ▨ *red*

Château L'Église-Clinet
Pomerol
Another tiny property on the Pomerol plateau, Château L'Église-Clinet has achieved star status over the past decade. The recipe for success has been a large portion of old vines (some dating

Most of the "châteaux" of the Pomerol region are little more than modest farmhouses

back to the 1930s), an interesting proportion of Cabernet Franc (up to 30 per cent) in the blend, and the winemaking skills of owner Denis Durantou. The results are rich and concentrated wines, with distinctive balance and refinement. ⊗ *Pomerol • 05 57 25 96 59*
• www.eglise-clinet.com ⬤ 🖼 *red*

Château L'Évangile
Pomerol

The Rothschilds of Lafite-Rothschild *(see p26)* have been co-owners of L'Évangile since 1989 but only took on sole ownership in 1999. Since then a heavy programme of investment has been under way, including replanting vines and the construction of new cellars. The vineyard is located on the Pomerol plateau, with châteaux Pétrus and Cheval Blanc as neighbours. The wines – rich, powerful, and already impressive – can only improve further. ⊗ *Pomerol • 05 57 55 45 56*
• www.lafite.com ☐ *by appt* 🖼 *red*

Château Pétrus
Pomerol

Although virtually unknown in Britain and the USA before the 1960s, Pétrus is one of Bordeaux's legendary wines. Almost 100 per cent Merlot is grown on a unique soil of heavy, blue clay that is known as the Pétrus "buttonhole", producing wines of power, volume, and rich extract with firm but fine tannins. The technical expertise of *négociant* owner Jean-Pierre Moueix, and his ability to harvest at optimum ripeness in little more than a day, also count for a lot. ⊗ *Pomerol • 05 57 51 78 96*
⬤ 🖼 *red*

Château Trotanoy
Pomerol

Purchased in 1953, Château Trotanoy, like Château Pétrus, is now part of *négociant* Jean-Pierre

Moueix's stable. It benefits from the same highly skilled technical team, and its vineyards, too, have a high percentage of Merlot, grown on clay-gravel soils. The red wines come closest to Pétrus in terms of their power and weight. Replanting of vines during the 1980s caused a slight dip in quality, but it is now back on top form. ⊗ *Pomerol • 05 57 51 78 96* ⬤ 🖼 *red*

Vieux Château Certan
Pomerol

Although a close neighbour of Château Pétrus, this estate makes a style of wine that is anything but similar. Vieux Château Certan is more svelte than fleshy, and its aromatic charm and firm, taut structure make it more like a wine of the Médoc than a Pomerol. The presence of Cabernet Franc (30 per cent) and Cabernet Sauvignon (10 per cent) explain why. The property has been owned by the Belgian Thienpont family since 1924. ⊗ *Pomerol • 05 57 51 17 33 • www.vieux-chateau-certan. com* ☐ *by appt* 🖼 *red*

VINCENT GASNIER'S TOP 10
Magnificent Red Bordeaux

1. **Château Latour** Pauillac *p26*
2. **Château Lafite-Rothschild** Pauillac *p26*
3. **Château Haut-Brion** Pessac-Léognan *p29*
4. **Château Margaux** Margaux *p29*
5. **Château Montrose** St-Estephe *p26*
6. **Château Léoville-Barton** St-Julien *p28*
7. **Château Pétrus** Pomerol *left*
8. **Château Cheval Blanc** St-Émilion Grand Cru *p36*
9. **Château Angélus** St-Émilion Grand Cru *p36*
10. **Château Ausone** St-Émilion Grand Cru *p36*

Over the last 25 years Château Pétrus has been the world's most expensive wine – only 2,500 to 4,000 cases are produced each year

39

Wine Areas of Entre-Deux-Mers

Entre-Deux-Mers is both a geographical region, between the Garonne and Dordogne rivers, and an appellation for dry, white wines. This is also Bordeaux's production engine room, turning out huge quantities of red Bordeaux and Bordeaux Supérieur *(see right)*, in addition to a little sweet white.

Old windmill among rows of vines in Haut-Benauge

Entre-Deux-Mers & Haut-Benauge

Within the greater Entre-Deux-Mers region lies the appellation Entre-Deux-Mers, known for dry, white wines made from a blend of the classic white Bordeaux varieties Sauvignon Blanc, Sémillon, and Muscadelle. These are crisp, fresh, fruity wines to be drunk young, normally representing good value. The production area covers around 1,600ha. AOC Haut-Benauge is a delimited zone in the south of Entre-Deux-Mers. The wines are similar, and production is negligible, most producers preferring the more marketable Entre-Deux-Mers or Bordeaux labels.  silt, sand, gravel, limestone-and-clay Sauvignon Blanc, Sémillon, Muscadelle white

Graves de Vayres

This small AOC has nothing to do with the Graves region but is a small enclave in the north of Entre-Deux-Mers, centred on the town of Vayres. As the name suggests, the soils are mainly gravel. Light, fruity reds are the main product, with a limited amount of dry white. gravel, sand Merlot, Cabernet Sauvignon, Cabernet Franc, Malbec Sauvignon Blanc, Sémillon, Muscadelle red, white

Premières Côtes de Bordeaux

This AOC forms a long, narrow strip of land in the south of Entre-Deux-Mers. It consists of a limestone scarp that follows the

Clairet

Clairet is a Bordeaux speciality which is steadily growing in popularity. It pays homage to the style of wine that was probably exported to Britain in the Middle Ages, giving us the English word "claret". Clairet is a dark pink colour, fruity and easy to drink. More characterful and vigorous than rosé, but less tannic than a red wine, it is ideal as an *apéritif* or with certain grills and starters. The wine is made by macerating the grape skins with the juice for up to two days, rather than the four or five hours that rosé is given. Merlot is the favoured grape variety, but both Cabernets are also used. Occasionally the wine is aged for a short spell in oak barrels. It is best drunk young and chilled, in the year following the harvest.

meandering path of the Garonne River, with a tumble of hills behind. The area was once known for its semi-sweet and sweet whites, however the main staple today is red wine. The dominant variety is Merlot, but these are blended wines, with both Cabernet Sauvignon and Cabernet Franc playing an important role. These lively, fruity, medium-bodied wines are intended for drinking over three to five years. Some special *cuvées* will age longer.

🌧 *limestone-and-clay, gravel* 🍇 *Merlot, Cabernet Sauvignon, Cabernet Franc, Malbec* 🍇 *Sauvignon Blanc, Sémillon, Muscadelle* 🍷 *red, white*

Cadillac, Loupiac & Ste-Croix-du-Mont

These three sweet white wine AOCs face Sauternes and Barsac across the Garonne River. Like their illustrious cousins on the Left Bank of the river, Cadillac, Loupiac, and Ste-Croix-du-Mont have the propensity to produce botrytized grapes *(see p24)* with autumnal morning mists provoking the onset of this fungus that helps concentrate the juice. The wines are less powerful and concentrated than Sauternes but represent excellent value for money, particularly with the recent spate of top vintages (in 1996 1997, 1999, and 2001).

Ste-Croix-du-Mont (425ha) is historically the most important of the three AOCs, and considered capable of producing wines that rival all but the very best Sauternes. Loupiac (400ha) is a little fresher, with more apparent acidity, while the smaller Cadillac varies from rich and exotic to semi-sweet styles. The human factor also plays an important role with regard to style and quality. 🌧 *limestone-and-clay, gravel* 🍇 *Sémillon, Sauvignon Blanc, Muscadelle* 🍷 *white, dessert*

Generic Bordeaux

The generic AOC Bordeaux encompasses over 50,000ha of vineyards and accounts for 50 per cent of production in the Bordeaux area. Generic Bordeaux is produced throughout the Gironde *département*, but Entre-Deux-Mers provides 75 per cent of it. Two thirds of generic Bordeaux is red, with white, rosé, clairet, and sparkling making up the rest. Given the extent and volume of the appellation, quality and style can vary, with everything from low-yielding garage-style wines to high-volume "plonk". Seventy-five per cent of Bordeaux AOC rouge is bulk-commercialized, feeding brand names like Mouton Cadet and own-label supermarket wines. At its best, red Bordeaux has a grassy fruitiness; the white is crisp, dry, and refreshing. Ste-Foy-Bordeaux is a delimited zone

in the east of Entre-Deux-Mers, where producers may bottle their wines using the Ste-Foy label, but most prefer to use the appellation Bordeaux.

Bordeaux Supérieur

The AOC Bordeaux Supérieur is predominantly for red wines, although there is also a tiny amount of sweet white. The appellation covers the same geographical area as generic Bordeaux (and a similar amount of its wine comes from Entre-Deux-Mers), but demands higher minimum alcohol (10 per cent instead of 9.5) and a slight reduction in maximum yield. The wines are not allowed on the market until the September following the harvest, so have a longer period of maturation. The implication is that these wines have more structure and depth than regular Bordeaux. Just over 10,000ha of red Bordeaux Supérieur are declared each year, with 75 per cent of the wine bottled at the property – the opposite of appellation Bordeaux. Standards vary, but these wines are generally more reliable.

Vineyards around an old church in Entre-Deux-Mers

Major Producers in Entre-Deux-Mers

Château Ste-Marie
Entre-Deux-Mers

Château Ste-Marie is a white wine specialist; the Entre-Deux-Mers Vieilles Vignes (vines over 25 years old) and barrel-fermented Madlys are Sauvignon Blanc-dominated, but both have a percentage of grapes from 100-year-old Sémillon vines. The former is classically fresh and fruity; the latter a little rounder and fuller. There is also a Premières Côtes de Bordeaux Alios and a red Bordeaux Supérieur, which are both soft and fruity. ◈ 51 rte de Bordeaux, Targon • 05 56 23 64 30 ☐ by appt ◪ red, white ★ Entre-Deux-Mers Vieilles Vignes

Château Reynon label

Château Reynon
Premières Côtes de Bordeaux

Château Reynon belongs to Denis Dubourdieu, a professor of oenology at Bordeaux University, who has put considerable effort into upgrading the Reynon red. The wine is beautifully balanced with an elegant expression of red fruits, gentle use of oak, and a long, fresh finish. It is best drunk at two to five years old. The white Bordeaux Vieilles Vignes has a citrusy aroma and flavour, and lovely depth of fruit. There is also a little sweet white Cadillac. ◈ 21 rte de Cardan, Beguey • 05 56 62 96 51 • www.denis dubourdieu.com ☐ by appt ◪ red, white, dessert ★ Premières Côtes de Bordeaux, Vieilles Vignes

Château Suau
Premières Côtes de Bordeaux

Monique Bonnet is one of the leading producers in the Premières Côtes de Bordeaux. Her 60-ha vineyard has been restructured over the past 10 years, and there has also been considerable investment in this château's winery and cellars. She makes two *cuvées*, each with red and white versions: Tradition and Cuvée Prestige. Of most interest is the sturdy, ripe red Cuvée Prestige made from a blend of Merlot, Cabernet Sauvignon, and Cabernet Franc aged in 30 per cent new oak barrels. ◈ Capian • 05 56 72 19 06 • www.chateausuau.com ☐ by appt ◪ red, white, rosé ★ Cuvée Prestige

Château Bonnet
Bordeaux

André Lurton's Château Bonnet has led the field in upgrading the quality of Bordeaux's generic wines. There is always a good level of ripeness and extraction of fruit. The red Réserve is aged in *barriques* for 12 months and has a little more volume and definition than the Cuvée Classique. The white Entre-Deux-Mers is always crisp, clean, and fruity. A recent addition is the garage-style *(see p38)* Divinius. ◈ Grézillac 05 57 25 58 58 • www.andrelurton.com ☐ ◪ red, white, rosé ★ Réserve, Entre-Deux-Mers

Château de Fontenille
Bordeaux

The three wines that Stéphane Defraine produces at the 36-ha Château de Fontenille are all of a regular and consistent quality. The red Bordeaux is round, soft, fruity, and drinkable early on. The white Entre-Deux-Mers is lighter-bodied than some but wonderfully aromatic with an almost exotic, New World character. The Cabernet Franc-led clairet is fruity and fun. ◈ *La Sauve* • 05 56 23 03 26 • www.chateau-fontenille.com ▢ by appt ▨ red, white, clairet ★ Bordeaux, Entre-Deux-Mers, Bordeaux Clairet

Château Thieuley
Bordeaux

Former oenology teacher Francis Courselle has spent the past 30 years placing this family-owned château at the top of its class. The vineyard is immaculately run, and technically the estate is on a par with many a *grand cru*. The standard red and white *cuvées* are regularly good, while the barrel-aged Cuvée Francis Courselle (which appears in both red and white) has more depth and ageability. ◈ *La Sauve-Majeure* • 05 56 23 00 01 ▢ by appt ▨ red, white, clairet ★ Cuvée Francis Courselle

Château Tour de Mirambeau
Bordeaux

Jean-Louis Despagne owns six different properties in the Bordeaux area, with a total of 300ha. Château Tour de Mirambeau is the flagship estate, which produces a range of wines including a consistently good Entre-Deux-Mers and a wholesome Bordeaux Supérieur. The Cuvée Passion is a special oak-aged selection in both red and white. ◈ *Naujan et Postiac* • 05 57 84 55 08 ▢ by appt ▨ red, white, rosé ★ Entre-Deux-Mers, Cuvée Passion

Château de Reignac
Bordeaux Supérieur

Château de Reignac and its park resemble a magnificent stately home. The wines have benefited from the investment and technical expertise of owner Yves Vatelot since 1990. Château de Reignac is the second label, an easy-drinking, fresh, aromatic wine. The top wine, Reignac, is rich, concentrated, and chocolaty, aged in new oak barrels. There is also a limited edition micro-*cuvée*, Balthus, and a little barrel-fermented white Reignac. ◈ *St-Loubès* • 05 56 20 41 05 ▢ by appt ▨ red, white ★ Bordeaux Supérieur

Château Penin
Bordeaux Supérieur

Owner Patrick Carteyron has made Château Penin one of the safe bets of generic Bordeaux. There are three red *cuvées* – Tradition, Grande Sélection, and Les Cailloux – all made from a high proportion of Merlot. Les Cailloux, which is aged for 12 months in new oak barrels, is as good as, if not better than, many St-Émilions. Also exceptional is the clairet. ◈ *Génissac* • 05 57 24 46 98 • www.chateaupenin.com ▢ ▨ red, white, rosé, clairet ★ Grande Sélection, Les Cailloux, Clairet

Domaine de Courteillac
Bordeaux Supérieur

Talented winemaker Stéphane Asseo, now making a name for himself in California, set up the estate in the 1980s. Now owned by *négociant* Dominique Meneret, it still sets high standards. The red Domaine de Courteillac is a classic Bordeaux with well-integrated oak and a firm but fine structure for ageing up to 10 years. The tiny volume of white is aromatic and finely textured. ◈ *Ruch* • 05 57 40 79 48 ▢ by appt ▨ red, white ★ Domaine de Courteillac

BURGUNDY

BURGUNDY

M ORE THAN ANY OTHER WINE REGION IN FRANCE, *Burgundy has distilled the wisdom and experience of its history into winemaking. Established by powerful monasteries from the 7th century onwards, the vineyards have been cultivated by people who came to understand every nuance of the soil and every natural factor acting upon it – rainfall, wind conditions, sunlight and temperature. Burgundian wine, patronized by royalty through the ages, is celebrated for its elegance and subtlety.*

The vineyards of Burgundy (Bourgogne) lie mostly in a narrow strip running south from Chablis to the suburbs of Lyon. Over the years they have been placed in a hierarchy, beginning with those producing simple *vins de Bourgogne* from the most basic soils, ascending to sites whose wines bear the names of villages or communes, and continuing to the *premiers* and *grands crus* that deliver Burgundy's finest, most long-lived, and expensive wines.

It is not always easy to see why one vineyard should be designated *grand cru* while its neighbour may be a mere village, but these distinctions have stood the test

Key

■ Burgundy

of time. It comes down to *terroir*, a somewhat baffling combination of soil type, microclimate, exposure, susceptibility to frost, and countless other factors, each of which affects the performance of any given patch of earth.

Complex inheritance laws, determined by the Napoleonic code, require estates to be divided equally among the children of the deceased. As a result, properties have been broken up among numerous heirs, and vineyards have been split into tiny parcels of land, often with no more than one or two rows of vines in the region's venerable *grand cru* sites. Burgundian estates therefore tend to be small (just 5 to 15ha) and

Harvesting grapes in the famous winemaking village of Nuits-St-Georges

  Preceding pages **Patchwork of tiny parcels of Burgundian vines**

Château de Corton-André, Côte de Beaune

fragmented, and most producers vinify and sell wines from a dozen or more appellations. Some of the largest vineyard holdings are in the hands of *négociants*, businesses that supplement their own harvests by buying from small growers in order to create sizeable volumes of sought-after wines.

The only simple factor about Burgundian wine is that just three grape varieties are cultivated. Chardonnay accounts for virtually all of the whites; Pinot Noir is the red grape found in most vineyards, while the juicy, if less refined, red Gamay thrives in Beaujolais.

As a general rule, the simpler the wine, the younger it can – and usually should – be consumed. A basic Burgundy can be drunk on release, while village wines benefit from three years in the bottle, and *premiers* and *grands crus* invariably benefit from ageing to give aromatic complexity. A top red Burgundy can be kept for up to 30 years, although 10 years is a more reliable limit; a good white can usually be drunk with pleasure at five years of age. In the past, grapes that were not fully ripe tended to give hard tannins that needed years to soften. Today, later harvesting and modern winemaking techniques deliver softer tannins, leaving the wine tasting richer and more supple, and allowing it to be drunk earlier.

VINCENT GASNIER'S TOP 10 Superb Celebration Wines

1. **Domaine Raveneau** (white) Chablis Grand Cru *p52*
2. **Domaine Leflaive** (white) Côte de Beaune *p66*
3. **Domaine Chave** (red or white) Hermitage *p91*
4. **Château Margaux, 1982** (red) Margaux *p29*
5. **Château Latour, 1982** (red) Pauillac *p26*
6. **Romanée-Conti: DRC** (red) Côte de Nuits *p59*
7. **Guigal: La Turque** (red) Côte Rôtie *p90*
8. **Château Cheval Blanc** (red) St-Émilion Grand Cru *p36*
9. **Louis Roederer: Cristal** Champagne *p132*
10. **Château Haut-Brion, 1982** (red) Pessac-Léognan *p29*

Wine Map of Burgundy

Burgundy covers some 175km from Chablis in the north to Beaujolais in the south. With the exception of Chablis, which is isolated from the rest of the region, the vineyards are virtually continuous. There are various AOCs, each with its own distinctive character. The most prestigious sites lie in the Côte de Nuits and the Côte de Beaune, which together form the Côte d'Or, Burgundy's famous "Golden Slope" between Dijon and Chagny.

WINE AREAS & MAJOR PRODUCERS

Chablis pp50–51
Billaud-Simon p52
Bouchard p53
Brocard p53
Chablisienne, La p53
Dauvissat p53
Droin p52
Fèvre p53
Laroche p52
Michel p53
Raveneau p52

Bacchus plinth at Louis Jadot, Côte de Nuits

Côte de Nuits pp54–5
Clair p56
Dugat-Py p56
Dujac p57
Gouges p58
Grivot p58
Jadot p58
Lambrays p57
Leroy p58
Méo-Camuzet p58
Mortet p57
Romanée-Conti p59
Roumier p57
Rousseau p56
Vogüé p56
Vougeraie p57

Côte de Beaune pp62–3
Armand, Comte p65
Bonneau du Martray p64
Bouchard p64
Bouzereau p67
Chandon de Briailles p65
Chorey p65
Clair p66
Coche-Dury p66
Colin p67

Girardin p67
Jobard p65
Lafarge p67
Lafon, Comtes p65
Leflaive, Domaine p66
Leflaive, Olivier p67
Maltroye p64
Morot p64
Prieur p66
Sauzet p66

Côte Chalonnaise & Mâconnnais pp70–71
Bongran p73
Faiveley p72
Ferret p73
Fuissé p73
Guffens-Heynen p73
Jacqueson p73
Juillot p73
Lumpp p72
Rodet p72
Salomon, Clos p72

Beaujolais pp74–5
Burgaud p77
Calot p76
Cheysson p76
Desvignes p77
Duboeuf p77
Jacques p76
Janin p77
Madone p76
Mommessin p77
Terres Dorées p76

Walled vineyard in the Côte de Nuits

Producers are listed by their surname or common name here. Their full house names appear in the main listings

Regional Information at a Glance

Latitude 45.5–48°N.

Altitude 175–500m.

Topography The most famous vineyards line the 50km stretch of the Côte d'Or. The escarpment is broken up by streams which run down the hills to join the Saône River. The exposure and angle of the slope are critical in this region.

Soil Limestone soils dominate, with some clay, granite, and sand.

Climate Moderate continental, with cold, dry winters and warm summers. Balmy Septembers help to bring grapes to full ripeness.

Temperature July average is 20°C.

Rainfall Annual average is 690mm. Heavy rainfall in May, June, and October.

Viticultural Hazards Frost; mildew; hail; harvest rain.

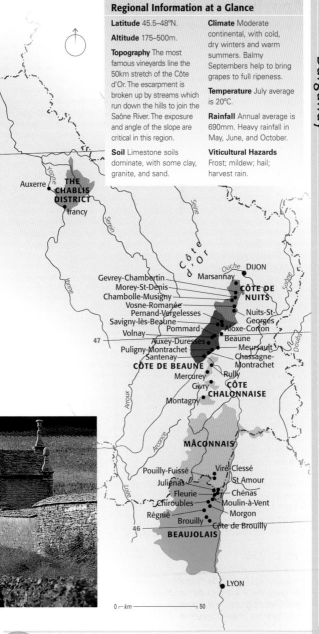

Auxerre

THE CHABLIS DISTRICT

Irancy

Yonne

Serein

Yonne

Côte d'Or

Ouche   DIJON

Marsannay

Gevrey-Chambertin
Morey-St-Denis
Chambolle-Musigny
Vosne-Romanée
Pernand-Vergelesses
Savigny-lès-Beaune
Volnay

CÔTE DE NUITS

Nuits-St-Georges

Aloxe-Corton

Pommard

Beaune

Auxey-Duresses   Meursault

Puligny-Montrachet   Chassagne-Montrachet

Santenay

CÔTE DE BEAUNE

Mercurey   Rully

Givry   CÔTE CHALONNAISE

Montagny

Arroux

Seine

Saône

Doubs

MÂCONNAIS

Pouilly-Fuissé   Viré-Clessé

Juliénas   St Amour

Fleurie   Chénas

Chiroubles   Moulin-à-Vent

Régnié   Morgon

Brouilly   Côte de Brouilly

BEAUJOLAIS

Loire

Arconce

LYON

47

46

0 ⊢ km ⎯⎯⎯⎯⎯ 50

Appellations of the Chablis Region

In the far north of Burgundy lies Chablis, which exclusively produces the famous white wine. An important wine region for at least 1,400 years, by the late 19th century Chablis had over 40,000ha under vine. However, phylloxera, disease, and competition caused a dramatic decline. Despite a turnaround in recent decades, the total vineyard area today is still only around 5,000ha.

Made only from the Chardonnay grape, Chablis should be bone-dry but not harsh; steely without being austere; rich, not heavy. The wine derives its characteristics from the northerly climate, which encourages high acidity, and from the chalky limestone soils on which the best grapes are grown. Like the rest of Burgundy, Chablis is divided by the AOC into a hierarchy of vineyards, beginning with Petit Chablis and generic Chablis, and rising through to Premier Cru Chablis and Grand Cru Chablis. ▨ *Kimmeridgian limestone* ▧ *Chardonnay* ▤ *white*

La Chablisienne label

Chablis

Generic Chablis is produced from around 3,000ha of vineyards, making it by far Burgundy's most important appellation in terms of quantity. Although the zone has been extended considerably in recent decades, the wine's quality does not seem to have deteriorated as a consequence.

Petit Chablis

In the eyes of many Burgundy fanciers this is a slightly suspect category, since the soils on which Petit Chablis grapes are grown often lack the strong limestone content found elsewhere in the region. But even Petit Chablis is pure Chardonnay and can offer good value. It should be drunk young and fresh.

Chablis Premier Cru

Chablis becomes interesting at *premier cru* level. It also becomes complicated, because there are no fewer than 40 qualifying vineyards dispersed throughout the Chablis region, varying considerably in exposure and gradient. The number is so high because small sections within the 17 main *premier cru* vineyards are recognized as *premier cru* appellations, or *lieux-dits*, in their own right. Growers with vines in Fourchaume, for example, can choose whether to label their wine with the name of the whole vineyard (Fourchaume) or the name of their section (Vaupulent, Côte de Fontenay, Vaulorent, or L'Homme Mort). In practice, most growers, conscious of the marketing implications, opt to use the bigger name.

A Chablis *premier cru* will show more mineral complexity – bracing acidity, tanginess, flintiness and almost a stoniness – than a simple Chablis, and it may need two or three years in the bottle to bring out its aromatic complexity. A top vintage can age well for a decade, becoming golden in colour and more mellow in flavour.

The other *premiers crus* are Montée de Tonnerre (including Chapelot and Pied d'Aloup); Mont de Milieu (including Morein, Fourneaux, and Côte des Prés Girots); Vaucoupin, Beauroy (including Troesmes); Côte de

Léchet; Vaillons (including Châtains, Sécher, Beugnons, Les Lys, Mélinots, Roncières, and Les Épinottes); Montmains (including La Forest and Butteaux); Vosgros (including Vaugiraut); Vau Ligneau; Vau-de-Vey (including Vaux Ragons); and a handful of others rarely identified on the labels.

Chablis Grand Cru

Grand cru Chablis wines show similar characteristics to those of *premier cru*, but to an even greater degree. These are the boldest, richest, most complex wines of the region, and they repay keeping – ideally for 10 years. Yields are lower for *grands crus* than for other Chablis sites, and with only 106ha of vineyard – accounting for just three per cent of the total production in Chablis – the wines are relatively scarce and so command high prices.

The northerly location of Chablis means that getting the grapes to ripen can be rather problematic. While the *premier cru* vineyards are dispersed, the *grands crus* are in a single band, along a southwest-facing slope where the climate encourages the grapes to ripen relatively early.

Jean-Marc Brocard's vineyard and the church of Préhy, Chablis

There are only seven *grands crus* vineyards: Les Clos is the largest and best known; the others are Bougros, Les Preuses, Vaudésir, Grenouilles, Valmur, and Blanchot.

Irancy & Sauvignon de St-Bris

Officially outside the Chablis AOC, between Chablis and Auxerre to the southwest, is a small region of Pinot Noir vineyards. The best known is Irancy, which has its own AOC; wines made elsewhere are sold as Bourgogne Rouge or vinified as sparkling wines and labelled Crémant de Bourgogne. Wines here can be charming and delicate in good years, but distinctly lean in cooler vintages. There is also a local anomaly, known as Sauvignon de St-Bris, made from Sauvignon Blanc, not Chardonnay. This wine is zesty and good value.

Left **Stainless steel tank at Jean-Marc Brocard** Right **Chablis Grand Cru label**

Major Producers of Chablis

Domaine Billaud-Simon

This 20-ha estate is blessed with one of the most complete ranges of *premiers* and *grands crus* in Chablis. Bernard Billaud and his nephew Samuel have a technically advanced winery, in which most of their wines are aged in stainless steel. One or two *crus*, including Mont de Milieu and Blanchot, receive some oak-ageing. These are wines marked by purity and mineral complexity. ◈ *1 quai de Reugny • 03 86 42 10 33 • www.billaud-simon.com* ▢ *by appt* ▨ *white* ★ *Vaillons, Blanchot*

Domaine François & Jean-Marie Raveneau

Raveneau owns only 8ha of vineyards, but everything is *premier* or *grand cru*. The wines are fermented in tanks but partly

VINCENT GASNIER'S Best Chablis Labels

1. Dauvissat: Les Clos *opposite*
2. Raveneau: Butteaux *above*
3. William Fèvre: Montée de Tonnerre *opposite*
4. Droin: Vaucoupin *right*
5. Laroche: Réserve de l'Obédience *right*
6. La Chablisienne: Vieilles Vignes *opposite*
7. Billaud-Simon: Vaillons *above*
8. Louis Michel: Montmains *opposite*
9. Domaine du Chardonnay *www.domaine-du-chardonnay.com*
10. Jean-Marc Brocard *opposite*

aged in older wood. Before bottling, different lots of the same wine are blended to ensure that the balance is consistent. The result is classic Chablis: mineral and even austere in its youth, but flowering with age into a rich, nutty complexity. Les Clos is usually the finest and most long-lived of the wines, but production is limited and demand is high. ◈ *9 rue de Chichée • 03 86 42 17 46* ▨ *white* ★ *Butteaux, Les Clos, Blanchot*

Domaine Jean-Paul & Benoît Droin

Jean-Paul Droin is one of the region's most thoughtful winemakers, and the fortunate possessor of plots in four *grands crus*: Blanchot, Les Clos, Valmur, and Vaudésir. For many years he used new oak for fermentation and ageing, but in the 1990s he changed his methods and today the wines are better balanced, with oak as a nuance rather than a flavour component. They are expensive, but beautifully made and infinitely complex. ◈ *14 bis rue Jean-Jaurès • 03 86 42 16 78 • www.jeanpaul-droin.fr* ▢ *by appt* ▨ *white* ★ *Vaucoupin, Les Clos*

Domaine Laroche

Michel Laroche is a man of prodigious energy and ambition. He owns around 100ha in Chablis and successfully combines sound commercial sense with top quality at all levels – from his generic Chablis brand (St-Martin) to the parade of *grands crus*. Laroche

Its blend of ripe fruit and mineral nuances makes Chablis sublime with seafood and grilled fish

ages his top wines in old oak and since 1991 has made Réserve de l'Obédience, a wine that uses some of Blanchot's oldest vines and is released at a high price. ✆ 22 rue Louis Bro • 03 86 42 89 00 • www.michellaroche.com ☐ ◙ white ★ St Martin, Fourchaume, Réserve de l'Obédience

Domaine Louis Michel et Fils

Louis Michel and his son Jean-Loup own some 20ha in Chablis, and most of their holdings are in the *premiers crus* of Montmains and Montée de Tonnerre. All wines are aged solely in stainless steel, which helps preserve the primary fruit and vigour. The absence of oak-ageing also helps maintains the individuality of each *cru*. All the wines are fairly priced. ✆ 9 blvd de Ferrières • 03 86 42 88 55 ☐ ◙ white ★ Montmains, Vaudésir

Domaine Vincent Dauvissat

The enthusiastic Vincent Dauvissat has inherited his father's winemaking skills, and this remains one of the region's finest and most traditional producers. Dauvissat believes that a long maturation period accentuates mineral nuances, and all his wines are fermented and aged in old oak. Consequently there is a loss of overt grapey fruitiness, but these are wines for ageing, and after five years they reveal fully their immaculate balance and complexity. ✆ 8 rue Émile Zola • 03 86 42 11 58 ◉ ◙ white ★ La Forest, Vaillons, Les Clos

Domaine William Fèvre

With 16ha, William Fèvre owned more *grand cru* vines than any other grower in Chablis. In 1998, he sold his holdings to Bouchard Père & Fils *(see p64)*, who within a few years transformed the wines into some of the most

exuberant in the region, richly fruity and wonderfully varied from *cru* to *cru*. ✆ 21 ave d'Oberwesel • 03 86 98 98 98 ☐ by appt ◙ white ★ Montée de Tonnerre, Blanchots

Jean-Marc Brocard

Having inherited 2ha, Jean-Marc Brocard has astutely built up a substantial 80-ha estate. His wines are aged entirely in stainless steel, and, as well as very reliable Chablis, Brocard also produces good-value Bourgogne Blanc from outside the Chablis zone.The large production allows Brocard to maintain fair prices. ✆ 3 rte de Chablis, Préhy • 03 86 41 49 00 • www.brocard.fr ☐ ◙ white ★ Montée de Tonnerre, Beauregard

La Chablisienne

With a production of some 500,000 cases, this co-op is a major player, and quality is consistently high. In addition to a wide range of *premiers* and *grands crus*, La Chablisienne produces blends such as the Vieilles Vignes (produced from old vines), which is given some oak-ageing and released ready to drink. Prices, although not low, offer good value. ✆ 8 blvd Pasteur • 03 86 42 89 89 • www.chablisienne.fr ☐ by appt ◙ white ★ Vieilles Vignes, Beauroy

Maison Pascal Bouchard

This is one of the largest estates in Chablis, with ownership of (or contracts with) around 100 ha of vines. Only some of the *grands crus* are treated to a touch of barrel-fermentation and oak-ageing. Generally, the wines are enjoyable young for their rich fruit and firm minerality, but the finest *crus* are best kept for a few years. ✆ Parc des Lys • 03 86 42 18 64 • www.pascalbouchard.fr ☐ ◙ white ★ Fourchaume Vieilles Vignes, Les Clos

Wine Villages of the Côte de Nuits

For many Burgundy lovers, the Côte de Nuits produces the area's finest red wines. Almost all the red *grands crus* lie here in Burgundy's heartland, tucked among the mighty monastic estates that once dominated the east-facing slopes. Nowhere else in the world does Pinot Noir attain such heart-stopping complexity and elegance. Its delicate red-fruit aromas are married to a firmness of structure that allows a well-made example to age for decades, developing ever more subtle aromas and flavours. Burgundians insist that the greatness of their wines comes from the soil rather than the grape – that Pinot Noir is merely a vehicle through which the rich, mineral limestone soils of the Côte de Nuits express themselves most brilliantly.

The vineyards begin just south of Dijon, rising from the plains onto the renowned east-facing slopes of the Côte d'Or. The AOC Côte de Nuits Villages is used mostly for villages on a plateau behind the slopes, where the cooler climate makes it more difficult for grapes to ripen. The major AOCs of the region are as follows. ▨ *limestone* ▧ *Pinot Noir* ▨ *Chardonnay* ◪ *red, white, rosé*

Marsannay

Until the 1980s, Marsannay was mostly known for its rosés. Made from Pinot Noir, these can be delicious, but are really thought to be a waste of good *terroir*. Bruno Clair is the best-known producer, but others, such as Charlopin, also take their winemaking seriously, and produce rich, enjoyable, and quite inexpensive wines, of which the reds are most worthwhile.

Domaine des Lambrays

Fixin

This somewhat obscure village makes the most of its authentic connections with Napoleon. One of his closest associates came from here, and returned from accompanying the emperor into exile to name a vineyard after him, erect a statue, and open a small museum about the man. The best vineyard is the Clos du Chapître, on the slopes behind the village. The wines here are solid in style rather than elegant, but can be good value.

Gevrey-Chambertin

The largest wine-producing village in the Côte de Nuits, Gevrey-Chambertin is richly endowed with nine *grands crus*, of which the best known (and usually the finest) is Le Chambertin. Vineyard status is not an infallible guide to quality: some of the *grand cru* producers are always disappointing, while growers like Denis Mortet make wonderful wines from mere village sites. Among the *premiers crus* here, Clos-St-Jacques reigns supreme. The wines of Gevrey-Chambertin tend to be muscular and very long-lived, yet the best ones can have surprising finesse.

Morey-St-Denis

The swathe of *grand cru* vineyards heading south from Gevrey-Chambertin continues into Morey-St-Denis, and some of those vineyards, notably Clos de la Roche and Clos St Denis, can be of truly outstanding quality. Unlike most Burgundian *crus*, which are divided into numerous parcels of vines with equally numerous owners, two of Morey-St-Denis' *grands crus* – Clos des Lambrays

The Côte de Nuits and adjoining Côte de Beaune **(see pp62–63)** *are collectively known as the Côte d'Or*

and Clos de Tartare – are actually monopolies with single owners. Both now produce delicious wines after decades of mediocrity.

Chambolle-Musigny

Morey-St-Denis segues so subtly into Chambolle-Musigny that the two villages share the *grand cru* Bonnes Mares. Chambolle-Musigny delivers the most elegant wines of the Côte de Nuits. They are perfumed and delicate, yet can age well. The other *grand cru* site, Le Musigny, is one of the most prized in all Burgundy.

Vougeot

This hamlet is best known for its large Clos de Vougeot *grand cru*, which sweeps up from the main road to a celebrated château. Because of its size and varied soils, this site produces wines ranging from unexceptional to magnificent. Buy only from the best growers, such as Château de la Tour and domaines Anne Gros, Denis Mortet, Jean Grivot, and Méo-Camuzet.

Vosne-Romanée

The wines of Vosne-Romanée are sturdy yet supple, perfumed yet rich, and full of body and vigour. Like Gevrey-Chambertin, this area is richly endowed with *grands*

The Négociants

Until about 50 years ago, almost all Burgundian vine growers sold their wines to merchants, known as *négociants*, who blended and sold them under their own name. Over the years, more and more growers have vinified and sold their own wine. Nonetheless, as Burgundian estates are so small, *négociants* still play an important role in supplying large volumes of good Burgundy. Many are mediocre, but a handful, including Louis Jadot, Joseph Drouhin, and Bouchard Père & Fils, produce truly fine wines. These tend to be the *négociants* that also have their own vineyard holdings.

---

crus and superb *premiers crus*. Not surprisingly, the wines are highly sought after and expensive, but they are rarely disappointing.

Nuits-St-Georges

It is something of an anomaly that this famous village has no *grands crus*. (Historically, its growers were reluctant to pay the higher taxes due from such sites.) Spreading southwards through the hamlet of Prémeaux, Nuits-St-Georges is a large commune where quality can be variable. The name of the producer tends to count for more than the name of the vineyard.

Clos de Vougeot's *grand cru* vineyard and château, Vougeot

 Côte d'Or translates literally as "golden slope," but the name is actually an abbreviation for Côte d'Orient, or "east slope"

Left **Charles Rousseau** Centre **Village sign** Right **Winemaking at Domaine de la Vougeraie**

Major Producers in the Côte de Nuits

Domaine Armand Rousseau
Few growers are as respected as the venerable Charles Rousseau. For decades he has produced some of the most profound wines of Gevrey-Chambertin, adapting his winemaking process to suit the structure of each one. His Clos St Jacques and Clos de Bèze are rich and oaky; but other wines have a lighter touch, with an intrinsic delicacy, aroma, and finesse. Sometimes simple in their youth, these wines often require 10 years to show their elegance. ◈ *1 rue de l'Aumônerie, Gevrey-Chambertin • 03 80 34 30 55 • www.domaine-rousseau.com* ▢ *by appt* ▨ *red* ★ *Gevrey-Chambertin Clos St Jacques, Ruchottes Chambertin, Chambertin*

Domaine Bernard Dugat-Py
The unassuming Bernard Dugat-Py is, alongside Charles Rousseau and Denis Mortet, one of the best growers in Gevrey-Chambertin. Most of his vines are very old, he intervenes as little as possible during vinification and ageing, and he lets the grapes and soils speak for themselves. ◈ *rue de Planteligone, Gevrey-Chambertin • 03 80 51 82 46 • www.dugat-py.com* ◐ ▨ *red* ★ *Bourgogne Cuvée Halinard, Gevrey-Chambertin Coeur de Roy, Chambertin*

Domaine Bruno Clair
Clair is based in unfashionable Marsannay, but has vines in many of the best sites in the Côte d'Or. His red Marsannays reveal just how good the area's wines can be, but his top bottlings are usually from Gevrey-Chambertin's Clos St Jacques and Clos de Bèze. The whites, from Morey-St-Denis and Marsannay, can be delicious too. With 21ha in as many communes, Bruno Clair has a fine range to offer his enthusiastic aficionados. ◈ *5 rue du Vieux College, Marsannay • 03 80 52 28 95* ▢ ▨ *red, white, rosé* ★ *Marsannay Longeroies, Gevrey-Chambertin Clos St Jacques*

Domaine Comte Georges de Vogüé
No domaine can match this one for the quality of its holdings in Chambolle-Musigny, which include the *premier cru* sites Le Musigny, Les Amoureuses, and Bonnes Mares. Some 70 per cent of Le Musigny is owned by this one estate. So high are its standards that the wines from vines under 20 years old are bottled under the lesser Chambolle *premier cru* appellation. De Vogüé aims for perfection and frequently attains it. ◈ *7 rue Ste Barbe, Chambolle-Musigny • 03 80 62 86 25* ▢ ▨ *red* ★ *Chambolle-Musigny Amoureuses, Bonnes Mares, Le Musigny*

Domaine de la Romanée-Conti
See p59.

Domaine de la Vougeraie
No merchant has been more astute than Jean-Claude Boisset when it comes to acquiring properties in this region. By the late 1990s he had assembled some 37ha of vineyards. He then hired a brilliant French-Canadian

The wines of the AOC Côte de Nuits Villages are less highly esteemed than those of the Côte de Nuits itself

winemaker, Pascal Marchand, and created this new domaine to produce and market the wines. From the outset, La Vougeraie has produced rich, modern-style Burgundies, boldly flavoured and built to last. ◈ *rue de l'Eglise, Prémeaux • 03 80 62 48 25 • www. domainedelavougeraie.com* ▢ *by appt* 🖪 *red, white* ★ *Pinot Noir Terres de Famille, Gevrey-Chambertin Les Évocelles, Bonnes Mares*

Domaine Denis Mortet

Within a few years of his father's retirement in 1991, Denis was acclaimed for his rich, dense wines that often had more punch than elegance. Today his wines have finesse and vigour as well as power. Most of his vineyards are village sites in Gevrey-Chambertin, but the vines are old and the quality sensational, so wines are priced at *premier cru* levels. ◈ *22 rue de l'Eglise, Gevrey-Chambertin • 03 80 34 10 05* ◼ 🖪 *red* ★ *Gevrey En Motrot, Gevrey En Champs, Clos de Vougeot*

Domaine des Lambrays

Except for one tiny parcel, this 9-ha *grand cru* domaine is owned by the German tycoon Günter Freund. Its exceptional site allows Thierry Brouin, who oversees the domaine and the winemaking, to produce equally exceptional wine. Anything he considers unworthy of the Lambrays label is bottled, modestly, as Morey-St-Denis Premier Cru. ◈ *31 rue Basse, Morey-St-Denis • 03 80 51 84 33* ▢ 🖪 *red* ★ *Morey-St-Denis Premier Cru, Clos des Lambrays*

Domaine Dujac

The "jac" in Dujac is Jacques Seysses, who abandoned banking for wine production in 1969 and created this outstanding estate based in Morey-St-Denis. As an outsider who was anxious to learn, he followed the best growers. Now he himself shares his knowledge with winemakers the world over. As for his own wines, they demonstrate finesse rather than pure power, which does not prevent the best of them from ageing for 30 years. ◈ *7 rue de la Bussière, Morey-St-Denis • 03 80 34 01 00 • www.dujac.com* ▢ *by appt* 🖪 *red, white* ★ *Gevrey-Chambertin Combottes, Bonnes Mares, Clos de la Roche*

Domaine Georges Roumier

Christophe Roumier is a superstar of Chambolle-Musigny. There is no hi-tech equipment in his winery; the winemaking is simple and traditional; and he takes care not to cosset his wines in too much new oak. The *premier cru* Chambolle-Musigny Les Amoureuses and the *grand cru* Bonnes Mares are usually his best wines, but even his simple Bourgogne Rouge has distinction. ◈ *rue de Vergy, Chambolle-Musigny • 03 80 62 86 37 • www.roumier.com* ▢ *by appt* 🖪 *red* ★ *Chambolle-Musigny, Les Amoureuses, Bonnes Mares*

VINCENT GASNIER'S TOP 10 Côte de Nuits Labels

1. **Armand Rousseau: Gevrey-Chambertin** *opposite*
2. **Dujac: Gevrey-Chambertin** *left*
3. **Romanée-Conti: La Tâche** *p59*
4. **Roumier: Chambolle-Musigny** *above*
5. **Lambrays: Clos des Lambrays** *left*
6. **Comte Georges de Vogüé: Chambolle-Musigny** *opposite*
7. **Leroy: Vosne-Romanée Brûlées** *p58*
8. **Anne Gros: Vosne-Romanée** *www.anne-gros.com*
9. **Grivot: Vosne-Romanée Beaux Monts** *p58*
10. **Méo-Camuzet: Vosne-Romanée Cros Parantoux** *p58*

Domaine Henri Gouges

For many years Gouges was acknowledged as the top estate in Nuits-St-Georges. Then it lost its way, and it was only in the 1990s, with a new generation in charge, that the domaine regained its supremacy. All the wines are from Nuits-St-Georges, offering a cross-section of the best *premiers crus*. Gouges also produces tiny quantities of remarkably spicy white wine from its vineyards.

⊗ *7 rue du Moulin, Nuits-St-Georges* • *03 80 61 04 40* ☐ *by appt* 🖻 *red, white • Nuits-St-Georges: Pruliers, Les St Georges*

Domaine Jean Grivot

For a time Étienne Grivot followed the advice of an oenologist called Guy Accad, whose techniques resulted in very dark wines that lacked true Burgundian character. Some years ago Grivot abandoned the system and has been producing wonderful wines, full of richness and style, ever since. They are perfect expressions of the great *terroirs* of Nuits-St-Georges and Vosne-Romanée.

⊗ *6 rue de la Croix-Rameau, Vosne-Romanée* • *03 80 61 05 95* ☐ *by appt* 🖻 *red* ★ *Vosne-Romanée Beaux Monts, Échézeaux, Richebourg*

Domaine Leroy

Lalou Bize-Leroy, a determined woman of a certain age whose favourite recreation is rock-climbing, has assembled this magnificent estate, which she runs alongside her renowned *négociant* business Maison Leroy. She was one of the first proprietors in Burgundy to convert her vineyards to biodynamism *(see p66)*, a somewhat esoteric regime that aims to restore health and vigour to the over-fertilized soils of Burgundy and other regions. The wines, developed from a wide range of excellent vineyards, are marvellous – and, not surprisingly, very expensive.

⊗ *rue du Pont Boillot, Auxey-Duresses* • *03 80 21 21 10* • *www.domaineleroy. com* 🖻 *red* ★ *Vosne-Romanée Brûlées, Pommard Vignots, Musigny*

Domaine Méo-Camuzet

Nicolas Méo could have followed his father into the advertising business, but chose instead to devote himself to the family domaine. Working closely with legendary Burgundian grower Henri Jayer, he soon began producing wines every bit as good as those from better known estates in Vosne-Romanée. These are not wines for the faint-hearted: they are rich and dense, and often remain closed for five years or more. Patience is, however, rewarded with some of the most complex red wines in the whole of Burgundy.

⊗ *11 rue des Grands Crus, Vosne-Romanée* • *03 80 61 11 05* • *www.meo-camuzet.com* 🖻 *red* ★ *Vosne-Romanée Cros Parantoux, Richebourg*

Louis Jadot

Directed for many years by the Gagey family, this famous merchant house consistently produces firm, tannic, long-lived wines from the Côte de Nuits. (It is also well known for its sumptuous whites from the Côte de Beaune.) Jacques Lardière has been the house winemaker for over 30 years, which accounts for the even and consistently high quality of the wines. Even in very difficult vintages such as 1994, Lardière's touch resulted in an impressive range of wines.

⊗ *21 rue Eugène Spuller, Beaune* • *03 80 22 10 57* • *www.louisjadot.com* ☐ *by appt* 🖻 *red, white* ★ *Fixin, Clos de Vougeot, Clos St Denis*

Domaine de la Romanée-Conti

With a production of just 7,500 cases a year, Domaine de la Romanée-Conti's ultra-silky red wines are some of the most sought after in the world. Anyone who has tasted the wines from the 1999, 1996, or 1990 vintages would have to agree that the estate merits its reputation and exorbitant prices. With overall standards of winemaking improving, however, the gap between other Burgundian estates and this one is narrowing all the time.

Its status as Burgundy's greatest wine estate may be open to challenge, but what is beyond doubt is that it boasts the finest collection of vineyards: nothing but grands crus, mostly in Vosne-Romanée, but also a precious parcel in Montrachet. The domaine is run with unobtrusive brilliance by co-owner Aubert de Villaine. The wines here impress with subtlety and elegance rather than with power and tannin. They are rich, even sumptuous, but they are also wonderfully perfumed: initially an amalgam of violets and raspberries, with wet leaves and truffles and many other aromas developing with age.

The Estate
This simple stone gatepost at the Romanée-Conti estate is an understated marker for one of the most famous, and valuable, vineyards in the world.

Contact Information
1 rue Derrière-la-Four, Vosne-Romanée
03 80 62 48 80

Wine Information

red ★ Domaine de la Romanée-Conti: La Tâche, Richebourg, Romanée-Conti, Échézeaux

The Wines
Four of the estate's *grand cru* sites are shared with other growers, but two – La Tâche and Romanée-Conti – are monopolies. There are no direct sales to the public from the vineyards, but Romanée-Conti, by far the estate's most expensive wine, retails in the UK at over £650 per bottle. Of all their wines, only one – Échézeaux – is released at under £100 per bottle.

Burgundy – Côte de Nuits – Producers

View over the village of Vosne-Romanée from the *grand cru* site of La Tâche

 Good recent vintages of Domaine de la Romanée-Conti include 1993, 1995, 1996, 1997, 1999, and 2001

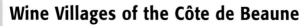

Wine Villages of the Côte de Beaune

Beginning a few miles south of Nuits-St-Georges in the Côte de Nuits *(see p55)*, the vineyards of the Côte de Beaune curve gracefully around the small city of Beaune and continue south into Pommard, Volnay, and Meursault. These are Burgundy's only *grand cru* white vineyards outside Chablis, and the region is as famous for its whites as for its elegant reds. Rising above the town of Aloxe-Corton is the great hill of Corton, with its celebrated Corton-Charlemagne vineyard. South of Beaune, set back from the villages of Puligny-Montrachet and Chassagne-Montrachet, are some other equally famous *grands crus*.

Côte de Beaune reds are quite varied: Pommard tends to be powerful and tannic; Volnay is more graceful. The wines of Chorey-lès-Beaune and Savigny-lès-Beaune are usually medium-bodied and best drunk in the medium term. Wines hailing from villages up on the plateau sell as Hautes Côtes de Beaune, and wines from less prestigious villages such as Ladoix are sometimes labelled Côte de Beaune Villages. 🗻 *limestone* 🍇 *Pinot Noir* 🍇 *Chardonnay* 🍷 *red, white*

Chorey-lès-Beaune, Ladoix & Pernand-Vergelesses

These villages are grouped around the hill of Corton. Chorey-lès-Beaune is on fairly flat land and delivers reds that lack complexity but are enjoyable when drunk young. Ladoix and Pernand-Gergelesses produce whites as well as reds. Very little wine is bottled as Ladoix as there are only about 100ha in production.

Aloxe-Corton

This pretty village has a great sweep of *grands crus*, all known as Corton. Originally planted with red grapes, Corton is today equally known for its magisterial white wine: Corton-Charlemagne. Only Montrachet *(see opposite)* can rival this wine for power and minerality. Reds from Corton can be tough in their youth, but acquire a haunting mellowness as they age.

Beaune & Savigny-lès-Beaune

The vineyards flanking the town of Beaune are relatively obscure, though many have *premier cru* status. Of greater fame is Beaune's annual charity wine auction, hosted by the Hospices de Beaune *(see p69)*. Savigny produces sound,

Parcels of vines owned by various growers in Savigny-lès-Beaune

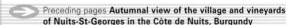
Preceding pages **Autumnal view of the village and vineyards of Nuits-St-Georges in the Côte de Nuits, Burgundy**

Tending grapes on the hill of Corton

moderately priced wine, most of it red. Clos des Mouches is Beaune's most remarkable white. It is worth paying the slight premium for a *premier cru* from these places.

Pommard

Generally, the Côte de Beaune gives lighter wines than the Côte de Nuits, but Pommard is the exception. Its richer soils deliver heady, dark, tannic reds, some of which never lose their initial toughness. The best *premiers crus* are usually Rugiens and Épenots: these often need eight years or more to mature.

Volnay & Monthélie

The hillside village of Volnay is crammed with excellent estates whose wines tend to be perfumed and stylish. The similar wines from neighbouring Monthélie lack the staying power of Volnay, but they are great value at roughly half the price of Volnay.

Auxey-Duresses, St-Romain & St-Aubin

These three villages lie in side valleys traversing the Hautes Côtes de Beaune. Auxey gives robust reds and whites for

medium-term drinking, while St-Romain, at a higher elevation, produces white wine that can be tart in tricky vintages. In general, the whites of St-Aubin are far better than its reds, and offer an inexpensive alternative to wines from the grander villages nearby.

Meursault

This large village is renowned for its sumptuous white wines; great Meursault is not just rich and hedonistic, it is also invigorating. There are some exceptional *premiers crus* such as Les Perrières, and even those without *premier cru* status are often named on labels because they have an individual character.

Puligny-Montrachet & Chassagne-Montrachet

Many of these wonderful *premier* and *grand cru* vineyards adjoin one another, and it is not easy to tell them apart. The wines are the quintessence of great white Burgundy: noble, elegant, and profound. The greatest sites of all, the *grands crus* of Montrachet and Bâtard-Montrachet, are divided between Puligny and Chassagne. The high quality – and scarcity – of these wines mean they sell at a premium, so top *premiers crus* from both villages are better value. Whereas Puligny produces only whites, almost half the production of Chassagne is of red wine.

Santenay & Maranges

Santenay comprises a range of vineyards just west of Chagny, and Maranges is its extension to the south, making it the most southerly vineyard of the Côte de Beaune. At their best, the wines from these sites are rich and fleshy, and, with quality steadily improving, they offer good value as both villages are little known.

Barrels in the cellar of Bouchard Père & Fils

Major Producers in the Côte de Beaune

Bouchard Père & Fils

For decades Bouchard Père et Fils was one of Beaune's most celebrated merchant houses, blessed with a magnificent array of top vineyards. In the 1980s, however, quality slipped and scandals damaged the house's reputation. In 1995 it was bought by Champagne producer Joseph Henriot *(see p132)*, who improved quality across the board and restored Bouchard as one of Burgundy's top *négociants*. ✆ *15 rue du Château, Beaune • 03 80 24 80 24 • www.bouchard-pereetfils.com* ◻ *by appt* 🖼 *red, white* ★ *Beaune Grèves Vigne de l'Enfant Jésus, Chevalier-Montrachet*

VINCENT GASNIER'S
TOP 10 Good Côte de Beaune Labels

1. **Bonneau du Martray** Corton-Charlemagne *right*
2. **Comtes Lafon** Meursault *opposite*
3. **Jean-Marc Pillot** Chassagne-Montrachet *p63*
4. **Jean-Marc Morey** Chassagne-Montrachet *p63*
5. **Comte Armand: Pommard Clos des Épeneaux** *opposite*
6. **Coche-Dury** Meursault *p66*
7. **Leflaive** Puligny-Montrachet *p66*
8. **Sauzet** Puligny-Montrachet *p66*
9. **Jean-Noël Gagnard** Chassagne Montrachet *p63*
10. **Domaine Germain** Meursault & Chassagne-Montrachet *p63*

Château de la Maltroye

The handsome Château de la Maltroye has been owned by Jean-Pierre Cornut since 1992. Its 15-ha property has a fine selection of *premiers crus*, and the wines are aged in one-third new oak in unusually cold medieval cellars. The whites are rich and spicy, and the top *crus* have tremendous power. Some red Chassagne-Montrachet is also made. ✆ *16 rue Murée, Chassagne-Montrachet • 03 80 21 32 45* ◻ *by appt* 🖼 *red, white* ★ *Chassagne-Montrachet: Clos de Château, La Romanée, Dent du Chien*

Domaine Albert Morot

This property was owned and run for years by Françoise Choppin who was succeeded in 2000 by her nephew Geoffroy. All the vineyards are *premier cru*, either in Beaune or Savigny. For a long time these wines were known only to insiders, but that is set to change. Geoffroy has been modernizing the winemaking and introducing more new oak. Quality remains as high as ever, and the style is increasingly sophisticated. ✆ *Ave Charles Jaffelin, Beaune • 03 80 22 35 39* ◻ *by appt* 🖼 *red* ★ *Beaune: Marconnets, Teurons, Bressandes*

Domaine Bonneau du Martray

Jean-Charles Le Bault de la Morinière's 200-year-old family estate produces red Corton and white Corton-Charlemagne. This makes it, together with Domaine de la Romanée-Conti, one of only two Burgundian estates to produce nothing but *grand cru* wines. With 9.5ha in Corton-Charlemagne, it is that *grand cru's* largest producer and best point of reference. The white offers richness, mineral complexity, persistence, and a capacity to age for many years. The reds, as yet, do not scale the same heights. Ⓢ *Pernand-Vergelesses • 03 80 21 50 64* 🏠 *red, white ★ Corton-Charlemagne*

Domaine Chandon de Briailles

Run by a mother-and-daughter team, Chandon de Briailles makes wines with a feminine touch. The whites from Pernand-Vergelesses and Savigny can be exquisite, and the red Savigny Lavières is minerally and elegant. The top wines come from the *grand cru* of Corton, with the emphasis on finesse and subtlety rather than power. Ⓢ *1 rue Soeur Goby, Savigny-lès-Beaune • 03 80 21 52 31* ❑ *by appt* 🏠 *red, white ★ Savigny Lavières, Pernand-Vergelesses Île de Vergelesses, Corton*

Domaine Charles & Rémi Jobard

François Jobard, renowned for his rather austere wines, is better known than his nephew Rémi, but since 1997 Rémi has been making sensational white Burgundies from his vineyards in Meursault. The wines that come out on top are usually Genevrières and Charmes: both *premiers crus*, they are vibrant, juicy and tightly structured. Ⓢ *12 rue Sudot, Meursault • 03 80 21 20 23* ❑ *by appt* 🏠 *white ★ Meursault: Genevrières, Charmes*

Domaine des Comtes Lafon

Some experts consider Dominique Lafon the world's greatest producer of white wine, and it is hard to disagree. Meursault from elsewhere can often be soft and buttery; delicious, maybe, but not intrinsically Burgundian. With its vigour and raciness, and abundant rich, ripe fruit, Lafon's Meursault cannot be mistaken for anything but a Burgundy. He is equally dexterous when it comes to red wine: his Volnay Santenots is one of the finest and best-balanced wines from that village. Ⓢ *5 rue Pierre Joigneaux, Meursault • 03 80 21 22 17* 🏠 *red, white ★ Meursault: Clos de la Barre, Perrières; Volnay Santenots*

Domaine du Château de Chorey

Chorey is usually overlooked because the village lies on the "wrong" (eastern) side of the main road, the N74, away from the prestigious slopes of the Côte d'Or. The Germain family, whose wine formerly sold under the name Germain Père & Fils, is based at the village's château, and makes delicious Chorey for early drinking, and a fine range of oaky Beaune *premiers crus*. Ⓢ *Chorey-lès-Beaune • 03 80 22 06 05 • www.chateau-de-chorey. com* 🏠 *red, white ★ Chorey-lès-Beaune, Beaune: Vignes Franches, Les Cras*

Domaine du Comte Armand

The glory of this Pommard property is its 5-ha Clos des Épeneaux, a top *premier cru* site. It produces one of Burgundy's most powerful and tannic reds, and needs many years to reveal its multi-layered depths. Any wine not considered worthy of the appellation is sold as simple Pommard and can be excellent value. Some less densely concentrated wine from Volnay and Auxey-Duresses is also produced here. In 2003 the estate converted all its vineyards to biodynamism *(see p66)*. Ⓢ *Place de l'Eglise, Pommard • 03 80 24 70 50* ❑ *by appt* 🏠 *red ★ Pommard, Pommard Clos des Épeneaux*

Burgundy – Côte de Beaune – Producers

Biodynamic Viticulture

Traditional French winemakers have always timed their racking and bottling according to lunar phases. In the 1920s philosopher Rudolf Steiner propounded ideas about lunar and cosmic rhythms that form the basis for biodynamic viticulture today – a holistic form of organic farming that utilizes astrology in the timing of soil treatments and winery processes. First adopted in 1980 by Nicolas Joly in the Loire, biodynamism is now used by more than 20 leading estates in Burgundy and the Rhône Valley. While many other estates are sceptical – especially of the homeopathic doses of animal compost, valerian, and boiled horsetail – most growers and buyers do accept that wines from these estates have improved.

Domaine Étienne Sauzet

This estate has produced some of the most consistent wines of Puligny. Winemaker Gérard Boudot likes a good acidity, and so the wines can take a few years to become harmonious. Boudot has a wonderful range of *premiers crus*, as well as old vines in the *grands crus* Bâtard-Montrachet and Chevalier-Montrachet. 🕙 *11 rue de Poiseul, Puligny-Montrachet • 03 80 21 32 10 • www.etienne-sauzet.com* ☐ *by appt* 🍷 *white* ★ *Puligny-Montrachet: Combettes, Champs Canet; Bâtard-Montrachet*

Domaine Françoise & Denis Clair

The Clairs' 11-ha property is divided between Santenay and St-Aubin, and excellent wines are made from both. Typical of his generation of Burgundian growers, Denis both cares for his vines and knows how to handle the grapes once they are brought into the cellars. Emerging from those cellars are succulent reds and

spicy, lightly oaked, and good-value whites. 🕙 *14 rue de la Chapelle, Santenay • 03 80 20 61 96* ☐ *by appt* 🍷 *red, white* ★ *St-Aubin: En Remilly, Murgers des Dents de Chien*

Domaine Jacques Prieur

The 1970s and 80s were a frustrating period for Burgundy aficionados who knew about this domaine. It had sensationally good vineyards (including Montrachet, Musigny, and Chambertin), but made very dull wines. Then in 1990 the Prieur family went into partnership with the *négociant* house of Antonin Rodet *(see p72)* and quality soared. The wines are now dark, rich, and gutsy. 🕙 *6 rue des Santenots, Meursault • 03 80 21 23 85* ☐ *by appt* 🍷 *red, white* ★ *Corton Bressandes, Vosne Clos des Santenots, Le Montrachet*

Domaine Jean-François Coche-Dury

This has been a legendary estate for some years. Owner Jean-François Coche-Dury has vines in many appellations, so quantities of each wine are limited and can be costly. Devotees from all over the world admire the Meursault and powerful Corton-Charlemagne, which benefits from prolonged ageing in oak barrels. 🕙 *9 rue Charles-Giraud, Meursault • 03 80 21 24 12* ● 🍷 *red, white* ★ *Meursault Perrières, Corton-Charlemagne, Volnay Clos des Chênes*

Domaine Leflaive

Vincent Leflaive was the first name to come to mind when speaking of white Burgundy in the 1970s and 80s. In the 1990s the domaine came into the hands of his daughter Anne-Claude, who converted the vineyards to biodynamism *(see above)*. Bottles from the *premiers* and *grands crus* of Puligny-Montrachet are now

66 The 8-ha site of Le Montrachet is the most famous white wine vineyard in the world

among the most profound and concentrated of all white Burgundies. ◈ place des Marronniers, Puligny-Montrachet • 03 80 21 30 13 • www.leflaive.fr ● ▨ white ★ Puligny-Montrachet Les Pucelles, Chevalier-Montrachet

Domaine Marc Colin & Fils

The genial Marc Colin and his three sons produce a range of wines from the underrated village of St-Aubin, as well as a tiny quantity of splendid Le Montrachet. All their St-Aubin vineyards are *premiers crus*, and the best are usually En Remilly and Chatenière. The wines are barrel-fermented and show exuberant fruit and a well-judged use of new oak.
◈ Gamay, St-Aubin • 03 80 21 30 43 ◻ by appt ▨ white ★ St-Aubin: En Remilly, Chatenière; Le Montrachet

Domaine Michel Bouzereau & Fils

Although not as well known as some other Meursault producers, Michel Bouzereau and his son Jean-Baptiste produce impeccable wines both from their *premiers crus* and from their prized village sites such as Tessons and Limozin. The wines have richness and concentration, but also a sleek elegance complemented by skilful use of oak, and a spiciness that keeps them lively on the palate.
◈ 3 rue de la Planche-Meunière, Meursault • 03 80 21 20 74 ◻ by appt ▨ white ★ Meursault: Limozin, Charmes, Genevrières

Domaine Michel Lafarge

For 30 years the quiet Michel Lafarge has been making some of Volnay's most elegant wines, rich in fruit but never dense. His top bottlings are usually from *premiers crus* Clos des Chênes and Clos du Château des Ducs, the latter of which is under Lafarge's sole ownership. By 2001 Michel had handed the reins to his son Frédéric, and the estate had become fully biodynamic. ◈ rue la Combe, Volnay • 03 80 21 61 61 ◻ by appt ▨ red, white ★ Volnay: Vendanges Sélectionées, Clos des Chênes, Clos du Château des Ducs

Domaine Vincent Girardin

From his base in the village of Meursault, Vincent Girardin has created a small but high-quality *négociant* business, supplementing the production of his own 14-ha estate with wines purchased from sites all over the Côte de Beaune. His Santenay reds are rich and supple; the wines from Corton-Charlemagne and Pommard are also impressive. Girardin likes a good deal of new oak, and so, it seems, do his numerous customers. ◈ Les Champs Lins, BP 48, Meursault • 03 80 20 81 00 ◻ ▨ red, white ★ Santenay Gravières, Corton-Charlemagne, Pommard Rugiens

Olivier Leflaive

With Anne-Claude Leflaive running the family domaine, also in Puligny-Montrachet *(see opposite)*, her cousin Olivier has set up this small *négociant* business specializing mostly in white wines, both from Puligny-Montrachet and Meursault, and from lesser-known villages such as St-Aubin and Rully, which offer exceptional value. These are modern-style Burgundies, full in colour, creamy in texture, and accessible young.
◈ place du Monument, Puligny-Montrachet • 03 80 21 37 65 • www.olivier-leflaive.com ◻ by appt ▨ red, white ★ Rully Rabourcé, Puligny-Montrachet Les Folatières, Bienvenues Bâtard-Montrachet

Domaine Michel Lafarge

Producers who own vines at Le Montrachet include Romanée-Conti, Lafon, Drouhin, Jacques Prieur and the two Leflaives

A Wine Tour of Burgundy

Burgundy is a fascinating region that offers the visitor a beguiling combination of scenic beauty and attractions ranging from wine-tasting and other forms of gastronomy to magnificent medieval architecture. The prettiest part of the area lies in the south, among the rolling hills of the Côte Chalonnaise and the Mâconnais. Small villages such as St-Aubin and Chambolle-Musigny, which lie tucked among their vineyards in the Côte de Beaune and Côte de Nuits, are also full of charm.

1 Dijon

Dijon was the ancient capital of the powerful dukes of Burgundy, who took a keen interest in the region's wine. In 1385 they forbade the planting of the Gamay grape in Burgundy's vineyards, as they considered it inferior. Their former palace, which is now crammed with the fine collections of the Beaux-Arts Museum, is open to visitors.

2 Route des Grands Crus

This narrow road follows the mid-slope from Gevrey-Chambertin southwards to Morey-St-Denis *(right)*, passing through the most famous *grands crus* of northern Burgundy, including Le Chambertin.

Visitors' Tips

Route: *This 150km-tour begins in the north at Dijon and ends at the Duboeuf wine museum at Hameau en Beaujolais just to the north of Villefranche-sur-Saône. A motorway runs parallel to the Route Nationale.*
Duration: *A full day.*
Wineries: *In Beaune and Nuits-St-Georges, many négociant houses welcome visitors, but private wine estates are rarely open without an appointment.*
Château du Clos de Vougeot: *03 80 62 86 09 • www.closdevougeot. com*
Hameau en Beaujolais: *Romanèche-Thorins • 03 85 35 22 22 • www.hameauen beaujolais.com*
Restaurant-Hotel: *36 Place d'Armes, Chagny-en-Bourgogne • 03 85 87 65 65 • www.lameloise.fr*

3 Château du Clos de Vougeot

Visit the medieval Château du Clos de Vougeot *(above)* where Burgundian growers traditionally hold their ceremonies and banquets.

4 Citeaux

The famous Abbaye Nôtre-Dame de Citeaux is where the Cistercian order of monks was founded in 1098. In medieval times the monks controlled most of Burgundy's finest vineyards. Only vestiges of the medieval abbey remain, but the interior can be visited.

N81

AUT

D906

D80

LE CREUSOT

Arroux

MONTCEAU
LES-MINE

N70

Arconce

Charolles

Loire

N7

0 ⊢ km ⊣ 25

Key

▬ Tour route

5 Beaune

An enchanting walled town, Beaune is crammed with churches, wine shops, restaurants, and tranquil squares. The unmissable sight is the Hôtel-Dieu *(left)* with its strikingly patterned roof of colourful tiles. Also worth a visit are some of the local wine merchants such as Patriarche.

6 Le Montrachet

From Beaune, take the Chagny road, which passes alongside Puligny-Montrachet *(see p63)*. Behind the village lies the world's most famous white wine vineyard, Le Montrachet, identifiable from its stone gateposts.

7 Côte Chalonnaise Villages

Notable AOC villages of the Côte Chalonnaise include Mercurey, Rully, and Givry. Many producers here welcome visitors who make an appointment.

8 Tournus

The main reason to visit this pretty little town is to tour the remarkable Romanesque abbey. Tournus is also a famous gastronomic centre, and an excellent base for visiting the villages and vineyards of the Mâconnais.

9 Mâconnais

The Mâconnais district includes the Pouilly-Fuissé appellation and is known for its fruity Chardonnays.

10 Hameau en Beaujolais

Located on the edge of the Beaujolais in the village of Romanèche-Thorins is the HQ of famous wine producer Duboeuf *(see p77)*. He has created a splendid wine museum here, with well-presented exhibits relating to the history of wine and its production process, plus the opportunity to purchase the entire range of Duboeuf wines.

The Hospices de Beaune

Founded in 1443, Beaune's magnificent Hôtel-Dieu is home to the Hospices de Beaune, which owns 58ha of vineyards. The charitable activities of the hospice are financed by the proceeds from wines made by the hospice. The charity auction takes place in November and is attended by wine lovers from around the world. After the sale, the oak barrels are taken to cellars, where the wine is aged until it is ready for resale. The auction prices are closely monitored as a guide to market trends for the new vintage.

Map labels:
CÔTE D'OR
DIJON
Sombernon
A38
Gevrey-Chambertin
Morey-St-Denis
CÔTE DE NUITS
Nuits-St-Georges
Vougeot
Ouche
A36
Puligny-Montrachet
BEAUNE
CÔTE DE BEAUNE
Chagny
Doubs
Chalon-sur-Saône
CÔTE CHALONNAISE
Tournus
SAÔNE ET LOIRE
MÂCONNAIS
A40
MÂCON
Romanèche-Thorins
BEAUJOLAIS
Villefranche-sur-Saône
LYON
D518

Wine label:
GEORGES DUBŒUF
FLEURIE
APPELLATION FLEURIE CONTRÔLÉE
MIS EN BOUTEILLE PAR
LES VINS GEORGES DUBŒUF
71570 ROMANÈCHE-THORINS
FRANCE
PRODUCE OF FRANCE

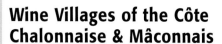

Burgundy – Côte Chalonnaise & Mâconnais

Wine Villages of the Côte Chalonnaise & Mâconnais

CÔTE CHALONNAISE

The landscape of the Côte Chalonnaise is markedly different to that of the Côte d'Or to the north. Amid gently rolling hills, viticulture here shares the land with other forms of farming. Until recently the district had a reputation for rusticity, but quality-conscious *négociants* and a handful of excellent growers have raised standards considerably, and today the Côte Chalonnaise offers both good quality and good value. In addition to the basic Côte Chalonnaise appellation, there are the following AOCs. 🎞 *limestone* 🦋 *Pinot Noir* 🍇 *Chardonnay* 🍷 *red, white*

Bouzeron

A tiny commune of only about 60ha, Bouzeron is best known for its acidic white grape variety, Aligoté *(see box)*. In 1997, the village was bestowed with its own appellation, promoted from Aligoté de Bouzeron to simple Bouzeron.

Rully

This village is dominated by its splendid château, and its 300ha of vineyards are divided almost equally between Pinot Noir and Chardonnay. Much of the wine is produced by *négociant* houses such as Antonin Rodet, Domaine Drouhin, and Olivier Leflaive, but private estates are beginning to produce excellent wines too. The *premiers crus* (both red and white) from growers such as Domaine Henri & Paul Jacqueson, are fruity, succulent, and excellent value.

Mercurey

Of around 600ha in cultivation, about one third of Mercurey's vineyards enjoy *premier cru* status. The wines – of which 90 per cent are red – used to be rather coarse, but the ambition of local growers such as Michel Juillot and *négociants* such as Domaine Faiveley has led to a marked improvement. White wines here are getting better, but Mercurey's strength lies in robust, fruity reds.

Givry

The quiet village of Givry is the smallest of the area's AOCs. The efforts of a handful of ambitious and enthusiastic local growers, such as Domaine François Lumpp, Michel Sarrazin, and Parizé & Fils, are showing that Givry is capable of producing supple Pinots and attractively aromatic Chardonnay (although only 10 per cent of its production is white).

Montagny

The southernmost village in the Côte Chalonnaise, Montagny produces only white wine. Its vineyards are

Handling Chardonnay grapes at the Buxy co-op in Montagny

Cliffside vineyard in Pouilly-Fuissé

all designated *premier cru*, but the wine is often dull. Much of it is produced by a sound co-operative in Buxy, but the best examples come from *négociants* such as Olivier Leflaive and Chartron & Trébuchet.

MÂCONNAIS

The strength of this large district lies in its fruity whites made from Chardonnay; the reds, usually from Gamay, are invariably inferior. Basic wines are sold as Mâcon or Mâcon Supérieur; of much greater character are the Mâcon-Villages, the *villages* often being replaced on the label by the name of one of the 43 villages entitled to the appellation. The top wines of Pouilly-Fuissé and nearby villages are characteristically broad, quite high in alcohol, and fleshy in texture. Although very different in style, they can rival some of the best from Chablis and the Côte de Beaune. The following are the main AOCs. 🗻 *limestone* 🍇 *Gamay* 🍇 *Chardonnay* 🍷 *red, white*

Viré-Clessé

This new AOC, created in 1999, replaced the two Mâcon-Villages appellations of Mâcon-Viré and Mâcon-Clessé. Around 400ha are in production and there are many good growers.

Pouilly-Fuissé

This is by far the best-known appellation within the Mâconnais, and with good reason, as its 850ha produce some of the area's most exciting wine. The vineyards lie beneath impressive cliffs, which help trap heat and project it onto the vines. The Chardonnay grown on these limestone soils tends to be rich and fat, and vinification varies from unoaked (for clean fruity wines) to heavily new-oaked *cuvées*, which, in the hands of good winemakers, can be sumptuous and opulent.

Pouilly-Vinzelles & Pouilly-Loché

These lesser appellations lie on the eastern fringes of Pouilly-Fuissé. Pouilly-Loché is often (legally) labelled as Pouilly-Vinzelles. Local co-operatives dominate production, which is limited to just 81ha in the two districts.

St-Véran

This 500-ha appellation unites the wine of seven communes, and before 1971, when the AOC was created, it was usually sold as Beaujolais blanc. The wines of St-Véran are fresh and attractive, and can be good value.

The Case for Aligoté

Few wine lovers have a good word to say about Aligoté, other than as an essential ingredient in Kir, in which its asperity is softened by cassis liqueur. However, Aubert de Villaine – co-owner of Domaine de la Romanée-Conti *(see p59)* – was quick to recognize the grape's potential when he bought a property here in the 1970s. Aubert helped establish Bouzeron's AOC and a better reputation for Aligoté, which, when fully ripe, is delicious and a refreshing alternative to the ubiquitous Chardonnay in Burgundy.

Co-operatives make most of the wine from the Mâconnais. Some are well equipped and produce wine to a good standard

71

Left **Château de Rully in the Côte Chalonnaise** Right **Château de Fuissé**

Major Producers in the Côte Chalonnaise & Mâconnais

Antonin Rodet
Côte Chalonnaise
Rodet is a well-run *négociant*, with 160ha in various parts of Burgundy. The company owns the Château de Mercey, which produces Mercurey and generic Burgundy, and leases the Château de Rully in Rully and Château Chamirey in Mercurey. In good vintages Rodet's wines can be sensational and represent excellent value.
🌐 *Mercurey • 03 85 98 12 12 • www. rodet.com* ⬜ 🔲 *red, white* ★ *Rully Blanc (Château de Rully), Mercurey (Château Chamirey), Mercurey (Château de Mercey)*

Domaine du Clos Salomon
Côte Chalonnaise
Clos Salomon was once the most highly esteemed vineyard in Givry, but over time its wines became less impressive. However, Ludovic du Gardin and his brother have made enormous efforts to raise standards and are now successfully

producing robust wines aged in around 20 per cent new oak to allow the richness of fruit to shine.
🌐 *Givry • 03 85 44 32 24* ⬜ 🔲 *red*
★ *Givry Clos Salomon*

Domaine Faiveley
Côte Chalonnaise
This major *négociant* has well-sited vineyards throughout Burgundy, including six in Mercurey. La Framboisière and Les Mauvarennes are intended for early drinking when their charm and fruit are most apparent, while their most serious wine, partly aged in new oak, is Clos du Roi. 🌐 *8 rue de Tribourg, Nuits-St-Georges, Mercurey • 03 85 61 04 55 • www.bourgognes-faiveley.com* ⬛ 🔲 *red, white* ★ *Mercurey: La Framboisière, Clos du Roi*

Domaine François Lumpp
Côte Chalonnaise
François Lumpp's wines respect the character of the Givry fruit, which is delicate rather than rich. This gives his whites an attractive herbal quality, and his reds a raspberry-scented fragrance. The best *cru* for red wine is usually Crausot, which has both freshness and concentration.
🌐 *36 ave de Mortières, Givry • 03 85 44 45 57 • www. francoislumpp.com* ⬜ *by appt* 🔲 *red, white* ★ *Givry: Crausot, Petit Marole*

VINCENT GASNIER'S TOP 10 Best Côte Chalonnaise & Mâconnais Labels

1. **Michel Juillot: Clos des Barraults** *opposite*
2. **Bongran: Cuvée Tradition** *opposite*
3. **Ferret: Les Ménétrières** *opposite*
4. **Faiveley: Clos du Roi** *above*
5. **Jacqueson: Grésigny** (white) *opposite*
6. **J M Boillot** Rully *p70*
7. **Fuissé: Cuvée Vieilles Vignes** *opposite*
8. **François Lumpp: Crausot** *above*
9. **Guffens-Heynen: Pierreclos** *opposite*
10. **Domaine Thibert** Pouilly-Fuissé *p71*

Domaine Henri & Paul Jacqueson
Côte Chalonnaise

Henri and his son Paul are regarded by many as the best producers in Rully. They have vines in some good *premiers crus*: Les Pucelles and Grésigny for whites, and Les Cloux and Chaponnière for reds. Although Jacqueson is best known for its rich spicy whites, the red Les Cloux can be outstanding.
⊗ *5 rue de Chèvremont, Rully*
• *03 85 91 25 91* ☐ *by appt* ▨ *red, white* ★ *Rully: Grésigny, Les Cloux*

Domaine Michel Juillot
Côte Chalonnaise

Michel Juillot was the first locally based producer to put Mercurey on the map. Today the 27-ha domaine is run by his son Laurent, with prized sites at Champs Martin, Clos de Tonnerre, and Clos des Barraults. Juillot's reds are fantastic, with red-fruit perfume and a sturdiness that is never rustic.
⊗ *59 Grande rue, Mercurey* • *03 85 98 99 89* • *www.domaine-michel-juillot.fr* ☐ ▨ *red, white* ★ *Mercurey: Champs Martin, Clos des Barraults*

Château de Fuissé
Mâconnais

For decades this property, owned by Jean-Jacques Vincent, set the pace for winemaking in Pouilly-Fuissé. Different parcels of vines are handled separately, and new oak is used sparingly, resulting in flavourful, good-structured wines that age well. The best known is Cuvée Vieilles Vignes. ⊗ *Fuissé* • *03 85 35 61 44* • *www.chateau-fuisse.fr* ☐ ▨ *white* ★ *Pouilly-Fuissé: Cuvée Vieilles Vignes, Le Clos*

Domaine de la Bongran
Mâconnais

The mischievous Jean Thévenet sees his methods as traditional. Yields are much lower than the

Sweet Chardonnay

Chardonnay is always dry, right? Not when Jean Thévenet of Domaine de la Bongran has a hand in it. Thévenet's vineyards sometimes attract botrytis, and in 1983 he decided to allow it to run riot. By selecting only those grapes that had been affected by botrytis, he produced a rich, honeyed wine, which attracted attention worldwide. Ever since, Thévenet has continued to make this wine whenever climatic conditions permit.

official maximum, and he picks late. Consequently, the wines are enormously rich, often with a high percentage of alcohol. ⊗ *Quintaine, rue Gillet, Clessé* • *03 85 36 94 03* • *www.bongran.com* ☐ *by appt* ▨ *white* ★ *Cuvée Tradition, Cuvée Botrytis*

Domaine Guffens-Heynen
Mâconnais

As well as running the *négociant* house Verget, Belgian-born Jean-Marie Guffens-Heynen also has vines in Mâcon Pierreclos and Pouilly-Fuissé. These are tended by his wife, while he takes care of the winemaking. The wines are exceptionally rich and profound.
⊗ *Vergisson* • *03 85 35 84 22* ☐ *by appt* ▨ *white* ★ *Mâcon Pierreclos, Mâcon Pierreclos en Chavigne*

Domaine J A Ferret
Mâconnais

One of the strengths of this 15-ha property is that most of its vines are at least 30 years old. All the grapes are picked by hand and mostly fermented in *barrique*. Some parcels of vines are vinified and marketed separately, and the star turn, Les Ménétrières, is aged in new oak and exceptionally rich.
⊗ *Le Plan, Fuissé* • *03 85 35 61 56* ☐ *by appt* ▨ *white* ★ *Pouilly-Fuissé: Le Clos, Les Ménétrières*

Burgundy – Côte Chalonnaise & Mâconnais – Producers

Good vintages in the Mâconnais have included 1996, 1997, 1999, 2000, 2002, and 2004

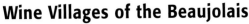

Burgundy – Beaujolais (side tab)

Wine Villages of the Beaujolais

The southern district of Burgundy is a large and exceptionally pretty area, with small villages and slopes planted almost exclusively with Gamay vines. It is often regarded as distinct from the rest of Burgundy in wine terms because its soil and grape variety, and therefore its wines, are markedly different in style from those found elsewhere in the region.

Beaujolais made its reputation decades ago as a popular quaffing wine in the bistros of Paris and Lyon. Endlessly enjoyable and with no pretensions, it is all freshness and vivid, zesty fruit – a style that has been taken to a profitable extreme with Beaujolais Nouveau. Like some more "serious" Beaujolais, this is made by a method known as carbonic maceration, which involves fermenting whole bunches of grapes under a protective layer of gas. The process emphasizes bright fruitiness at the expense of structure. At the same time, certain producers continue to vinify and age their wines in a traditional Burgundian fashion, aiming to create something more serious and age-worthy.

It seems that Beaujolais may have lost its way in recent years: in addition to the clusters of small family domaines – some excellent, others mediocre – it is dominated by co-operatives and merchants, some of whom have dragged down the quality of the wine. Markets have been shrinking, and in 2002 the region saw part of its crop sent for distillation for lack of customers. Yet Beaujolais at its best is a unique wine that, if well made and well priced, will always find an enthusiastic following.

The basic appellation is AOC Beaujolais, of which on average some 80 million bottles are produced annually; a step up is AOC Beaujolais Villages, of which 45 million bottles are released. The rest of the production, around 48 million bottles, carries the AOCs of the 10 *crus* entitled to their own appellation, each with its own character. These *crus (below)* all lie in the granitic north of the region.
🗻 granite 🍇 Gamay 🍷 red

Juliénas
This is not usually one of the most immediately appealing of *crus*, as its 560ha give wines that are very high in tannins and acidity. On the other hand, it ages quite well, developing spiciness as it matures. In vintages where acidity levels are low, Juliénas shows a welcome vigour.

St-Amour
The most northerly *cru*, St-Amour fetches a premium thanks to its romantic name. It can indeed be a charming wine, offering a

Gamay grapes ripening by a windmill at Moulin-à-Vent

mouthful of sweet, ripe fruit. However, it has less personality than some other Beaujolais *crus*.

Chénas
Granitic subsoils beneath this village yield wines with more ageing potential than many other Beaujolais *crus*. The wines are less overtly fruity and quaffable, but have weight and density, which give them added complexity.

Moulin-à-Vent
This 640-ha appellation is the most serious of the Beaujolais *crus*. It produces wines that do not really conform to the stereotype of juicy purple wines to be knocked back with abandon. Its character derives from manganese in the soil. It also tends to be aged longer, and with a higher proportion of oak barrels than the other *crus*. It can keep well, and after 10 years or so comes to resemble Pinot Noir. Some wines from this *cru* can be slightly too serious and extracted, giving less pleasure than simpler, fruitier examples.

Fleurie
The Fleurie appellation is one of the most fragrant and elegant wines of Beaujolais. This, combined with its charming name, has made Fleurie one of the most expensive wines of the district, even though there is plenty of it to go round, with over 800ha in production. Fortunately there are fair number of reliable producers.

Chiroubles
With its 300ha of vineyards located on some of the highest spots in the region, Chiroubles produces wine that is relatively light, though none the worse for that. It is best enjoyed young when its fruit is at its most vivid.

The Nouveau Phenomenon

Beaujolais Nouveau is Beaujolais that has been vinified and bottled as fast as possible – within a few weeks of harvesting – to ensure the wine is bursting with youthful fruitiness. An excess of mediocre Nouveau has led to declining interest in the wine, but it can be delicious. The process begins with a few days of carbonic maceration, then the Gamay grapes are pressed and fermentation is finished in a vat, without grape skins to minimize astringency. The technique emphasizes colour and fruitiness, and keeps tannin to a minimum.

Morgon
With over 1,000ha under vine, Morgon is an important *cru*, as well as one of the most distinctive, thanks to the schist and granite in the soil. It is not always the most appealing of wines when very young, but can age well. Beaujolais fanciers look out for wines from the sub-district called the Côte du Py, where Morgon's best fruit is grown.

Régnié
The most recent village to be promoted to *cru* status, Régnié became an AOC in 1988. With 640ha in the appellation, the wine should be more in evidence. However, it has been slow to catch on, and a good deal of it is bottled as simple Beaujolais Villages.

Brouilly & Côte de Brouilly
These are the most southerly *crus* of Beaujolais. Brouilly is quite a large village, with 1,200ha under vine; Côte de Brouilly, with just 300ha, is usually of slightly superior quality, since the vines are planted on slopes. Both wines often have an abundance of fruit and can be drunk with pleasure relatively young.

Left **Harvesting Gamay grapes** Right **Maison Mommessin label**

Major Producers in the Beaujolais

Château des Jacques
In 1996 Louis Jadot *(see p58)* acquired this Moulin-à-Vent property and imposed a Burgundian style of vinification, with no carbonic maceration and discreet use of new-oak ageing. The 27-ha estate is divided into various sectors, which are vinified separately, and sometimes bottled, separately to demonstrate the varied styles and flavours of which Beaujolais is capable. ◈ *Romanèche-Thorins* • 03 85 35 51 64 • www.louis-jadot.com ◘ by appt ▣ red ★ *Moulin-à-Vent: Roche, Clos du Grand Carquelin*

Domaine Calot
Jean Calot is one of a growing number of Beaujolais winemakers who no longer use carbonic

maceration. He wants instead to highlight the depth of fruit from his 10ha. His vines' average age is 40 years, and there are even some centenarians. The latter are the source of his blackberry-scented Morgon Cuvée Vieilles Vignes. ◈ *Villié-Morgon* • 04 74 04 20 55 ◘ ▣ red ★ *Morgon: Cuvée Vieilles Vignes, Cuvée Jeanne*

Domaine de la Madone
La Madone is one of a handful of good producers in Fleurie. Fleurie should be floral and charming, and Jean-Marc Desprès makes wines that are very true to type. The regular bottling is simple and straightforward; the Cuvée Vieilles Vignes is more concentrated. ◈ *La Madone, Fleurie* • 04 74 69 81 51 ◘ ▣ red ★ *Fleurie, Fleurie Vieilles Vignes*

Domaine des Terres Dorées
Jean-Paul Brun is the region's most individual producer. In a Burgundian fashion, he opts for natural yeasts and a long period of fermentation. Appropriately, he calls this wine Cuvée à l'Ancienne. Brun does not confine himself to Gamay; he produces Chardonnay, both oaked and unoaked, as well as rich, late-harvest wines. ◈ *Crière, Charnay* • 04 78 47 93 45 ◘ by appt ▣ red, white ★ *Cuvée à l'Ancienne, Moulin-à-Vent*

Domaine Émile Cheysson
The 26ha of vineyards here are dispersed among various sectors of Chiroubles. The wines can be muted when young, but reveal

violet scents and especially silky textures if kept for a year or two.
🜲 Chiroubles • 04 74 04 22 02 • vins-du-beaujolais.com/chiroublescheysson ⬚ 🔳 red ★ Chiroubles: Traditionnelle, Cuvée Prestige

Domaine Louis-Claude Desvignes

Louis-Claude Desvignes likes to harvest as late as possible for maximum ripeness, and then give the wine a long fermentation to extract colour and richness. Although these wines can be drunk young, they are among the few that benefit from two or three years in bottle. 🜲 135 rue de la Voute, Villié-Morgon • 04 74 04 23 35 ⬚ by appt 🔳 red ★ Morgon: Javernières, Côte du Py

Duboeuf

Over 50 years ago Georges Duboeuf began his career by peddling his wines to local restaurants. Before long he was established as a major négociant, working closely with 400 growers and 15 co-operatives, producing three million cases per year. Duboeuf has remained firmly planted on Beaujolais soil and still tastes for three hours daily with his son Franck to select wines for his reliable range. 🜲 BP12, Romanèche-Thorins • 03 85 35 34 20 • www.duboeuf.com ⬚ 🔳 red, white ★ Fleurie, Morgon, Moulin-à-Vent Prestige

Jean-Marc Burgaud

Along with a few other growers, Jean-Marc Burgaud has moved towards a more substantial and subtle form of Beaujolais that nevertheless retains its fruity charm. The Morgon Les Charmes is light and fresh, and the more serious wine, aged for 12 months in oak casks, comes from the renowned Côte du Py.
🜲 Villié-Morgon • 04 74 69 16 10

A Return to Tradition

By the early 21st century, Beaujolais was in crisis. Although its top wines were highly prized, run-of-the-mill Beaujolais was failing to attract buyers. The solution, many traditionalists argued, was to revert to more authentic forms of production with less reliance on high yields, chaptalization, and carbonic maceration. Today, conscientious Beaujolais producers are returning to less hurried practices, working with lower yields, selecting with care in the vineyard, and ageing in old oak barrels to give more harmony and depth to their wines.

• www.jean-marc-burgaud.com ⬚ by appt 🔳 red ★ Morgon: Côte du Py, Vieilles Vignes ⬚ by appt

Maison Mommessin

Founded in 1865, this is a high-quality négociant that blends and sells wines from all the Beaujolais crus. The basic bottlings are of sound quality, but there is a major step up to single-vineyard cuvées such as the Moulin-à-Vent Réserve. 🜲 Pont des Samsons, Quincié-en-Beaujolais • 04 74 69 09 30 • www.mommessin.com ● 🔳 red ★ Brouilly, Fleurie, Moulin-à-Vent Réserve

Paul Janin et Fils

This is a very traditional 12-ha domaine that, unusually for Beaujolais, is partly cultivated biodynamically (see p66). Janin vinifies and ages numerous parcels separately before blending them. These are certainly complex wines, with aromas of cherry and liquorice, and the estate's top wine is usually the Moulin-à-Vent Clos du Tremblay, made from its oldest vines. 🜲 Romanèche-Thorins • 03 85 35 52 80 ⬚ by appt 🔳 red ★ Beaujolais-Villages, Moulin-à-Vent Clos du Tremblay

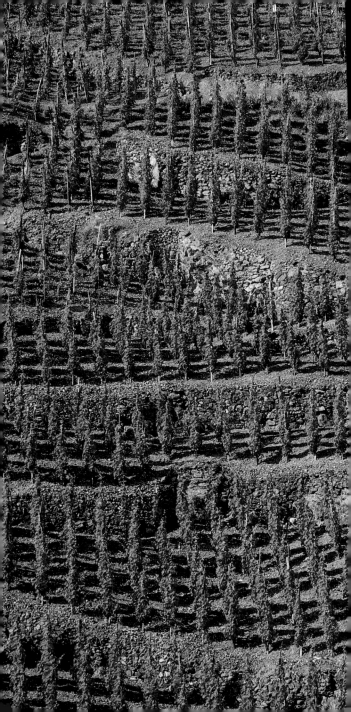

RHÔNE VALLEY

RHÔNE VALLEY

THIS IS A REGION OF EXTREME CONTRASTS. *The north is cool, discreet, noble, and expressed in different shades of just one red grape, Syrah; the south is warm, exuberant, heartily earthy, with wines from myriad grape varieties. The unifying factors are the Rhône River and the enduring appeal of all its wines, many produced under the umbrella AOC Côtes du Rhône.*

The Northern Rhône

As the Rhône flows south from Lyon, it passes through a landscape of high, rocky hills, a mass of granite, schist, and gneiss, with vineyards clinging to the sides. The slope and erosion here necessitate dry-stone terraces and wooden stakes for trellising, and on this patchwork landscape just one red grape variety, Syrah, is allowed expression in five different vineyard areas or *crus*: Côte Rôtie, Hermitage, Cornas, St-Joseph, and Crozes-Hermitage. The tiny volume of white is produced from fragrant Viognier and subtle Marsanne and Roussanne.

Key

■ The Rhône Valley

In the 1960s Côte Rôtie, Hermitage, Cornas, and the Viognier-made white wine appellations Condrieu and Château Grillet were threatened with extinction through lack of interest and investment. They survived, regaining lustre and prestige as their true quality was recognized, but production remains tiny.

The Southern Rhône

In the southern part of the region the Rhône Valley opens out into a broad panorama of river plain, rocky *garrigue*, oak and olive trees, and bush-grown vines offset by mountains. Over 90 per cent of the Rhône's 80,000ha is cultivated here. Estates are larger than in the north, and as well as Syrah, the south is free to grow Grenache, Mourvèdre, and other red grapes.

Châteauneuf-du-Pape, with its warm, generous, mostly red wines, is the largest and most famous *cru*. The other major regions for red wine are Gigondas and Vacqueyras; rosé region Tavel and tri-coloured Lirac complete the list of *crus*. The bulk of production, though, comes in the form of Côtes du Rhône and Côtes du Rhône Villages, and "younger" districts like Côtes du Ventoux.

Côtes du Rhône

Côtes du Rhône, a name often used to refer to the whole Rhône Valley, is also the label given to a broad base of generic wines. AOC Côtes du Rhône accounts for over

The chapel that gives its name to Paul Jaboulet's Hermitage vineyard, la Chapelle

 Preceding pages **Individually staked Syrah vines on the steep terraces of the Côte Blonde, Ampuis, Côte Rôtie**

View across the Rhône to vineyards on the hill of Hermitage

40,000ha of vines and nearly two million hectolitres of wine in an average year, most of it red. The appellation extends to parts of the Northern Rhône, but the south has the lion's share. Over such a large area there are naturally great variations in style, from light and fruity to richer, fuller wines with lovely dark fruit character. Price is often the best indicator of quality. Grenache is the principal red variety and, in accordance with AOC rules, represents 40 per cent of the total plantings. Other red varieties include Syrah, Mourvèdre, Cinsaut, and Carignan, while whites are produced from Grenache Blanc, Clairette, Bourboulenc, Marsanne, and Viognier. Co-operatives account for around 70 per cent of production.

Côtes du Rhône Villages is a step up from generic Côtes du Rhône, implying limestone-and-clay or stony soils, stricter rules of production, and wines of greater depth. The percentage of Grenache, Syrah, and Mourvèdre in the blend is higher, and permitted yields lower. The *villages* appellation covers 96 Southern Rhône communes, of which 16 are allowed to print their village names on the labels. Côtes du Rhône Villages is almost always red; the one per cent of white is soft, round, and floral for early drinking. The village of Rasteau also makes a sweet, fortified *vin doux naturel (see p102)* from Grenache, as does Beaumes-de-Venise from Muscat.

VINCENT GASNIER'S TOP 10 Finest French Reds

1. **Côte Rôtie** Northern Rhône *p84*
2. **Châteauneuf-du-Pape** Southern Rhône *p88*
3. **Hermitage** Northern Rhône *p85*
4. **Vosne-Romanée** Côte de Nuits, Burgundy *p55*
5. **Gevrey-Chambertin** Côte de Nuits, Burgundy *p54*
6. **St-Émilion** Bordeaux Right Bank *p32*
7. **Margaux** Bordeaux Left Bank *p23*
8. **Pauillac** Bordeaux Left Bank *p22*
9. **Pessac-Léognan** Bordeaux Left Bank *p24*
10. **Chambolle-Musigny** Côte de Nuits, Burgundy *p55*

Wine Map of the Rhône Valley

The vineyards of the Northern Rhône follow the course of the river south from Vienne to Valence – Côte Rôtie, Condrieu, Château Grillet, St-Joseph, Cornas, and St-Péray on the left bank, with Hermitage and Crozes-Hermitage on the right. A distance of approximately 100km separates these Northern Rhône AOCs from the main southern group of Châteauneuf-du-Pape, Gigondas, Vacqueyras, Lirac, and Tavel situated just north of Avignon.

View across the Rhône to Tain l'Hermitage with Hermitage vineyards on the hill beyond

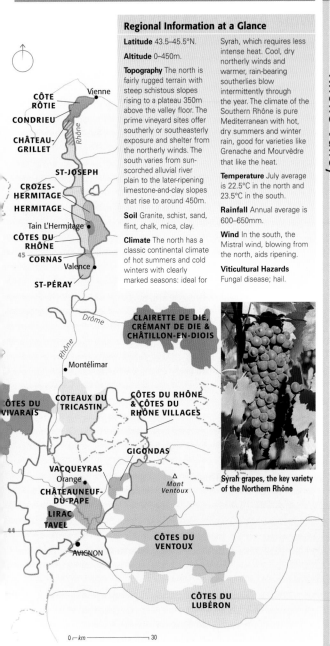

Regional Information at a Glance

Latitude 43.5–45.5°N.

Altitude 0–450m.

Topography The north is fairly rugged terrain with steep schistous slopes rising to a plateau 350m above the valley floor. The prime vineyard sites offer southerly or southeasterly exposure and shelter from the northerly winds. The south varies from sun-scorched alluvial river plain to the later-ripening limestone-and-clay slopes that rise to around 450m.

Soil Granite, schist, sand, flint, chalk, mica, clay.

Climate The north has a classic continental climate of hot summers and cold winters with clearly marked seasons: ideal for Syrah, which requires less intense heat. Cool, dry northerly winds and warmer, rain-bearing southerlies blow intermittently through the year. The climate of the Southern Rhône is pure Mediterranean with hot, dry summers and winter rain, good for varieties like Grenache and Mourvèdre that like the heat.

Temperature July average is 22.5°C in the north and 23.5°C in the south.

Rainfall Annual average is 600–650mm.

Wind In the south, the Mistral wind, blowing from the north, aids ripening.

Viticultural Hazards Fungal disease; hail.

Syrah grapes, the key variety of the Northern Rhône

CÔTE RÔTIE · CONDRIEU · CHÂTEAU-GRILLET · ST-JOSEPH · CROZES-HERMITAGE · HERMITAGE · CÔTES DU RHÔNE · CORNAS · ST-PÉRAY · Vienne · Tain L'Hermitage · Valence

CLAIRETTE DE DIE, CRÉMANT DE DIE & CHÂTILLON-EN-DIOIS · Montélimar · CÔTES DU VIVARAIS · COTEAUX DU TRICASTIN · CÔTES DU RHÔNE & CÔTES DU RHÔNE VILLAGES · GIGONDAS · VACQUEYRAS · Orange · CHÂTEAUNEUF-DU-PAPE · LIRAC · TAVEL · AVIGNON · Mont Ventoux · CÔTES DU VENTOUX · CÔTES DU LUBÉRON

0 — km — 30

Wine Areas of the Rhône Valley

Côte Rôtie

The hillsides of Côte Rôtie AOC, or the "roasted slope", are an imposing sight – stairways of narrow terraced vineyards rising at vertiginous angles from the river below. These are the most northerly vineyards in the Rhône, strung along 8km of the right bank of the river. Economic constraints and the physical difficulties of working the vineyards nearly led to their abandonment in the 1960s, but a revival of interest from a younger generation led to renewed planting. There are now 200ha under vine, producing just over a million bottles a year of this fabulous red wine. Deeply coloured, it has an exuberant aroma of dark fruits, violet, and spice, intensity of flavour, velvety texture, and lithe, rather than heavy, form. Although appealing when young, it also has the ability to age. All this is down to Syrah, grown on heat-retaining schistous soils at the limits of a continental climate. Up to 20 per cent of white Viognier can officially be blended with Syrah in this appellation, but it rarely is.

Côte Rôtie is divided into two parts. South of the town of Ampuis, the silica-limestone soils of the Côte Blonde produce wines of great elegance, while to the north in the Côte Brune, which has darker, ferruginous clay soils, the emphasis is on structure. Seventy-two specific vineyard sites have been officially designated within these zones, leading to a trend for single-vineyard bottlings that sell at a premium. The bulk of Côte Rôtie, however, is from vineyards owned in small parcels by 100 or so growers who either bottle their own wine or sell to a major *négociant*. 🗻 *schist, gneiss, limestone, clay* 🍇 *Syrah* 🍇 *Viognier* 🍷 *red*

Condrieu

Condrieu AOC has a similar aspect and history to neighbouring Côte Rôtie: steep slopes running to the river's edge, terraced vineyards, and a revival from virtual demise in the late 1970s. The big difference is that it is white wine that is made here, from Viognier. This variety has been grown in the region for centuries and seems to favour the continental climate and sandy, granite slopes to produce one of the world's most original wines. Unctuous and heady, the aromatic spectrum hovers around a mix of apricot, peach, pear, and rose water for dry Condrieu, and candied citrus flavours for the rarer, sweeter wines. The volume and texture on the palate is provided by an imposing level of alcohol and low acidity. These sought-after whites are best drunk young at two to three years. The problem is that Viognier in these climes is also a fickle variety, prone to difficult fruit set and with a history of low levels of production. This means that with only 100ha under vine, Condrieu is a rare wine and the price is consequently high. Of the 100 or so growers in the district, 30 make and bottle their own wines, the rest sell to the region's *négocians*. E Guigal is the most important of these, accounting for a third to a half of the district's output. 🗻 *granite, sand* 🍇 *Viognier* 🍷 *white*

Château Grillet

With only 4ha under vine, Château Grillet AOC is one of the smallest appellations in France. It is actually an enclave within Condrieu and forms a south-facing amphitheatre that offers shelter from the northerly winds. The wine is again

Steep terraces of Château Grillet

made from Viognier but lacks the exuberance of Condrieu, being rather more reserved and austere and in need of bottle age. This is possibly due to the earlier harvesting date practised by the single owning family (Neyret-Gachet) and lengthy time (20 to 22 months) in oak cask. Its high price is related to its rarity. *granite, sand* *Viognier* *white*

St-Joseph

St-Joseph runs for 60km along the right bank of the Rhône. The wines are over 90 per cent red, varying from light, fruity styles to a fuller, firmer, tannic form. Much depends on the aspect of the vineyard – as in Côte Rôtie the south-facing slopes are preferred – and on the techniques of the winemaker. Ideally, the wines should display the delicious dark fruit purity of the Syrah, making them good for drinking at two to five years. St-Joseph is one of the largest districts in the Rhône, with over 900ha, which means the wines are readily available. The small percentage of white is made mainly from Marsanne, with just a hint of Roussanne; the best of it is full-bodied with a lively acidity and faint floral bouquet. *granite, schist, sand, gravel* *Syrah* *Marsanne, Roussanne* *red, white*

Hermitage

Hermitage AOC is the blue-blooded peer of the Northern Rhône, famous for its long-lived reds and complex whites. The reputation of these wines dates from the 18th century, when they became as highly prized as Bordeaux's classed growths. Indeed Rhône wines were sometimes added to Bordeaux wines to give extra strength, depth, and colour. The appellation Hermitage applies to a single granite hill that towers above the town of Tain l'Hermitage on the left bank of the Rhône. The origin of the name lies in the story of a wounded knight returning from the crusades who ended his days living as a hermit on the hill; a tiny chapel on the summit, owned by *négociant* Paul Jaboulet Aîné, commemorates the legend.

As in Côte Rôtie, aspect and soil can vary over the 140ha – leading to a number of different *climats*, or designated vineyards, producing wines of varying nuance. Red Hermitage (75 per cent of the production) is a wine revered for its power and intensity. It needs at least a decade in bottle and can age for as long as the great wines of Bordeaux. White Hermitage, made from Marsanne and Roussanne, is full-bodied with a honeyed bouquet in youth, acquiring a more mineral finish with bottle age. The co-operative in Tain l'Hermitage accounts for a third of Hermitage's output. The *négociant* houses of Chapoutier and Paul Jaboulet Aîné are next in terms of production, and about 20 individual growers bottle their own wines. *granite, clay, loess* *Syrah* *Marsanne, Roussanne* *red, white*

Rhône Valley

Crozes-Hermitage

The largest appellation in the Northern Rhône by some way, with 1,280ha under production, Crozes-Hermitage lies mostly on the flatlands surrounding the famous hill of Hermitage on the left bank of the Rhône. Essentially a red wine producing area, with only 10 per cent white, this is the value-for-money wine of the Northern Rhône. Softer and fruitier than Hermitage, but with some of its august neighbour's robust intensity, Crozes-Hermitage is generally consumed young. Styles do vary with the soils, though: grapes grown on granite and the stony soils to the south produce longer-ageing wines than the norm. The efficient co-operative at Tain l'Hermitage accounts for 60 per cent of the production, and the rest comes from *négociants* like Paul Jaboulet Aîné and good individual producers. White Crozes-Hermitage is full bodied and floral with the potential for a little more complexity at five to six years. 🎞 *granite, gravel, sand, clay* 🍇 *Syrah* 🍇 *Marsanne, Roussanne* 🍷 *red, white*

Cornas

Cornas is the black sheep of the Northern Rhône. The Syrah-based wines from this district had a solid reputation in the 18th century but have recently been left out on a limb, stranded between acclaimed Côte Rôtie and Hermitage and "good value" Crozes-Hermitage and St-Joseph. The size of the appellation (90ha) and lack of a superstar producer are perhaps part of the reason the wines have been a little underrated. The south-facing granitic vineyards, an amphitheatre of vines sheltered from the wind, provide the potential for good ripeness, and the wines are generally concentrated and of a solid disposition. They have also been labelled as tannic in the past, but riper fruit and less extraction has helped round out the tannins to a greater degree. A more modern style using destemming, rapid fermentation, and ageing in new-oak barrels also evolved in the late 1980s, following the arrival of controversial consultant oenologist Jean-Luc Colombo, who set up the Centre Oenologique here in 1984. In terms of ageability, a decade is the ideal, providing a wine with satisfying expression and complexity. 🎞 *granite, sand, limestone* 🍇 *Syrah* 🍷 *red*

St-Péray

This is the last stop on the voyage south down the Northern Rhône. The tiny volume of wine produced in this AOC is white, both still and sparkling, from Marsanne and Roussanne grapes. The sparkling wine is made by the traditional method and is sold mainly locally. It tends to lack the refreshing zip of good sparkling wines. The still white is soft and round with a floral fragrance, not dissimilar to white St-Joseph and appealing when drunk young. 🎞 *granite, limestone* 🍇 *Marsanne, Roussanne* 🍷 *white*

Syrah vineyards in Cornas

Clairette de Die, Crémant de Die & Châtillon en Diois

About 40km east of the Rhône in the Drôme Valley lies the region of Diois. The best-known wine from the three AOCs here is the light, sweet, grapey, sparkling Clairette de Die. This is made from Muscat Blanc à Petits Grains and Clairette grapes by the *méthode dioise*. With this method, there is a secondary fermentation of the wine in the bottle that is provoked by residual grape sugars rather than by the addition of sugar as used in the traditional method. The more regular dry white sparkling Crémant de Die is made exclusively from Clairette by the traditional method. A little still red and white is made in the zone of Châtillon en Diois. These wines are light in weight and frame: the red comes mainly from Gamay and the whites from Aligoté and Chardonnay. 🎞 stony 🍇 Gamay, Pinot Noir, Syrah 🍷 Muscat Blanc à Petits Grains, Clairette, Aligoté, Chardonnay 🍾 red, white, rosé

Coteaux du Tricastin

A fairly extensive AOC of 2,500ha, Coteaux du Tricastin is located just to the south of Montélimar. Red wines, which represent 90 per cent of the area's production, are like a lighter styled Côtes du Rhône and should be drunk young. The high, open landscape is exposed to the full blast of the Mistral and grapes like Grenache do not ripen easily. Syrah does better and, by AOC regulations, must represent 20 per cent of the plantings. A fruity, rosé accounts for another eight per cent of production, while

Vineyards in the Côtes du Rhône

white is scarce but improving in quality. 🎞 limestone-clay, sand 🍇 Grenache, Syrah, Cinsault, Carignan, Mourvèdre 🍷 Grenache Blanc, Clairette, Marsanne, Roussanne, Viognier 🍾 red, white, rosé

Côtes du Vivarais

This little-known district in the Ardèche was given full appellation status in 1999. The climate is cooler and wetter than in the rest of the Southern Rhône, and the wines are therefore leaner in style. Reds are in the majority, made principally from blends of Syrah and Grenache, which together must account for 90 per cent of the plantings. Co-operatives produce 85 per cent of the volume. 🎞 limestone 🍇 Syrah, Grenache, Cinsault, Carignan 🍷 Clairette, Grenache Blanc, Marsanne 🍾 red, white, rosé

VINCENT GASNIER'S TOP 10 French Wines for Everyday Drinking

1. **Touraine Sauvignon** (white) Loire Valley *p118*
2. **Côtes du Rhône Villages** (red) Southern Rhône *p81*
3. **Faugères** (red) Coteaux du Languedoc *p100*
4. **Menetou-Salon** (white) Central Loire *p119*
5. **Vin de Pays d'Oc Merlot** (red) Languedoc-Roussillon *p97*
6. **Bergerac Sec** (white) Southwest *p25*
7. **Mâcon-Villages** (white) Mâconnais, Burgundy *p71*
8. **Saumur-Champigny** (red) Anjou-Saumur *p117*
9. **Minervois** (red) South of France *p100*
10. **Côtes du Frontonnais** (red) Southwest *p25*

Gigondas

Gigondas, like Vacqueyras, lies in the shadow of the Dentelles de Montmirail hills. The two AOCs have similar soils, but Gigondas has the greater percentage of its vineyards on the limestone-clay slopes, which rise as high as 400m. These soils and the slightly cooler temperatures give additional intensity and volume, and a tighter structure to the Grenache-based blends, making them firmer and longer ageing. A decade presents no problem to these powerful wines, and although the price has risen in recent years, Gigondas still represents excellent value.

limestone, clay, sand **Grenache, Syrah, Mourvèdre, Cinsaut** *red, rosé*

Vacqueyras

Vacqueyras is the most recent of the Rhône's *crus*, promoted from Côtes du Rhone Villages to full appellation status in 1990. Essentially a red wine district, it produces one of the great value wines of the region, with more weight and concentration than regular *villages* offerings. Grenache is the dominant grape variety, imparting a rich, warm, full-bodied generosity to the wine, which is best drunk at between three and six years. A small amount of white is also produced. *limestone, clay, sand* **Grenache, Syrah, Mourvèdre, Cinsaut** *Grenache Blanc, Clairette, Bourboulenc, Marsanne, Viognier* **red, white, rosé**

Châteauneuf-du-Pape

The Rhône's most celebrated wine takes its name from the location of a summer residence for the pope, built in the 14th century when the papal seat was temporarily moved to Avignon.

Châteauneuf-du-Pape is a sizeable appellation of 3,200ha producing over 100,000hl of wine yearly, by far the largest *cru* in the Rhône. Many of the vineyards here are covered with *galets* – large, smooth pebbles that retain heat, ensuring full ripeness and flavour.

The wine itself, essentially red, is a powerful, heady libation, the best sweet and smooth, packed with summer fruits and fine tannins, a mineral freshness on the finish, and the ability to age. There is even a hint of top red Burgundy about some of it. That said, no fewer than 13 different grape varieties are allowed in the appellation, and winemaking techniques vary enormously, as do soils and exposures. This means that style and quality are not set in stone. The present vogue for special *cuvées* – old vine fruit, less traditional blends (for example, higher percentages of Syrah), or wines aged in new oak – is even more irregular. The district is on a roll, however, with several great vintages (1998 to 2001 inclusive) and a new generation of producers entering the fray. It is an ideal time to try these wines.

Chateau Beaucastel Châteauneuf-du-Pape

White Châteauneuf, usually a blend of four varieties – Grenache Blanc, Clairette, Bourboulenc, and Roussanne – is full and fruity with a delicate floral bouquet, and should be drunk young. *sandy red clay, stones, limestone* **Grenache, Syrah, Mourvèdre, Cinsaut, Counoise** *Grenache Blanc, Clairette, Bourboulenc, Roussanne* **red, white**

Lirac

On the opposite bank of the Rhône to Châteauneuf-du-Pape, the appellation of Lirac has grown to nearly 700ha. Its Grenache-

Although 13 red grape varieties are permitted in Châteauneuf-du-Pape, Grenache accounts for 75 per cent of the plantings

Vineyards in Tavel

based red is robust and meaty; some of it, with a higher percentage of Mourvèdre, is firmer in style and has the ability to age. The rosé is similar to that of neighbouring Tavel, full and heady and good with food. Like the fruity white, it should be consumed young.  *limestone, sand, stones* Grenache, Syrah, Mourvèdre, Cinsaut *Grenache Blanc, Clairette, Bourboulenc* red, white, rosé

Tavel
The reputation of this district is based on rosé. And with nearly 950ha under production, there is a lot of it. Grenache provides the base grape variety, supplemented, according to producer, by a mix of other red and white grapes. This is a strong, full-bodied, fruity wine that finishes dry and is best drunk chilled with food. The name usually commands a higher price than other rosés. *limestone, sand, clay* Grenache, Syrah, Mourvèdre, Cinsaut, Carignan *Clairette, Bourboulenc* rosé

Côtes du Ventoux
By far the largest of the "young" Rhône appellations, with over 7,700ha under production, Côtes du Ventoux is again dominated by red wine. The 1,900m-high Mont Ventoux is its focal point, with vineyards planted as high as 500m on its slopes. The altitude means a generally cooler than average climate with greater variation

between day- and night-time temperatures, resulting in fresh and fruity wines with a marked point of acidity. As a whole they are made for drinking young, but a growing number of producers are providing wines of greater structure that will age well for up to five or six years. The small percentage of white wine is usually light-bodied with a floral bouquet. *limestone, clay, sandstone* Grenache, Carignan, Syrah, Cinsault, Mourvèdre *Clairette, Ugni Blanc, Bourboulenc, Grenache Blanc, Roussanne* red, white, rosé

Côtes du Lubéron
The profile of Côtes du Lubéron AOC is similar to that of Côtes du Ventoux, with the added allure of a magical Provençal setting. Its vineyards are planted on the slopes of the Lubéron hills, surrounded by lavender, fruit orchards, and picture-postcard villages. The climate is slightly cooler here, and the red wines are generally light, fruity, and easy drinking, although they occasionally display greater weight and frame. The cooler climate appears conducive to white varieties, and indeed Côtes du Lubéron produces more white wine than any other Rhône district. This tends to be round and fruity, although it is crisper than other whites from the Rhône region. *limestone, sand* Grenache, Syrah, Carignan, Cinsaut, Mourvèdre *Grenache Blanc, Ugni Blanc, Vermentino, Clairette, Bourboulenc* red, white, rosé

Costières de Nîmes
This AOC just west of the mouth of Rhône is sometimes considered part of the Rhône region. It is covered in this book as part of Languedoc-Roussillon *(see p100).*

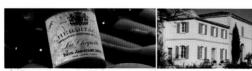

Left **Hermitage by Paul Jaboulet Aîné** Right **Château de Beaucastel**

Major Producers in the Rhône Valley

Domaine Jamet
Côte Rôtie

Brothers Jean-Luc and Jean-Paul Jamet make outstanding, long-ageing Côte Rôtie from 25 parcels of vines scattered around the district. Enjoy the lively fruit aspect of the wine up to five years of age or cellar for eight years for greater complexity. Unfortunately, production is limited to just 30,000 bottles each year. 🕲 *Le Vallin, Ampuis* • *04 74 56 12 57* ☐ *by appt* 🍷 *red* ★ *Côte Rôtie*

Guigal
Côte Rôtie / Condrieu

Marcel Guigal is one of the key figures, if not the key figure, responsible for the revival of Northern Rhône wines. With quiet authority (and assisted by his son Philippe), he oversees a now burgeoning empire that includes the *négociant* wines of E Guigal, Vidal Fleury, and de Vallouit as well as the domaine wines from his own vineyards. Best known of these are the richly intense but expensive single-vineyard Côte Rôtie wines La Mouline, La Landonne, and La Turque, as well as Château d'Ampuis from six different sites, and the voluptuously fragrant Condrieu La Doriane. There is also a very fine St-Joseph from vineyards acquired from Jean-Louis Grippat. 🕲 *Ampuis* • *04 74 56 10 22* • *www. guigal.com* ☐ *by appt* 🍷 *red, white* ★ *Côte Rôtie La Mouline, Côte Rôtie La Landonne, Côte Rôtie La Turque, Condrieu La Doriane*

Domaine Georges Vernay
Condrieu

Georges Vernay is Mr Condrieu. Back in the 1950s and 60s, when the district was being abandoned, he was the one stoically replanting the terraces. Today, the domaine extends to 16ha and is run by George's daughter, Christine, producing some much-improved Côte Rôtie and St-Joseph as well as three *cuvées* of Condrieu. The Côte Rôtie Maison Rouge is an ample but elegant wine; Condrieu Chaillés de l'Enfer and Coteau de Vernon are rich, full, and exotic, the latter with greater depth; both should be drunk at three to six years. 🕲 *1 rte nationale, Condrieu* • *04 74 56 81 81* • *www.georges-vernay.fr* ☐ *by appt* 🍷 *red, white* ★ *Condrieu Coteau de Vernon*

Cave Yves Cuilleron
Condrieu

This domaine has increased considerably in size and notoriety since Yves Cuilleron took over in 1987; it now totals 31ha. There is a complex catalogue of different *cuvées* from Condrieu, Côte Rôtie, and St-Joseph, all relating to specific parcels of vines. These are rich, dense, powerful wines, often marked by new oak in youth. The compellingly aromatic white Condrieu Les Chaillets is produced from the oldest parcels, and the sweet, citrus and marmalade Les Ayguets, also white, is made from late-harvested grapes. The top red *cuvées* include the St-Joseph Les Serines, and Côte Rôtie Terres

Good recent vintages for red wines from the Northern Rhône include 1997, 1998, 1999, 2000, and 2003

Sombres and Bassenon. ◈ *Verlieu, Chavanay* • *04 74 87 02 37* • *www. cuilleron.com* ☐ *by appt* 🍷 *red, white* ★ *Condrieu Les Ayguets, Côte Rôtie Terres Sombres, St-Joseph Les Serines*

Domaine Jean-Louis Chave
Hermitage

The neck labels of Chave bottles display the phrase "Vignerons de Père en Fils depuis 1481" (vignerons from father to son since 1481). When Gerard Chave took over from his father in the 1970s, the wines he produced became highly sought-after. Now with his son, Jean-Louis (the name appears every second generation), he continues to make firm, fine, long-ageing Hermitage. The secret is in the old vines located in seven different vineyard sites or *climats*, which are vinified separately and blended astutely. Whenever the Chaves consider it an exceptional year, they make the more intense Cuvée Cathelin. The white Hermitage is also a long-ageing wine, and there is a little rich, fruity red St-Joseph for more immediate consumption.
◈ *37 ave du St-Joseph, Mauves* • *04 75 08 24 63* ◖ 🍷 *red, white* ★ *Hermitage red, Hermitage white, Hermitage Cuvée Cathelin*

Paul Jaboulet Aîné
Hermitage / Cornas

Antoine Jaboulet established this legendary *négociant* house in the 19th century, and it remains very much a family affair. Although less consistent than in former years, it still has a number of eye-catching wines, particularly those from the company's own vineyards. The flagship wine is the powerful, long-ageing red Hermitage La Chapelle, produced from 21ha of vines dotted over the Hermitage hill. Crozes-Hermitage has always been a strong Jaboulet line and

includes the well structured *cuvées* Domaine de Thalabert and Raymond Roure. The Domaine de St-Pierre, from Cornas, is a richly concentrated wine. ◈ *Les Jalets, RN 7, La Roche de Glun, Tain l'Hermitage* • *04 75 84 68 93* • *www.jaboulet.com* ☐ *by appt* 🍷 *red, white* ★ *Hermitage La Chapelle, Crozes-Hermitage Domaine de Thalabert, Cornas Domaine de St-Pierre*

Domaine Alain Graillot
Crozes-Hermitage

A former marketing manager for a large French industrial concern, Alain Graillot quickly settled into the life of vigneron in the late 1980s and now turns out consistently good Crozes-Hermitage. The red is ripe and fruity; the top wine, La Guiraude, richly concentrated and age-worthy; and the white is fresh and aromatic. There is also a little spicy red St-Joseph and a tiny volume of supple Hermitage made from a parcel of vines in the Les Gréffieux part of the appellation.
◈ *Les Chênes Verts, Pont de l'Isère* • *04 75 84 67 52* ☐ *by appt* 🍷 *red, white* ★ *Crozes-Hermitage, Crozes-Hermitage La Guiraude*

Domaine Clape
Cornas

The reserved Auguste Clape has been a pillar of Cornas for many years. Along with his son, Pierre-Marie, he produces an authentic, traditional Cornas brimming with ripe fruit but also firm and concentrated, without a trace of new oak.The young vines are used for the *cuvée* Renaissance, while the older ones (25 to 60 years) make the top wine, simply called Cornas. Clape also produces a little generic Côtes du Rhône from Syrah, and some 1,200 bottles per year of delicious St-Péray. ◈ *146 rte nationale, Cornas* • *04 75 40 33 64* ☐ *by appt* 🍷 *red, white* ★ *Cornas*

Rhône Valley – Producers

Domaine Raspail-Ay
Gigondas
Dominique Ay is a down-to-earth, no-nonsense vigneron who makes a traditional, ageworthy Gigondas at his 18ha domaine. There is no artifice here, just good fruit, careful vinification, and ageing in the classic large oak *foudres*. The wines have a firm tannic frame and need a minimum of four or five years bottle age. There is also a small amount of excellent rosé. *Gigondas • 04 90 65 83 01* ❑ *by appt* 🖼 *red, rosé* ★ *Gigondas*

Domaine de la Monardière
Vacqueyras
Martine and Christian Vache produce different expressions of Vacqueyras with a selection of *cuvées* from three soil types. All are Grenache-based. Les Calades from clay soils is warm and generous and drinks well young. Réserve des 2 Monardes shows the freshness and finesse gained from sandier soils, while the Vieilles Vignes from the stony clay-limestone plateau is richer, firmer, and for longer ageing. *Quartier les Grès, Vacqueyras • 04 90 65 87 20* ❑ *by appt* 🖼 *red, white* ★ *Vacqueyras Réserve des 2 Monardes, Vieilles Vignes*

Château de Beaucastel
Châteauneuf-du-Pape
This château's unique wine is one of the greatest in France. Rich, firm, concentrated, it has notes of dark fruits, spice, and game, and with age can have a tobacco-like complexity. The originality comes in the blend, where Grenache is reduced to 30 per cent and more prominence given to Mourvèdre (30 per cent) and Counoise (10 per cent) – the other 30 per cent is made up of a mix of varieties depending on the vintage. All 13 permitted grape varieties are cultivated at the 100-ha estate.

In exceptional years, the tannic *cuvée* Hommage à Jacques Perrin, (Jacques Perrin is the father of present owners François and Jean-Pierre), is produced from 60 to 70 per cent Mourvèdre. There are also two excellent white Châteauneufs, including the sumptuous Roussanne Vieilles Vignes, as well as red and white Côtes du Rhônes produced under the label Coudoulet de Beaucastel. *Courthézon • 04 90 70 41 00 • www.beaucastel.com* ❑ *by appt* 🖼 *red, white* ★ *Châteauneuf-du-Pape (red), Châteauneuf-du-Pape Hommage à Jacques Perrin, Châteauneuf-du-Pape Roussanne Vieilles Vignes*

Château la Nerthe
Châteauneuf-du-Pape
This magnificent estate is one of the oldest in Châteauneuf-du-Pape, and it was bottling its own wines as far back as 1784. The modern era dates from 1985 when the property was bought by the Richard family, Parisian coffee and wine merchants, and Alain Dugas was installed as manager. The vineyard has been completely overhauled, yields reduced, and the winemaking given a more contemporary approach. Both red and white wines are ripe, elegant, and polished. In exceptional vintages the longer-ageing special selection, Cuvée des Cadettes in red and Clos de Beauvenir in white are produced. *Rte de Sorgues, Châteauneuf-du-Pape • 04 90 83 70 11 • www.chateau-la-nerthe.com* ❑ *by appt* 🖼 *red, white* ★ *Châteauneuf-du-Pape (red and white), Châteauneuf-du-Pape Cuvée des Cadettes*

Château Rayas
Châteauneuf-du-Pape
An idiosyncratic domaine, Rayas is known for the eccentric manner of its former owner, Jacques Reynaud, and the quality and

originality of its wines. Jacques's nephew, Emmanuel, has introduced a little more order and consistency, but the 100 per cent Grenache wine remains essentially the same: rich, sweet, powerful, with the flavour of summer fruits. There is also an impressive second wine, Pignan, and a full, fresh white Rayas. Some delicious, concentrated red and white Côtes du Rhône is bottled under the label Château de Fonsalette. ◈ *Châteauneuf-du-Pape* • 04 90 83 73 09 ◾ ◾ *red, white* ★ *Châteauneuf-du-Pape (red), Châteauneuf-du-Pape Pignan, Côtes du Rhône Château de Fonsalette (red)*

Domaine Bosquet des Papes
Châteauneuf-du-Pape

This is a great address for classic Châteauneuf-du-Pape, made mainly from Grenache aged in large oak *foudres*, by the father and son team of Maurice and Nicolas Boiron. The regular *cuvée* has a cherry-raspberry fragrance, generous fruit, and a minerally freshness. There is greater intensity in the *cuvée* Chante le Merle, and it exudes old vine depth and concentration, while La Gloire de Mon Grand Père, introduced in 1998, has an elegance and freshness of fruit. The small percentage of white is round, fruity, and for early drinking. ◈ *18 rte d'Orange, Châteauneuf-du-Pape* • 04 90 83 72 33 ◻ *by appt* ◾ *red, white* ★ *Châteauneuf-du-Pape (red), Châteauneuf-du-Pape Chante le Merle*

Domaine de la Janasse
Châteauneuf-du-Pape

Aimé Sabon created this domaine in 1973, but it is since the arrival in 1991 of his son Christophe, who had completed viticultural studies in Burgundy, that the wines have really taken off. A new approach has given the essentially

Grenache-based wines more finesse while retaining the soft, round, plummy fruit character. There are three *cuvées* of varying intensity, Tradition, Chaupin (100 per cent Grenache, some planted in 1921), and Vieilles Vignes (60 to 100 years). There is also some good-value Côtes du Rhône, particularly Les Garrigues. The white Châteauneufs include the fleshy, Roussanne-based Prestige. ◈ *27 chemin du Moulin, Courthézon* • 04 90 70 86 29 • www.lajanasse.com ◻ ◾ *red, white* ★ *Châteauneuf-du-Pape (red), Châteauneuf-du-Pape Chaupin, Côtes du Rhône Les Garrigues*

Château d'Aquéria
Tavel

This large, rambling estate of over 60ha has been a regular source of good fruity Tavel rosé for a number of years. There is a freshness in Château d'Aquéria's wines that is not always evident elsewhere. The estate also produces Lirac, the red firmly structured and the white fresh and fragrant. ◈ *Tavel* • 04 66 50 04 56 • www.aqueria.com ◻ ◾ *red, white, rosé* ★ *Tavel*

Domaine Marcel Richaud
Côtes du Rhône Villages

The bustling Marcel Richaud is a master at producing succulent, thirst-quenching wines that are bursting with ripe fruit flavours. The pick are his good-value red Côtes du Rhône Garrigues, the firmer Cairanne, and the top of the range Cairanne l'Ebrescade made from a parcel of old-vine Grenache that has greater intensity and finer tannins, and can be aged five or six years. The lightly oaked white Cairanne is full, fat, and creamy. ◈ *Rte de Rasteau, Cairanne* • 04 90 30 85 25 ◻ ◾ *red, white* ★ *Côtes du Rhône Garrigues, Côtes du Rhône Villages Cairanne, Côtes du Rhône Villages Cairanne l'Ebrescade*

SOUTH OF FRANCE

SOUTH OF FRANCE

BLUE SKIES, DAZZLING SUNLIGHT, *cypress, pine, and olive trees bowed by the force of the mistral wind, rocky terrain, and tiny villages with medieval towers – the traditional picture of the South of France still holds true. Stretching the whole length of the Mediterranean coast between the Italian and Spanish borders, the area is also an enormous viticultural zone. Languedoc-Roussillon alone represents a third of France's total vineyard area.*

The history of wine in the South of France probably dates back to the 6th century BC, when Greek colonists first established settlements around Marseille and the mouth of the Rhône. The Greeks were followed by the Romans, who also cultivated vines here.

Key

■ South of France

Vines were very easy to grow in the reliable hot sunshine of France's Mediterranean coast, and Romans evidently appreciated the region's wines. It is clear from archaeological finds of amphorae that they shipped large quantities of the local wine back to Rome. Perhaps vines were just too easy to grow – for 1,500 years after the fall of the Roman Empire the South of France continued to produce a huge volume of wine, but none of it in any way distinguished.

Languedoc-Roussillon

Red wines reign in Languedoc-Roussillon, accounting for nearly 90 per cent of production. Almost all are made from the five classic southern varieties, and AOC regulations mostly demand a blend of all five grapes. Syrah, famous in the neighbouring Rhône Valley, is becoming increasingly fashionable; Catalan

Sign for Rivesaltes wines

varieties Mourvèdre and Carignan give dark, tannic, spicy wines; and Grenache and Cinsault are full of easy-going fruitiness.

The era of modern winemaking started up in the 1970s, when Languedoc-Roussillon producers began to recognize that quality wine was needed to replace the cheap, mass-produced, rough red that had previously given the area a dubious reputation. Over the last 30 years styles have changed beyond recognition. Hillside sites have been planted with Grenache, Syrah, and Mourvèdre, while mature vine Carignan has been nurtured to produce wine of greater character. With increased investment and the introduction of modern winemaking techniques, Languedoc-Roussillon appellations, especially Coteaux de Languedoc, now produce some of France's most exciting new wines – rich, characterful blends with the distinctive imprint of the region. This corner of the country has become France's answer to the New World. Not surprisingly, a fair number of Australian winemakers have been attracted to the region, giving an additional boost to the quality of its wines.

Preceding pages **Vines with first signs of spring growth, Provence**

Old farm buildings surrounded by Provençal vineyards

The *vin de pays* classification has allowed stringent appellation rules to be stretched, enabling non-local varieties like Merlot and Cabernet Sauvignon to be planted. Good-value, single varietal wines are the result, many of which are labelled under the handy regional umbrella category, Vin de Pays d'Oc.

White grapes do not do well in Languedoc or Roussillon. In Limoux, however, a hilly region some distance inland from the Mediterranean, there is a long tradition of making sparkling white wines. These are produced by various methods, including the *méthode champenoise*. The main grapes used are a local white variety, Mauzac, and Chardonnay.

The Wines of Provence

The story in Provence is a little different. The lifestyle, food, and warm climate maintain a flourishing tourist industry, and the wine that tourists have come to expect is rosé. The rosé wines of Provence are unlikely to win

many accolades, but they still account for over 50 per cent of the region's production.

Great reds can, however, be found in Mourvèdre-dominated Bandol, and increasingly from individual producers throughout the region who are making significant strides with a mix of Grenache, Syrah, Mourvèdre, and Cabernet Sauvignon grapes.

VINCENT GASNIER'S TOP 10 Refreshing Rosés

1. **Bandol** South *p103*
2. **Côtes de Provence** South *p102*
3. **Tavel** Southern Rhône *p89*
4. **Rosé de Loire** Anjou-Saumur, Loire *p117*
5. **Cabernet d'Anjou** Anjou-Saumur, Loire *p117*
6. **Sancerre Rosé** Central Loire *p119*
7. **Bergerac Rosé** Southwest *p25*
8. **Corbières Rosé** South *p100*
9. **Coteaux du Languedoc Rosé** South *p100*
10. **Lirac Rosé** Southern Rhône *p88*

Wine Map of the South of France

Bordered to the south by the Mediterranean and to the north by the foothills of the southern Alps and the Massif Central, the South of France is essentially one huge vineyard. To the east, Provence has some 26,000ha under vine, mostly in appellation Côtes de Provence. Moving west, the vineyards flow across the Rhône delta through Costières de Nîmes and on into the Languedoc and then Roussillon, which together are home to around 300,000ha of vines. In terms of wine production, the most important appellation is Coteaux du Languedoc.

WINE AREAS & MAJOR PRODUCERS

Costières de Nîmes *p100*

Coteaux du Languedoc *p100*
Domaine d'Aupilhac *p106*
Domaine Canet-Valette *p106*
Domaine Peyre Rose *p106*
Mas Bruguière *p106*
Mas de Daumas Gassac
　(vin de pays) *p107*
Mas Jullien *p107*
Prieuré de St-Jean de Bébian
　p107

Minervois *p100*

Wall decoration, Provence

Corbières & Fitou *p100*

Cabardès & Côtes de Malepère *p101*

Limoux *p101*

Côtes du Roussillon *p101*

Côtes du Roussillon Villages / Rivesaltes & Maury *pp101–102*
Domaine du Clos des Fées *p107*
Domaine Gauby *p107*

Banyuls & Collioure *p102*
Domaine du Mas Blanc *p108*
Domaine de la Rectorie *p108*

Regional Information at a Glance

Latitude 42.5°–44°N.

Altitude 0–500m.

Topography The most famous vineyards line the 50km stretch of the Côte d'Or. The escarpment is broken up by streams which run down the hills to join the Saône River. The exposure and angle of the slope are critical in this region.

Soil Rich alluvial soils in the valleys; schist and limestone on the hillsides.

Climate Mediterranean. Hot, dry summers and mainly winter rain.

Temperature Although the July average is 22°C, daytime highs are often above 30°C in summer months. Temperatures on the coast are more extreme than those inland, and hill sites experience the greatest variation between daytime and night-time degrees.

Rainfall Annual average is 500–700mm. In the west of the region, the Atlantic influence means rainfall is slightly higher.

Wind Northerly winds known locally as the cers and tramontane, along with the mistral, accentuate the dry climate and help to prevent rot. Sea breezes can moderate temperatures near the coast.

Viticultural Hazards Storms; humidity; weather fluctuation.

gnon

S BAUX DE
PROVENCE   *Lubéron*   BELLET
                                                                      Nice
   COTEAUX
   D'AIX EN   Aix-en-
   PROVENCE   Provence   Draguignan   Cannes
       PALETTE   COTEAUX
                              VAROIS
                    Brignoles   CÔTES DE
   MARSEILLE   PROVENCE
                                        St Tropez   *Côte d'Azur*
           CASSIS
           CORSICA   Toulon
           170km↓ BANDOL

Harvested grapes being delivered to the winery at Mas de Daumas Gassac

Wine Areas of the South of France

Costières de Nîmes

The name of the area was changed from Costières du Gard in 1989, since when investment has increased and the winemaking improved. The

Market stand selling wine in the Coteaux du Languedoc

climate is one of the hottest in France, the land low-lying and covered with stones or *galets roulés*, similar to those in Châteauneuf-du-Pape *(see p88)*, which radiate heat at night. Wines are similar in style to the powerful, fleshy reds of the Southern Rhône.

 *sandy soils covered with large, smooth galets roulés* 🔲 *Grenache, Syrah, Carignan, Mourvèdre* 🔲 *Grenache Blanc, Marsanne, Roussanne* 🔲 *red, white, rosé*

Coteaux du Languedoc

Now one of France's most exciting appellations, this is a huge, diverse region with 15,000ha under vine. The land varies from the cooler, inland zones in the foothills of the Cévennes, where the wines – 90 per cent red and rosé – are fresher in style, to warmer parts near the sea, where the style is bigger and bolder. Much of the landscape is sparse, rocky *garrigue*, covered in wild rosemary and thyme.

Historically, 12 *terroirs* have been allowed unofficially to put their name on the label. Some, like St-Georges d'Orques, are noteworthy, others obscure. To make sense of the region, a hierarchy is being established for red wines. The "generic" Coteaux du Languedoc appellation keeps existing rules for production like yield and grape variety. As the next step up, seven climatic zones (Grès de Montpellier, Terrasses de Béziers, Terres de Sommières, La Clape, Pic St-Loup, Terrasses de Larzac, and Pézenas)

have been defined as sub-regions with stiffer controls.

A host of talented winemakers have brought a sea change in quality over the last 20 years. Styles vary but the overall theme is of ripe concentration, vigour, and a nuance of herbs. AOCs within the region include fresh, minerally Faugères, slightly meatier Saint-Chinian, and dry and semi-sweet white Clairette du Languedoc. 🔲 *limestone, schist, stony galets roulés* 🔲 *Syrah, Grenache, Mourvèdre, Carignan, Cinsault* 🔲 *Grenache Blanc, Bourboulenc, Picpoul, Clairette, Roussanne* 🔲 *red, white, rosé*

Minervois

Minervois is like a huge, south-facing amphitheatre rising above the Canal du Midi. The west of the region experiences an Atlantic influence, but the east has a more Mediterranean climate. Co-operatives are influential here, although there are also good individual growers producing attractive fruity wines. Since 1997 Minervois La Livinière, in the centre of the district, has been awarded its own appellation. Its rocky soils, hilly terrain, and warm, dry climate produce wines that are fuller, firmer, and longer ageing, 96 per cent of them red.

🔲 *stony limestone, sandstone, schist* 🔲 *Syrah, Carignan, Grenache, Cinsault, Mourvèdre* 🔲 *Marsanne, Roussanne, Macabeo, Bourboulenc, Grenache Blanc* 🔲 *red, white, rosé*

Corbières & Fitou

Corbières is a dramatic mix of mountain and valley with sparse vegetation and rocky terrain. It is also huge – over 15,000ha under vine, with 11 zones of production to denote the varying influence of mountain, soil, and sea. Boutenac, Lagrasse, and Durban are areas of particular note for their meaty, full-bodied reds. The appellation Fitou is for red wines only; those from vines grown in the rugged, hilly interior are more structured and age-worthy. *red sandstone, clay, limestone, schist, gravel* 🥂 *Grenache, Syrah, Mourvèdre, Carignan, Cinsault* 🍇 *Grenache Blanc, Bourboulenc, Macabeo, Marsanne, Roussanne* 🍷 *red, white, rosé*

Cabardès & Côtes de Malepère

Cabardès and Côtes de Malepère (the latter a VDQS) are the two most westerly zones in the Languedoc-Roussillon. Wine styles vary considerably according to the blend: a greater percentage of Cabernet Franc or Cabernet Sauvignon gives wines a leaner, firmer, blackcurranty style more in tune with the wines of the southwest, whereas Grenache offers more of Mediterranean warmth. *limestone, schist, granite, clay* 🥂 *Merlot, Cabernet Franc, Grenache, Syrah, Cabernet Sauvignon* 🍷 *red, rosé*

Limoux

The cooler, Atlantic influence in this hilly zone gives good balance and acidity for white grapes and has played its part in establishing Limoux as the South's sparkling wine district. The best wines are made by the traditional

method; Blanquette de Limoux has a minimum 90 per cent Mauzac, while Crémant de Limoux has a generous amount of Chardonnay. The AOC Limoux is for still whites made mainly from Chardonnay; red AOC Limoux was officially recognized in 2003. *clay-limestone* 🥂 *Merlot, Malbec, Syrah, Grenache, Carignan* 🍇 *Mauzac, Chardonnay, Chenin Blanc* 🍷 *red, white, sparkling*

Côtes du Roussillon & Côtes de Roussillon Villages

The culture of the border region of Roussillon is Catalan, which sets it apart from the Languedoc. The climate is hot and dry, the land swept by the northwesterly Tramontane wind, resulting in rich, warm, plummy wines. Grapes for Côtes du Roussillon wines are grown in 118 communes throughout the district, whereas the superior Côtes du Roussillon Villages is sourced from hill sites in the valleys to the north. The Villages wines have more spice and concentration and a softer texture. Four communes can append their name to the Villages label: Caramany, La Tour de France, Lesquerde, and Tautavel. *limestone-clay, granite, schist, gneiss* 🥂 *Grenache, Carignan, Syrah, Mourvèdre, Cinsault* 🍇 *Grenache Blanc, Marsanne, Roussanne, Vermentino (Rolle), Macabeo* 🍷 *red, white, rosé*

Valley slopes and vineyards in Corbières

Blanquette de Limoux was invented by the monks of the Abbaye de St-Hilaire in 1531, making it an older sparkling wine than Champagne

Rivesaltes & Maury

Rivesaltes *vin doux naturel* comes in red, white, and occasionally rosé form and is made by many of the same producers that make Côtes du Roussillon and Côtes du Roussillon Villages – including a number of large co-operatives. Rivesaltes Ambré comes from white grapes, Rivesaltes Tuilé from a minimum of 50 per cent red Grenache, and both are aged in barrel for two years. "Hors d'Age" means the wine has been aged for at least five years. Maury is a strong, tannic, Grenache-based *vin doux naturel* produced in the north of the district. It is either bottled when young and fruity and usually labelled "Vintage", or aged for a few years before bottling.

🏔 limestone, schist 🍇 Grenache, Syrah, Carignan 🍇 Grenache Blanc, Grenache Gris, Macabeo, Bourboulenc 🍷 fortified

Banyuls & Collioure

On the Spanish border, where the steep, sun-baked foothills of the Pyrenees tumble down to the Mediterranean, terraced vineyards are held in place by 6,000km of dry stone walls. It is here that France's finest fortified wine, Banyuls, is produced. Vintage Banyuls, labelled Rimage, is bottled early to capture the power of the fruit. Banyuls aged for longer in oak barrels or glass *bonbonnes* has a maderized flavour. Banyuls *grand cru* indicates 75 per cent Grenache and at least 30 months ageing in barrel. There is also a small amount of white Banyuls. Collioure is produced in the same zone. Red and rosé are dry but full-bodied. Dry white Collioure was officially recognized in 2002.

🏔 schist 🍇 Grenache, Mourvèdre, Syrah, Carignan 🍇 Grenache Blanc, Grenache Gris, Malvoisie, Macabeo, Vermentino (Rolle) 🍷 red, white, fortified

Bellet

In the Alpine foothills behind Nice, a handful of producers, occupying around 50ha of vineyards, maintain the name of Bellet. The cool hill sites are suited to the production of fresh, aromatic white made mainly from Vermentino (Rolle). Nice's Italian past is evident in the use of the red grapes Folle Noire (Fuella) and Braquet (Brachetto). Most of the wine is consumed locally. 🏔 gravel, sand, clay 🍇 Folle Noire, Braquet, Grenache, Cinsault 🍇 Vermentino, Chardonnay 🍷 white, rosé

Côtes de Provence

Côtes de Provence has 20,000ha under vine, with zones ranging from the coastal area around St-Tropez to cooler hill sites north of Draguignan. Rosé, made mainly from Cinsault and Grenache, accounts for 80 per cent of production, though a growing number of producers offer interesting reds from blends that can include Syrah, Cabernet Sauvignon, and Mourvèdre.

🏔 sandstone, limestone, granite, schist 🍇 Cinsault, Grenache, Syrah, Carignan, Cabernet Sauvignon 🍇 Clairette, Vermentino, Sémillon, Ugni Blanc 🍷 red, white, rosé

Vin Doux Naturel

Golden *vins doux naturels* (VDN) are a Roussillon speciality. They are not naturally sweet, as the name suggests, but fortified wines made by the process of *mutage* (adding alcohol to partly fermented grapes). This stops fermentation, leaving residual sugar. Some of the powerful, sweet wines are bottled early to preserve the fruit character (Muscat de Rivesaltes, Vintage Maury, Banyuls Rimage); others are aged in large oak barrels to acquire a more maderized flavour and aroma (Rivesaltes Hors d'Age, Banyuls Grand Cru).

Typical vineyard in Côtes de Provence

Coteaux Varois

Upgraded to full AOC status in 1993, Coteaux Varois uses much the same grape varieties as Côtes de Provence. The vineyards are inland away from the coast at a higher, cooler altitude, making the wines a little more intense. *limestone* *Grenache, Cinsault, Syrah, Carignan, Cabernet Sauvignon* *Vermentino, Clairette, Grenache Blanc, Semillon, Ugni Blanc* *red, white, rosé*

Bandol

Provence's most serious appellation takes its name from the fishing port/holiday resort of Bandol. Rosé provides the volume, but it is the red that holds most interest: a steely, tannic wine with a herbal nuance, aged in cask for a minimum of 18 months. The vineyards form a terraced amphitheatre, rising to 400m, overlooking the sea. An annual average of 3,000 hours of sunshine and sea breezes to temper the heat are ideal for the awkward Mourvèdre, which makes up at least 50 per cent of the blend for the red. *limestone, clay* *Mourvèdre, Grenache, Cinsault, Syrah, Carignan* *Clairette, Ugni Blanc, Bourboulenc, Sauvignon Blanc* *red, white, rosé*

Cassis

Urban development poses the greatest threat to the pretty fishing port of Cassis and its wines. These are mainly whites, which are fresh but low in acidity, and much in demand locally. *limestone* *Grenache, Cinsault, Mourvèdre, Carignan* *Ugni Blanc, Clairette, Marsanne, Sauvignon Blanc, Grenache Blanc* *red, white, rosé*

Palette

The particularity of this tiny district of barely 35ha is a distinctive limestone soil called *calcaire de Langesse* and wines – red, white, and rosé – that benefit from bottle age. *limestone* *Grenache, Mourvèdre, Syrah, Cinsault* *Clairette, Grenache Blanc, Ugni Blanc, Muscat* *red, white, rosé*

Coteaux d'Aix en Provence

Coteaux d'Aix en Provence has some 3,500ha of vines planted at an altitude of anywhere between zero and 400m. A diverse range of grapes is permitted, including Cabernet Sauvignon, Mourvèdre, and the obscure Counoise, providing fresh, round rosés (55 per cent) and reds (40 per cent) that have a certain depth and intensity. *limestone with either clay or sand* *Grenache, Cabernet Sauvignon, Carignan, Syrah, Cinsault* *Bourboulenc, Vermentino, Clairette, Grenache Blanc, Ugni Blanc* *red, white, rosé*

Les Baux de Provence

This used to be part of Coteaux d'Aix but was given independent AOC status for reds and rosés in 1995 – whites produced here are still labelled Coteaux d'Aix en Provence. The vineyards in the foothills of the Alpilles range grow traditional southern grape varieties alongside Cabernet Sauvignon, which is permitted up to a maximum 20 per cent. There are only a dozen or so domaines, many of them run organically, producing fruity reds with a little tannic grip. *limestone* *Grenache, Cinsault, Syrah, Carignan, Mourvèdre* *red, rosé*

Left **Barrels at Mas de Daumas Gassac** Right **Chateaux Pradeaux label**

Major Producers in the South of France

Left margin: South of France – Producers

Domaine d'Aupilhac
Coteaux du Languedoc
Sylvain Fadat began with limited resources in 1989, initially vinifying in the reservoir of a wine tanker. He now has nearly 30ha of vines, including one vineyard developed at 350m. The range of wines includes the Coteaux du Languedoc Montpeyroux made from the five classic southern varieties (Syrah, Grenache, Mourvèdre, Carignan, Cinsault) and two *vins de pays*: Le Carignan from vines over 50 years old, and Les Plos des Baumes from Cabernet Sauvignon, Cabernet Franc, and Merlot planted in the highly prized region of Aniane.
⊗ *28 rue du Plô, Montpeyroux • 04 67 96 61 19 • www.aupilhac.com* ⬚ *by appt* 🍷 *red, white, rosé* ★ *Coteaux du Languedoc Montpeyroux, VDP Le Carignan*

VINCENT GASNIER'S Best-Kept Secrets in French Wine

1. **Montagny** (white)
   Côte Chalonnaise *p71*
2. **Touraine Sauvignon**
   (white) Loire Valley *p118*
3. **Gigondas** (red)
   Southern Rhône *p88*
4. **Chinon** (red) Touraine *p118*
5. **Côtes de Castillon** (red & white)
   Bordeaux Right Bank *p34*
6. **Madiran** (red) Southwest *p25*
7. **Faugères** (red)
   Coteaux du Languedoc *p100*
8. **Jurançon Sec** (red) Southwest *p25*
9. **Alsace Riesling** (white) *p133*
10. **Canon-Fronsac** (red)
    Bordeaux Right Bank *p34*

Domaine Canet-Valette
Coteaux du Languedoc
Marc Valette is an idealist whose dreams have come to fruition. He planted his vineyard between 1988 and 1992 while still a member of the local co-operative and added a new gravity-fed winery in 1999. He keeps his yields low, cultivates organically, and even physically treads most of the grapes. The wines are rich and concentrated and have more finesse since he began destemming in 1997. Maghani, made from Syrah and Grenache, is his top wine. ⊗ *Rte de Causses-et-Veyran, Cessenon • 04 67 89 51 83* ⬚ *by appt* 🍷 *red* ★ *Maghani*

Domaine Peyre Rose
Coteaux du Languedoc
The wines made by Marlène Soria from this isolated vineyard in the hinterland of La-Grande-Motte are very special. Syrah-dominated and from extremely low yields, the two reds, Clos des Cistes and Syrah Léone, are aged for three years or more in vat. Dense, concentrated, and perfumed, they both age well. ⊗ *Saint-Pargoire • 04 67 98 75 50* ⬚ *by appt* 🍷 *red, white* ★ *Syrah Léone, Clos des Cistes*

Mas Bruguière
Coteaux du Languedoc
Guilhem Bruguière is one of the region's early pioneers, replanting the family domaine with Syrah, Grenache, and Mourvèdre as far back as the 1970s. La Grenadière is his top red, matured in barrels and made to age. L'Arbouse is

Preceding pages **Patch of colourful blue phacelia planted in a vineyard in southern France**

attractively spicy, and the white, Les Muriers, made from Roussanne, is one of the most harmonious in the region. ◈ *La Plaine, Valflaunes* • 04 67 55 20 97 ☐ *by appt* ▣ *red, white, rosé* ★ *l'Arbouse, La Grenadière*

Mas de Daumas Gassac
Coteaux du Languedoc / VDP
This legendary domaine was created from nothing by former leather manufacturer Aimé Guibert in the 1970s with the help of consultant, Professor Emile Peynaud. The first vintage, 1978, was acclaimed as the Château Lafite of the south and the wine's reputation was made. Cabernet Sauvignon is the mainstay of the long-ageing red, and Viognier, Chardonnay, and Petit Manseng are used for the white, so the wines are labelled as *vins de pays*. The astonishing success of the wines has attracted others to buy plots around Aniane, including actor Gérard Depardieu. ◈ *Aniane* • 04 67 57 71 28 • www.daumas-gassac. com ☐ ▣ *red, white* ★ *VDP L'Herault*

Mas Jullien
Coteaux du Languedoc
In 1985 Olivier Jullien, then aged 20, created this domaine from a small parcel of family held vines. Smitten with the local soils and grape varieties, he is now a major reference point in the region. His wines include a serious top red, Coteaux du Languedoc, which ages well, an easier-drinking red, Les Etats d'Ame, and the quirky, late-harvested Clairette de Beudelle. ◈ *Route de St-André, Jonquières* • 04 67 96 60 04 ☐ ▣ *red, white, rosé* ★ *Coteaux du Languedoc, Les Etats d'Ame*

Prieuré de St-Jean de Bébian
Coteaux du Languedoc
A 12th-century chapel highlights the antiquity of the domaine, which made its mark in the 1980s, when former owner Alain Roux replanted with vines from top estates in Châteauneuf-du-Pape, Hermitage, and Bandol. Present owners, former wine writer Chantal Lecouty and her husband Jean-Claude Le Brun, arrived in 1994 and have continued Roux's legacy, producing rich, powerful, long-ageing wine. ◈ *Route de Nizas, Pézenas* • 04 67 98 13 60 • www.bebian. com ▣ *by appt* ▣ *red, white* ★ *Coteaux du Languedoc (red)*

Domaine du Clos des Fées
Côtes du Roussillon Villages
Former sommelier, restaurateur, and wine writer Hervé Bizeul has proved that he can also turn his hand to winemaking. The progress of this domaine has been meteoric since the first vintage in 1998. Three blends are produced from Grenache, Syrah, Carignan, and Mourvèdre: Les Sorcières is rich and fruity, while Vieilles Vignes and Le Clos des Fées are more serious. Petite Sibérie is an expensive limited edition of just 2,000 bottles made from Grenache grown on a single plot. ◈ *69 rue du Maréchal-Joffre, Vingrau* • 04 68 29 40 00 • www.closdesfees.com ☐ *by appt* ▣ *red* ★ *Vieilles Vignes, Le Clos des Fées*

Domaine Gauby
Côtes du Roussillon Villages
Gérard Gauby is the down-to-earth star of the Roussillon. He started bottling in the 1980s and his wines, once powerful and tannic, are now more refined in texture and quality of fruit. He has been cultivating the vines organically since 1996 and biodynamically since 2001. The red Vieilles Vignes and Syrah-dominated Muntada are superb, and there is also a very good range of whites. ◈ *Le Faradjal, Calce* • 04 68 64 35 19 ☐ ▣ *red, white* ★ *Vieilles Vignes, Muntada*

Domaine du Mas Blanc
Banyuls & Collioure

The larger-than-life Dr André Parcé put this family domaine firmly on the map in the 1970s. His son, Jean-Michel, has since maintained continuity. Collioure is produced,

Château de Roquefort label

but the real interest is in the range of Banyuls: Rimage and Rimage La Coume are bottled early to preserve the fruit; Cuvée du Docteur Parcé is a blend of various years; and Hors d'Age de Sostréra is produced by a sherry-like solera system. The white is made from Muscat, Grenache Blanc, and Malvoisie.
◈ *9 ave du Général-de-Gaulle, Banyuls-sur-Mer • 04 68 88 32 12 • www.domaine-du-mas-blanc.com* ❏ *by appt* ▣ *red, fortified* ★ *Banyuls La Coume Rimage*

Domaine de la Rectorie
Banyuls & Collioure

The hard-working Parcé brothers cultivate some 30 different terraced parcels at altitudes ranging from sea level to 400m. They then craft a range of wines: four Banyuls, three Collioures, two dry whites, and two rosés. The reds are made from a majority of Grenache, the long-ageing and elegant Collioure Coume Pascole with a little Syrah. The Banyuls cuvée Léon Parcé has a rich concentration of fruit and is aged in barrel for 12 months.
◈ *54 ave du Puig-Delmas, Banyuls-sur-Mer • 04 68 81 02 94* ❏ *by appt* ▣ *red, white, rosé, fortified* ★ *Collioure Coume Pascole, Banyuls cuvée Léon Parcé*

Château de Roquefort
Côtes de Provence

The emergence of this estate near Bandol is relatively recent. Raimond de Villeneuve spent his childhood years here and returned in 1994 to take over the reins. He

rapidly restructured the vineyard and continued the policy of organic cultivation. The wines are sumptuously fruity with a fine-grained texture. The white Les Genêts is fresh and floral, and the rosés Corail and Sémiramis have red berry fruit. The red blends, Les Murès and Rubrum Obscurum, are simply delicious, the latter with greater concentration and structure. In exceptional years La Pourpre is produced from Carignan and Syrah. ◈ *Roquefort La Bedoule • 04 42 73 20 84* ❏ *by appt* ▣ *red, white, rosé* ★ *Les Mûres, Rubrum Obscurum*

Domaine Richeaume
Côtes de Provence

A job as lecturer at the University of Aix-en-Provence was the catalyst for Henning Hoesch establishing Richeaume in 1972. The domaine has now grown to 20ha, and Henning has been joined by his son Sylvain, whose training was at Ridge in California and Penfolds in Australia. There is an aromatic white Blanc de Blancs made from Vermentino (Rolle) and Clairette, and a selection of very good reds. The Cuvée Tradition, a Cabernet Sauvignon-Grenache blend, is dark, rich, and herbal, while the Cuvée Columelle (Cabernet Sauvignon, Syrah, Merlot) has greater depth and complexity.
◈ *Puyloubier • 04 42 66 31 27* ❏ *by appt* ▣ *red, white, rosé* ★ *Cuvée Columelle*

Château de Pibarnon
Bandol

In 1977 Henri de St Victor gave up his job in pharmaceuticals in Paris for the life of a wine producer in Bandol. The magnificent Château de Pibarnon estate, overlooking the Mediterranean, has grown to nearly 50ha. Run by Henri's son Eric, it produces one of the region's most elegant, complex, long-lived reds, made from Mourvèdre with just a splash of Grenache. The fruity rosé is a blend of Mourvèdre and Cinsault, the white a mix of Clairette, Bourboulenc, Marsanne, Roussanne, and Viognier. ⚘ *Chemin de la Croix-des-Signaux, La Cadière-d'Azur • 04 94 90 12 73 • www.chateaupibarnon. com* ☐ 🖾 *red, white, rosé* ★ *Bandol red*

Château Pradeaux
Bandol

The Portalis family has owned Château Pradeaux since 1752; Cyrille Portalis is the present custodian. Its success is due in part to old vines and low yields. The style of the Mourvèdre-dominated wine is totally uncompromising: firm, structured, and needing several years in bottle to soften and unwind, developing finesse and complexity with time. ⚘ *Chemin des Pradeaux, Saint-Cyr-sur-Mer • 04 94 32 10 21* ☐ *by appt* 🖾 *red, rosé* ★ *Bandol red*

Domaine Tempier
Bandol

Tempier has long been one of the leading lights of Bandol. Relaunched in the 1940s by Lucien Peyraud, it is still owned by his family, although it is now managed by Daniel Ravier. A number of different red wines are made here, from varying blends of Mourvèdre with a little Grenache, Cinsault, and Syrah. The Classique and Cuvée Speciale are sourced from different sites around the estate, while La Migoua, La Tourtine, and Cabassou are magnificent single-vineyard wines. ⚘ *Le Plan du Castellet, Le Castellet • 04 94 98 70 21 • www.domainetempier. com* ☐ 🖾 *red, white, rosé* ★ *Cuvée Speciale, La Tourtine, Cabassou*

Clos Sainte Magdeleine
Cassis

The terraced vineyards of the Clos Sainte Magdeleine step down to the sea at an idyllic spot. This is consistently one of the top producers in the district. Its wines, made from Marsanne, Clairette, and Ugni Blanc grape varieties, have a floral, honeyed bouquet and ample soft, round fruit. They are best consumed young. ⚘ *Cassis • 04 42 01 70 28* ☐ *by appt* 🖾 *white, rosé* ★ *Cassis white*

Château Simone
Palette

Owned for seven generations by the Rougier family, this unique estate is ultra-traditional. The organically cultivated vineyard has never been replanted – individual vines are replaced only when necessary. Three principal grape varieties are used: Grenache and Mourvèdre for the red and Clairette for the white. The latter has a minerally freshness and improves with bottle age. The red, matured for upwards of three years in oak barrels, is light in colour, fine, and the antithesis of modern, fruit-led wine. ⚘ *Meyreuil • 04 42 66 92 58* ☐ *by appt* 🖾 *red, white, rosé* ★ *Palette white*

Domaine de Trévallon
Les Baux de Provence / VDP

Eloi Dürrbach makes a truly original red wine from an equal blend of Cabernet Sauvignon and Syrah. The texture is fine, the aromas of laurel and garrigue, and the ageing potential long. However, the percentage of Cabernet Sauvignon exceeds that authorized by AOC Les Baux de Provence, so the wines are labelled *vins de pays*. The barrel-fermented white is a blend of Marsanne, Roussanne, and Chardonnay. ⚘ *Saint-Etienne du Grès • 04 90 49 06 00 • www.trevallon.com* ☐ *by appt* 🖾 *red, white* ★ *VDP red*

109

LOIRE VALLEY

LOIRE VALLEY

PARISIANS HAVE LONG DELIGHTED *in the wines of the Loire, but elsewhere in the world they tend to be undervalued. Yet, there is a fantastic diversity to be found in the region – from crisp, dry whites and good-value fizz to thirst-quenching rosé, light and food-friendly reds, and world-ranking sweet wines. The overall theme of wines from this region is one of harmony and easy drinkability.*

The proximity of France's capital city has historically provided a ready market for the wines of the Loire Valley. Ever since the Middle Ages, the area's numerous small growers have enjoyed a profitable trade with Paris. Links with Belgium and Holland were also established early on thanks to excellent river connections, while ports on the western seaboard facilitated export to England, where the wines of Anjou were once preferred to those of Bordeaux.

Key

■ Loire Valley

From Source to the Atlantic

The interconnecting thread through the whole region is the long, languorous Loire River, which covers a distance of some 1,000km from its source in the Massif Central. The upper reaches of the river are home to a handful of "country" wines (St-Pourçain, Côte Roannaise, Côtes du Forez) that are rarely seen outside France. Serious winemaking begins further north at Pouilly-sur-Loire and continues all the way west to Nantes. Along this stretch of the Loire some 13,000 family-run estates cultivate just over 50,000ha of Appellation d'Origine Contrôlée vines. The average holding is small – a little over 4ha – but with a total annual production of around three million

hectolitres the Loire Valley is the third largest producer of AOC wines in France, behind Bordeaux and the Rhône Valley.

The majority of the Loire's wines are white, representing 55 per cent of the total volume, with just 24 per cent red, 14 per cent rosé, and 7 per cent sparkling. The northerly latitude for winemaking and generally temperate climate ensure that the wines have good acidity and are refreshing in character. The geographical extent of the Loire Valley, the many grape varieties cultivated, and the effect of vintage variation, however, mean that the wines are very varied in character.

Grape Varieties and Wine Styles

The Loire produces truly original wines in a gamut of styles. White wines are made principally from Chenin Blanc (known locally as Pineau de la Loire) in Anjou-Saumur and Touraine, Melon de Bourgogne in the Pays Nantais, and Sauvignon Blanc in the Central Loire and Touraine. Chenin Blanc is a truly local grape, taking its name from Mont-Chenin in Touraine. It is used to make wines in many different styles, some more successful than others. Its high sugar content makes it ideal for sweet and sparkling wines,

Preceding pages **Château de Tracy, a historic estate in the celebrated Pouilly-Fumé region of the Central Loire**

Harvesting Sauvignon Blanc grapes outside the hill town of Sancerre

especially after a hot summer. Its most famous incarnation is in the wines of Vouvray.

Melon de Bourgogne, a grape, which, as its name suggests, originated in Burgundy, is synonymous with the bone dry refreshing Muscadet wines of the Pays Nantais. The grape itself does not possess strong fruit flavours and Muscadet wines are classically made *sur lie*, that is the wine is left in contact with its lees (sediment) over winter to give it a yeasty zest.

The most famous dry whites of the Loire Valley, however, are those from the Central Valley made from Sauvignon Blanc in Sancerre and Pouilly-Fumé. These have enjoyed such success in recent years that increased demand has led a few growers to overproduce. The larger yields mean that the fruit does not achieve sufficient ripeness to produce the wonderful pungent gooseberry aromas for which Sauvignon Blanc is famous. Good

Sauvignon Blanc is also produced in nearby Menetou-Salon.

Cabernet Franc (or Breton, as it is known in Touraine) is the dominant red grape of the region. It finds its most notable expression in the Chinon and Bourgeuil districts in Touraine and the Saumur-Champigny district in Anjou-Saumur. With a few notable exceptions, most of the red wines made here are best drunk young. The same is true of the rosés, particularly the Rosé d'Anjou. Whatever the wine style, the northerly climes of the Loire place the emphasis on delicacy and flavour rather than power and fruit-driven concentration.

VINCENT GASNIER'S TOP 10 Great French White Wines

1 Grand Cru Chablis Burgundy *p51*	**6 Condrieu** Northern Rhône *p84*
2 Puligny-Montrachet Côte de Beaune *p63*	**7 Sancerre** Central Loire *p119*
3 Meursault Côte de Beaune *p63*	**8 Bâtard-Montrachet** Côte de Beaune *p63*
4 Pessac-Léognan Bordeaux Left Bank *p24*	**9 Corton-Charlemagne** Côte de Beaune *p62*
5 Hermitage White Northern Rhône *p85*	**10 Alsace Riesling Grand Cru** Alsace *133*

Wine Map of the Loire Valley

The four main wine areas of the Loire Valley lie along the section of the river from Pouilly-sur-Loire in central France to its mouth on the Atlantic coast. The Pays Nantais on the Atlantic seaboard is home to Muscadet. Moving east, Anjou-Saumur produces luscious sweet wines and long-ageing Chenin Blanc. Touraine boasts the best Loire reds and sweet forms of Chenin Blanc, while the Central Loire is the hub for Sauvignon Blanc, produced under the appellations of Sancerre and Pouilly-Fumé.

WINE AREAS & MAJOR PRODUCERS

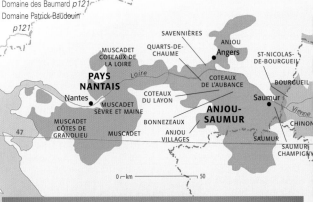

SAVENNIÈRES
QUARTS-DE-CHAUME
ANJOU
Angers
ST-NICOLAS-DE-BOURGUEIL

MUSCADET
COTEAUX DE
LA LOIRE

**PAYS
NANTAIS**
Loire

COTEAUX
DE L'AUBANCE

BOURGUEIL

Nantes

MUSCADET
SÈVRE ET MAINE

COTEAUX
DU LAYON

Saumur

Vienne

CHINON

**ANJOU-
SAUMUR**

MUSCADET
CÔTES DE
GRANDLIEU

47

BONNEZEAUX

MUSCADET

ANJOU
VILLAGES

SAUMUR

SAUMUR
CHAMPIGNY

0 ⊢km 50

Old vineyard in the Pays Nantais, the home of Muscadet

Sauvignon Blanc vineyards in Sancerre, Central Loire

Regional Information at a Glance

Latitude 47–48°N.

Altitude 0–350m.

Topography The Loire River creates one long valley from west to east. The area is relatively flat with some hilly countryside in Anjou-Saumur and Touraine, where the Loire's tributaries create river valleys with gentle slopes. In the east, Sancerre is on a hill at 300m.

Soil Schist, granite, gneiss, sand in the Pays Nantais; slate, schist, sandstone, tufa (limestone) in Anjou-Saumur; sand, clay, gravel, tufa in Touraine; kimmeridgian limestone soils similar to those of Chablis in the Central Loire.

Climate Generally cool and temperate. A maritime influence prevails on the Atlantic seaboard and persists in varying degrees inland as far as Orléans. In the Central Loire the climate is more continental.

Temperature July average is 19°C

Rainfall Annual average is 750mm.

Viticultural Hazards Spring frost.

Orléans

VOUVRAY

Tours • **TOURAINE**

MONTLOUIS

CENTRAL LOIRE

SANCERRE / POUILLY-FUMÉ & POUILLY-SUR-LOIRE

MENETOU-SALON

QUINCY

REUILLY

Cher

Indre

Loire

Food and Wine Pairing in the Loire

Known as the "Garden of France", the Loire has a great gastronomic tradition based on local produce combined with the region's many and varied wines. Oysters, mussels, and other shellfish from the Atlantic are perfect with a crisp, dry, tangy Muscadet. Asparagus, fried whitebait, chicken liver mousse, or goat's cheese are the ideal partners to a clean, aromatic

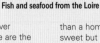

Fish and seafood from the Loire

Sancerre or Pouilly-Fumé. Poached carp or pike in a creamy sauce pairs well with a young, fruity red like Saumur-Champigny or a dry white Vouvray or Savennières. Game such as wild duck and pheasant are matched by older vintages of red Chinon and Bourgueil. For dessert, what better than a home-made fruit tart with a sweet but tinglingly fresh Coteaux du Layon to round things off?

Wine Areas of the Loire Valley

Pays Nantais

The most westerly of the Loire Valley wine areas is the Pays Nantais, home of Muscadet, the crisp, cautiously neutral, dry white so often served as an accompaniment to seafood. The wine is made from the rather neutral Melon de Bourgogne, a Burgundian grape variety introduced in the 17th century that had the fortitude to withstand a bitingly cold winter in 1709, which destroyed the previously dominant red varieties of the region.

The vineyards, some 13,000ha, are located around the city of Nantes and divided into four appellations. **Muscadet Sèvre et Maine** is by far the largest, accounting for over 80 per cent of the production. The best of these wines have a fine, floral bouquet, a mineral edge, and occasionally the ability to age. **Muscadet Coteaux de la Loire** is perhaps fuller bodied, while **Muscadet Côtes de Grandlieu**, the most recent designation – introduced in 1994 – is softer in style. There is also a small volume of ordinary AOC **Muscadet**.

Throughout the region there is the potential to bottle the wine *sur lie*, and the best examples of Muscadet usually are. This entails leaving the wine on its lees for four or five months over the winter in the tank or barrel in which it has been fermented without racking and then bottling directly. The process helps enhance flavour and, as the wine still contains a teasing sparkle of carbon dioxide, it emphasizes freshness and compensates for a generally low acidity. Even drier than Muscadet is the VDQS Gros Plant du Pays Nantais made from Folle Blanche. ▨ *schist, granite, gneiss, sand* 🏵 *Melon de Bourgogne, Folle Blanche* 🍷 *white*

Anjou-Saumur

The greatest expression of the Chenin Blanc grape in the world, with the exception of Vouvray in Touraine, is found in Anjou. A combination of maritime climate, sheltered valleys, schistous soils, and the grape itself produce superlative dry and sweet styles, some with the potential to age for years, even decades.

Southwest of the town of Angers on the north side of the Loire River, the vineyards of **Savennières** are planted on slate and schist soils that slope to the river's edge. A dry, minerally Chenin Blanc with great depth and persistence, Savennières needs at least four or five years to mellow. Medium-dry and sweet versions of the wine are occasionally produced in exceptional years.

Picking Melon de Bourgogne grapes in Muscadet, Pays Nantais

Within the district there are two sub-appellations considered *grands crus*, **Roche aux Moines** and the tiny **Coulée de Serrant**, a monopoly run in a resolute biodynamic *(see p66)* fashion by owner Nicolas Joly.

The best of the sweet styles come from tributary valleys on the south side of the Loire in the **Coteaux de l'Aubance** and **Coteaux du Layon** AOCs. The Chenin Blanc grape ripens to a fragrant sweetness on sites of varying aspect, assisted, when conditions are right, by the onset of botrytis *(see p24)*. Selective, late harvesting is thus essential. The top wines have luscious fruit and floral aromas when young, maturing to notes of honey and dried fruits, an unctuosity on the palate backed by a mouth-tingling acidity. Two sites, **Bonnezeaux** and **Quarts de Chaume**, in the Coteaux du Layon are considered superior for this style of wine and given individual AOC status.

Dry white and red is also produced throughout the AOC **Anjou**. The white invariably has an apple-quince flavour with a mineral note and is produced from Chenin Blanc, sometimes with a dash of Chardonnay and Sauvignon Blanc; the soft red is from Cabernet Franc. From a different red grape, light, quaffable **Anjou-Gamay** is mainly consumed within the region. **Anjou-Villages** and **Anjou-Villages Brissac** are uniquely red wine appellations from selected sites mostly south of the river. Produced from Cabernet Franc and Cabernet Sauvignon, they have a little more colour, intensity, and structure than regular Anjou and can represent excellent value.

Rosé is another staple of Anjou and comes in various styles. **Cabernet d'Anjou** and **Rosé**

Crémant de Loire

Sparkling wines *(crémants)* are another facet of the Loire showcase. The best are produced by the traditional method *(see p128)* in Saumur and Vouvray. Sparkling Vouvray and Montlouis are produced solely from Chenin Blanc, and with its bite of acidity are crisp and appley. A little bottle age adds a honeyed nuance. Saumur *brut* is based on Chenin  Blanc but allows other varieties like Chardonnay, Sauvignon Blanc, and Cabernet Franc to round out the wine. Crémant de Loire is made from a similar range of grapes grown in Anjou, Saumur, and Touraine. Regulations for production are stricter than those for Saumur, and the wine is usually

Crémant de Loire finer in style with a less aggressive fizz.

d'Anjou are medium to medium-sweet while **Rosé de Loire**, also produced in Touraine, is dry.

South of the river, the soft limestone or tufa soils of Saumur have made it a centre for sparkling wine *(see above)*. With its large companies and cellars cut into the calcareous tufa, the town of Saumur is reminiscent of Épernay in Champagne. **Saumur** is the generic appellation for still red and white made, as in Anjou, from Cabernet Franc and Chenin Blanc respectively, although the chalky soils make the wines a touch lighter. The best reds come from **Saumur-Champigny**, a more limited AOC zone. Raspberry or violet scented, they are usually fresh, fruity, and easy drinking.
🏔 *slate, schist, sandstone, tufa* 🍇 *Cabernet Franc, Cabernet Sauvignon, Grolleau, Gamay* 🍇 *Chenin Blanc, Chardonnay, Sauvignon Blanc* 🍷 *red, white, rosé, sparkling*

Barrels in the cellars of Domaine Huet in the Touraine region

Touraine

The best Loire reds come from Touraine and specifically the appellations **Chinon**, **Bourgueil**, and **St-Nicolas-de-Bourgueil**. They are generally fresh and fruity, produced from Cabernet Franc. These invigorating wines are digestible, convivial, not tiringly heavy, and above all food friendly. The lighter, youthful styles can, like Beaujolais *(see p74–75)*, be served slightly chilled (at 13 to 14°C) to emphasize the fruitiness. In great vintages (such as 1997 and 1996) and from certain soils, these wines can be firmer and longer lived and have the potential to age for at least 10 years.

Chinon is the largest of the three districts with 2,100ha located south of the Loire on either side of its tributary, the Vienne. The wines have a soft, rounded texture, the lighter styles coming from the sandy, alluvial soils close to the river, those with greater vigour and structure from the clay-gravel plateaux or south-facing tufa slopes. There is also a little rare, dry white Chinon made from Chenin Blanc. The tufa reappears north of the Loire at Bourgueil, giving firmness to the wines there, while grapes grown on the

predominantly alluvial soils at St-Nicolas-de Bourgueil make lighter, fruitier wine. In all three districts, producers often present a number of different *cuvées*, each reflecting the soil type and age of the vines.

Touraine is the generic appellation for simple, lightweight white, red, and rosé wines produced in a zone around the town of Tours. A multitude of grape varieties are permissible, but the two most common are Gamay and Sauvignon Blanc. Three specific sectors are allowed to add their names to the label: **Touraine Mesland**, **Touraine Amboise**, and **Touraine Azay-le-Rideau**, while **Touraine Noble-Joué** accounts for a tiny production of pale pink, fruity *vin gris* made from Pinot Meunier, Pinot Noir, and Pinot Gris.

Just east of Tours are the two great white wine AOCs of Touraine: **Vouvray** and **Montlouis**. The mercurial Chenin Blanc again comes into its own producing dry *(sec)*, medium-dry *(demi-sec)*, sweet *(moelleux)*, and sparkling wines *(see p117)*, all with an appley, honeyed nuance and sharp streak of acidity. Vintage can vary considerably in this mid-continental, mid-maritime zone, and with it the style of the wine. In ripe years, when noble rot takes hold, the pendulum swings towards the sweeter, quince and crystallized fruit styles, whereas in leaner years sparkling and dry prevail. Whichever, these wines have incredible endurance and can age for decades. Vouvray is located on the north bank of the Loire and, with its tufa slopes, produces a wine of greater weight and intensity than Montlouis on the south bank, where the soils are sandier. Carved into the tufa at Vouvray are some impressive wine cellars and troglodyte homes. 🗾 *tufa, sand, clay, gravel* 🍇 *Cabernet Franc, Gamay, Côt (Malbec), Cabernet Sauvignon* 🍇 *Chenin Blanc, Sauvignon Blanc, Chardonnay* 🍷 *red, white, rosé, sparkling*

Central Loire

The Central Loire is France's Sauvignon Blanc capital, as demonstrated by the famous wines of **Sancerre** and **Pouilly-Fumé**. The vineyards are 360km upstream from the Atlantic coast, the climate decisively continental, and the wines crisp, dry, and tangy with a piercing redcurrant, gooseberry, and occasionally citrus aroma and flavour.

The hill town of Sancerre on the south bank of the Loire gives its name to the larger of the two appellations, some 2,600ha planted on a hilly, limestone terrain. Pouilly-Fumé is produced on the opposite side of the river, where the land is flatter. Confusingly, there is also a white wine called Pouilly-sur-Loire, but it is made from Chasselas and is infinitely less memorable. Tasting the difference between Sancerre and Pouilly-Fumé is not easy. The former varies in quality but is generally fuller and fruitier, the latter more minerally and intense. Both are delicious when drunk young.

Whereas Pouilly-Fumé is a white wine-only district, Sancerre also produces a little red and rosé from Pinot Noir. The red is light-bodied with a cherry-like fragrance and is generally consumed locally or destined for Parisian bistros.

Three other districts of the Central Loire lie on the same side of the river as Sancerre. Just to the west **Menetou-Salon** AOC also produces pungent Sauvignon Blanc and light-bodied red and rosé. The wines are less well known but often represent excellent value. **Reuilly** AOC, too, produces all three colours from the same grape varieties as well as a little Pinot Gris for the rosé. The white is dry and a little more austere, the red lighter than Sancerre. Neighbouring **Quincy** AOC is a white wine-only district, the Sauvignon Blanc grown on sandy-gravel soils again producing fruity, aromatic wines. 🗾 *limestone, flint, sand, gravel* 🍇 *Pinot Noir* 🍇 *Sauvignon Blanc* 🍷 *red, white, rosé*

VINCENT GASNIER'S TOP 10 Excellent Crémants

1 **Bouvet-Ladubay** Loire
   www.bouvet-ladubay.fr

2 **Gratien-Meyer** Loire
   www.gratienmeyer.com

3 **Domaine des Baumard** Loire *p121*

4 **André Bonhomme** Burgundy
   Vire, 03 85 27 93 93

5 **Caves de Bailly** Burgundy
   www.caves-bailly.com

6 **Dopff au Moulin** Alsace
   www.dopff-au-moulin.fr

7 **Cave de Pfaffenheim** Alsace
   www.pfaffenheim.com

8 **Sieur d'Arques** Limoux
   www.sieurdarques.com

9 **Rolet Père et Fils** Jura
   www.rolet-arbois.com

10 **Domaine Raspail** Die (Rhône Valley)
   www.raspail.com

Crémant *is the French term for sparkling wine. For more details on Crémant de Loire* See p117 *& for the Top 10 Champagnes* See p127

Vineyards of Domaine Huet, one of the leading biodynamic producers in Touraine

Major Producers in the Loire Valley

Domaine de l'Écu
Pays Nantais /
Muscadet Sèvre et Maine
There could be no better publicity
for biodynamic cultivation *(see p66)*
than the Domaine de l'Écu. Guy
Bossard's Muscadet reaches
another plane with full, fragrant,
complex wines that can even be
aged. The regular Muscadet Sèvre
et Maine sur lie is a classic, and
there are three exceptional *cuvées*
named after the soils from which
they come. Bossard also makes a
traditional method sparkling wine,
Ludwig Hahn, from Melon de
Bourgogne, Folle Blanche, and
Chardonnay. ◉ *La Bretonnière, Le
Landreau • 02 40 06 40 91* ◘ *by appt*
🍷 *white* ★ *Expression d'Orthogneiss,
Expression de Gneiss, Expression de Granit*

Château de Villeneuve
Anjou-Saumur /
Saumur-Champigny
The grand 18th-century Château
de Villeneuve was built from the
local tufa. Jean-Pierre Chevallier's
wines are equally impressive,
in particular the rich, powerful,
deep-coloured reds made from
Cabernet Franc. The regular
cuvée is consistently good, and in
exceptional years the long-ageing
Le Grand Clos and Vieilles Vignes
are also produced. The Chenin
Blanc Saumur Les Cormiers is
rich and concentrated. ◉ *3 rue Jean
Brevet, Souzay-Champigny • 02 41 51 14
04 • www.chateau-villeneuve.com* ◘
🍷 *red, white* ★ *Saumur-Champigny,
Saumur-Champigny Le Grand Clos,
Saumur Les Cormiers*

Château Pierre Bise
*Anjou-Saumur / Savennières
& Coteaux du Layon*
Claude Papin knows the *terroir*
of his 54-ha estate like the back of
his hand. Selective late harvesting
gives his wines great generosity of
fruit. Of particular note are the firm
but succulent dry white Clos de
Coulaine, the sumptuous sweet
Coteaux du Layon Anclaie and
Quarts de Chaume, and the
red Anjou-Villages Sur Spilite.
◉ *Beaulieu-sur-Layon • 02 41 78 31 44*
◘ *by appt* 🍷 *white* ★ *Coteaux du Layon
Anclaie, Savennières Clos de Coulaine,
Anjou-Villages Sur Spilite*

Clos Rougeard
Anjou-Saumur /
Saumur-Champigny
The Foucault brothers, Charly
and Nadi, may be a roisterous pair,
but they know how to make good
Saumur-Champigny. Old Cabernet
Franc vines, low yields, and ageing
in oak *barriques* turn out rich,
concentrated wines. Les Poyeux
and Le Bourg are as elegant
and structured as many a fine
Bordeaux. ◉ *15 rue de l'Eglise, Chacé
• 02 41 52 92 65* ◘ *by appt* 🍷 *red, white*
★ *Les Poyeux, Le Bourg*

Coulée de Serrant
Anjou-Saumur / Savennières
Owner Nicolas Joly is the leading
proponent of biodynamic viticulture
(see p66) in France. The 7-ha
grand cru Coulée de Serrant is a
monopoly, one of various parcels
Joly owns in Savennières. The
wines rely on the quality of the

Chenin Blanc grapes. Coulée de Serrant is always dry and full bodied with firm acidity and the aroma of honey and quince. ◈ *Château de la Roche-aux-Moines, Savennières • 02 41 72 22 32 • www.coulee-de-serrant.com* ▢ ▨ *white ★ Coulée de Serrant, Roche aux Moines Clos de la Bergerie*

Domaine des Baumard
Anjou-Saumur / Coteaux de Layon & Savennières
Florent Baumard's domaine lies on both banks of the Loire. The dry white Savennières Clos St-Yves is firm but rounded. In exceptional years there is also the Trie Spéciale, which is even more intense. From the Coteaux du Layon the sweet Clos Ste-Catherine has wonderful elegance, while the Quarts de Chaume has a huge concentration of rich, succulent fruit. ◈ *8 rue de l'Abbaye, Rochefort-sur-Loire • 02 41 78 70 03 • www.baumard.fr* ▢ *by appt* ▨ *red, white, rosé ★ Coteaux du Layon Clos Ste-Catherine, Quarts de Chaume, Savennières Trie Spéciale*

Domaine Patrick Baudouin
Anjou-Saumur / Coteaux de Layon
Selective harvesting produces wines of great natural richness and fruit concentration. Depending on the vintage, a number of *cuvées* are produced from Chenin Blanc, with varying degrees of sugar potential. In order of richness, they are Après Minuit, Maria Juby, Grains Nobles, and Les Bruandières. The domaine also makes a soft, fresh, minerally dry Anjou blanc and some fruity red Anjou-Villages. ◈ *Princé, Chaudefonds-sur-Layon • 02 41 78 66 04 • www. patrick-baudouin-layon.com* ▢ *by appt* ▨ *red, white ★ Anjou Blanc, Coteaux du Layon: Grains Nobles, Maria Juby*

Domaine Bernard Baudry
Touraine / Chinon
Bernard Baudry began in 1977 with just 2ha, but has expanded the domaine, which he runs with his son Matthieu, to 30ha. The wines are aged in cellars excavated in the tufa rock. La Croix Boissée from Cabernet Franc grown on limestone soils and Grézeaux on gravel are structured and good for ageing, while Granges is a softer, fruitier Chinon. Fresh, white Chinon is also produced from Chenin Blanc. ◈ *13 coteau de Sonnay, Cravant-les-Coteaux • 02 47 93 15 79* ▢ *by appt* ▨ *red, white ★ Granges, Grézeaux, La Croix Boissée*

Domaine de la Taille aux Loups
Touraine / Montlouis
Former wine merchant Jacky Blot created this domaine in 1988. The carefully selected Chenin Blanc grapes are vinified in oak barrels. There are two dry wines: the elegant Les Dix Arpents and Cuvée Remus, which has an atypical toasted oak flavour. Depending on the vintage, there may also be a *demi-sec* and a sweet Cuvée des Loups as well as sparkling wines. ◈ *8 rue des Aitres, Husseau, Montlouis-sur-Loire • 02 47 45 11 11* ▢ *by appt* ▨ *white ★ Montlouis: Les Dix Arpents, Cuvée des Loups (demi-sec)*

VINCENT GASNIER'S
Best Organic Wine Producers TOP 10

Domaine du Clos Naudin
Touraine / Vouvray
Philippe Foreau describes the firm, minerally edge in older vintages of his Vouvray Chenin Blanc wines as almost "Chablisesque". Whether *sec*, *demi-sec*, *moelleux*, or – in exceptional years when botrytis appears – *moelleux réserve* (1997, 1995, 1990) all are ripe, crystalline pure, and age for a considerable length of time. Some splendid traditional method vintage and non-vintage sparkling Vouvray is also produced. ◈ *14 rue de la Croix Buisée, Vouvray* • *02 47 52 71 46* ☐ *by appt* ▨ *white, sparkling* ★ *Vouvray sec, réserve moelleux*

Domaine Henry Marionnet
Touraine / vin de pays
Henry Marionnet has been something of a pioneer in his native Touraine, replanting his 60-ha vineyard, producing clean, modern style Sauvignon Blanc and fruity Gamay nouveau. Now he has taken to reviving forgotten grape varieties such as white Romorantin (planted in 1850) in his Provignage, and Gamay de Bouze in Les Cépages Oubliés (both *vins de pays*). There is also a wine called Vinifera from ungrafted Gamay. All three reveal a superb purity of fruit. ◈ *Domaine de la Charmoise, Soings* • *02 54 98 70 73* • *www.henry-marionnet.com* ☐ *by appt* ▨ *red, white* ★ *Touraine Sauvignon Blanc, Provignage, Vinifera*

Domaine Huet
Touraine / Vouvray
Gaston Huet built the reputation of this Vouvray domaine after World War II. His son-in-law, Noël Pinguet, has turned the vineyard over to biodynamic cultivation. The wines,

Domaine Henry Marionnet label

made from Chenin Blanc, are produced from three superb sites: Le Mont, Le Haut-Lieu, and Le Clos du Bourg, and depending on the vintage can be dry, medium-dry, or sweet. The wines have tremendous ageing potential. ◈ *11 rue de la Croix Buisée, Vouvray* • *02 47 52 78 87* • *www. huet-echansonne.com* ☐ ▨ *white* ★ *Le Mont, Le Haut-Lieu, Le Clos du Bourg*

Domaine Philippe Alliet
Touraine / Chinon
Philippe Alliet is a reserved but determined man, who, with his wife Claude, has made his domaine the model for red winemaking in Chinon, employing techniques of the top Bordeaux estates such as ageing in *barriques*. Three wines are produced from Cabernet Franc: a light regular *cuvée* and the more structured and concentrated Vieilles Vignes and Coteau de Noiré. ◈ *L'Ouche-Mondé, Cravant-les-Coteaux* • *02 47 93 17 62* ☐ *by appt* ▨ *red* ★ *Coteau de Noiré, Vieilles Vignes*

Domaine Yannick Amirault
Touraine / Bourgueil
Yannick Amirault is one of those dedicated *vignerons* who still prunes the vines on his 18-ha estate himself. He produces a number of Cabernet Franc *cuvées* from different soils and ages of vine, all with a wonderful purity of fruit. From St-Nicolas-de-Bourgueil, there is Les Graviers and the firmer Les Malgagnes, while from Bourgueil he offers La Petite Cave as well as the finely textured Les Quartiers and Le Grand Clos, all from vines of an honourable age. ◈ *5 pavillon du Grand Clos, Bourgueil* • *02 47 97 78 07* ☐ ▨ *red* ★ *St-Nicolas-de-Bourgueil Les Malgagnes, Bourgueil: Les Quartiers, Le Grand Clos*

Château de Tracy
Central Loire / Pouilly-Fumé
Vines have been cultivated at Château de Tracy since 1396, and the owners, the d'Estutt d'Assay family, whose origins are Scottish, have been resident since the 16th century. Over the past 10 years Henry d'Estutt d'Assay has replanted two-thirds of the 29-ha vineyard and improved methods of cultivation. There is only one wine: produced from Sauvignon Blanc grapes grown on limestone and silex soils and vinified and aged in stainless steel and concrete vats. It has a classic mineral and citrus intensity and is best with a year's bottle age. ◈ 58150 Tracy-sur-Loire • 03 86 26 15 12 ☐ by appt ▨ white ★ Pouilly-Fumé Château de Tracy

Domaine Alphonse Mellot
Central Loire / Sancerre
There have been 19 Alphonse Mellots, including the domaine's present winemaker and manager. The *cuvée* Génération XIX, which comes as white (Sauvignon Blanc) and red (Pinot Noir), celebrates the fact. The other Sauvignon Blancs from the 48-ha estate are all beautifully crafted. Domaine de la Moussière is the regular *cuvée*, all freshness and citrus fruit. The intense Cuvée Edmond comes from old vines and, like Génération XIX, is aged in oak. Its red double is as good as Pinot Noir gets in Sancerre. ◈ Domaine de la Moussière, Sancerre • 02 48 54 07 41 • www.mellot. com ☐ by appt ▨ red, white ★ Domaine de la Moussière, Cuvée Edmond, Génération XIX (red)

Domaine Didier Dagueneau
Central Loire / Pouilly-Fumé
In contrast to his wild lion's mane and beard, Didier Dagueneau's wines are beautifully turned out. All are aged in oak barrels to create the finest expressions of Sauvignon Blanc in Pouilly-Fumé. En Chailloux is the softest and largest in volume, Buisson Renard citrusy, Pur Sang generous, and Silex minerally and pure. ◈ 1–7 rue Ernesto Ché Guevara, St-Andelain • 03 86 39 15 62 ☐ by appt ▨ white ★ Buisson Renard, Pur Sang, Silex

Domaine Henri Bourgeois
Central Loire / Sancerre
This dynamic domaine is located in the village of Chavignol, equally famous for its Sancerre as for its goats' cheese (Crotin de Chavignol). The company also has vineyards in Pouilly-Fumé, Quincy, and even Marlborough in New Zealand. A range of Sancerres is produced from specific sites, soils, and Sauvignon Blanc vines of varying age. Among these, les Baronnes is a crisp, fresh standard *cuvée*, Le MD de Bourgeois more minerally and intense, while La Côte des Monts Damnés is long and complex. ◈ Chavignol, Sancerre • 02 48 78 53 20 • www.bourgeois-sancerre.com ☐ ▨ red, white, rosé ★ Le MD de Bourgeois, La Côte des Monts Damnés

VINCENT GASNIER'S TOP 10 Good Producers of the Loire

1. **Coulée de Serrant** Savennières *p120*
2. **Baumard** Coteaux du Layon & Savennières *p121*
3. **Clos Rougeard** Saumur-Champigny *p120*
4. **Château de Villeneuve** Saumur-Champigny *p120*
5. **Château Pierre Bise** Coteaux du Layon *p120*
6. **Didier Dagueneau** Pouilly-Fumé *left*
7. **Alphonse Mellot** Sancerre *left*
8. **Huet** Vouvray *opposite*
9. **Yannick Amirault** Bourgueil *opposite*
10. **Henry Marrionet** Touraine *opposite*

CHAMPAGNE

CHAMPAGNE

AT ITS GLORIOUS BEST, *Champagne has no peers. It offers all the elements of a truly great sparkling wine: freshness and vivacity to lift the spirits, complexity of aroma, and richness on the palate balanced by fine acidity. While many wine regions produce good sparkling wine, Champagne has a monopoly of the most celebrated brands. With around 300 million bottles produced every year, it is the benchmark by which all other sparkling wines are judged.*

Champagne is France's most northerly wine region. The cool climate and long slow ripening of the fruit help to ensure high acidity. This is vital in the wine's long, slow ageing process. The unique complexity of Champagne, however, is the result of a magical combination of climate, chalky soil, and three centuries of human endeavour.

Key

▨ Champagne

Originally, Champagne was a red wine production area; wines were made in autumn and left to settle over winter, when the cold would halt fermentation. As spring arrived and the wines warmed up, they would begin to referment in the bottle – giving a slight spritz. These young, fizzy wines became fashionable in England in the mid-17th century. Later that century, Champagne's producers, led by Benedictine monk Dom Pérignon (who was in charge of the cellars at Hautvillier Abbey), found a way to refine and control this secondary fermentation. The modern era of Champagne was born.

Today, Champagne is usually a blend of three grape varieties (Pinot Noir, Pinot Meunier, and Chardonnay) and also a judicious mix from a number of vineyards *(crus)*. Additionally, unlike almost any other great wine, Champagne is largely a blend of grapes from more than one harvest. Single vintage wine is made, but only in the very best years.

In this marginal climate, slight *terroir* variations can affect the quality of grapes. For this reason, vineyards are rated on a scale known as the Échelle des Crus. All 301 villages in the appellation are classified, with the 17 *grands crus* all at 100 per cent, and 43 *premiers crus* with a rating between 90 and 99 per cent.

There are just over 12,000ha of Pinot Noir, around 10,900ha of Pinot Meunier, and just under 9,000ha of Chardonnay in the whole appellation. Only about an eighth of the vineyards are owned by the 264 *négociants*, who include the great houses whose names are synonymous with Champagne around the world. The *négociants* buy in grapes from growers all over the appellation. Blending the wines to maintain a specific house style is a complex process, with major firms using as many as 100 different *crus* (as Moët does in its Brut Impérial), to create the desired taste. No house grows all its own grapes; Bollinger and Louis Roederer are unusual in supplying around 75 per cent of their own needs. Some *négociants* buy in everything and have no vineyard holdings at all.

 Preceding pages **Moët & Chandon's Château de Saran in the Côte des Blancs**

Snow-covered Moët & Chandon vineyard on the Côte des Blancs

Champagne Areas

The Champagne appellation divides into five main production areas, each mainly associated with one of the three principal grape varieties. More a wide plateau than a mountain, the **Montagne de Reims** is best known for Pinot Noir (41 per cent), and the reputations of the famous *grand cru* villages of Mailly, Verzenay, Verzy, Ambonnay, and Bouzy are based on the quality of this variety. Differences in microclimate, aspect, and exposure of individual sites result in a large range of styles. Soil types may also vary, although all the *grands crus* are on the same chalky bed for which Champagne is famous.

In the **Vallée de la Marne** the majority of plantings are Pinot Meunier (63 per cent), which because of its late bud-break and early ripening is not as vulnerable in this low-lying, frost-prone valley. Less refined than Pinot Noir and Chardonnay, Meunier has a reputation for being Champagne's workhorse grape. Its fruitiness and early development help soften non-vintage blends, making them more approachable when young.

The **Côtes des Blancs**, which runs south from Épernay, takes its name from the fact that it is devoted to the cultivation of white grapes (Chardonnay 97 per cent). Grapes from the five *grands crus* – Cramant, Avize, Oger, Le Mesnil-sur-Oger, and Chouilly – are the most sought after and command the highest prices. They give freshness and finesse to any blend, and when used unblended – as in the wines of Salon – they can produce wines of great longevity and intensity. The small **Côte de Sézanne**, virtually a continuation of the Côte des Blancs, is also planted mainly with Chardonnay (62 per cent). Its wines tend to be more forward and fruitier than those in the Côte des Blancs. The most southerly area, the **Côte des Bar**, is an important source for vigorous, full-flavoured, ripe Pinot Noir. 🕸 chalky 🍇 Pinot Noir, Pinot Meunier 🍇 Chardonnay 🍷 sparkling

VINCENT GASNIER'S TOP 10 Great Champagne Houses

Wine Map of Champagne

The Champagne AOC embraces a total vineyard area of 32,000ha. It extends 150km north to south and 115km east to west and is made up of five distinct vineyard areas. Épernay sits at the heart of the three largest and most prestigious production zones: Montagne de Reims, Vallée de la Marne, and Côte des Blancs. Continuing south from the Côte des Blancs is the lesser-known Côte de Sézanne, while at the appellation's southerly extreme, some 100km from Épernay, is the Côte des Bar.

**MAJOR CHAMPAGNE
PRODUCERS**

Champagne Bollinger *p130*
Champagne Charles Heidsieck
    p130

Champagne Lanson *p130*
Champagne Perrier Jouët *p130*
Champagne Salon *p130*
Champagne Taittinger *p131*
Champagne Veuve Clicquot
    Ponsardin *p131*

Krug *p131*
Laurent-Perrier *p131*
Louis Roederer *p132*
Moët & Chandon *p132*
Pol Roger *p132*
Ruinart *p132*

Champagne: the Traditional Method

The traditional method (méthode traditionnelle) of producing sparkling wine was pioneered and developed in Champagne over many centuries. Though costly and labour-intensive, it is now used all over the world, although the label "Champagne" can, of course, only be applied to sparkling wine made in the region.

Grapes Acidity is very important in sparkling wine, so grapes may be harvested earlier than usual. If red grapes are used, hand harvesting is essential to avoid damaging the berries and staining the clear free-run juice.

Pressing The gentler the pressing, the better, to avoid harsh flavours and tannins.

First Fermentation The grape must, or juice, is fermented in stainless steel (or occasionally old oak casks) to produce an acidic white wine with moderate levels of alcohol.

Blending A range of wines is combined, either to achieve a consistent style or to create a wine far greater than the sum of its parts.

Second Fermentation The blended wine is bottled with a mixture of wine, sugar, and yeast, known as *liqueur de tirage*. This initiates a secondary fermentation inside the bottle, converting the sugar into alcohol and producing carbon dioxide – the fizz. A crown cap is added to seal the bottle.

Remuage of bottles in the cellars of Perrier-Jouet

Maturation During maturation the spent yeast cells or lees react with the wine, creating bready, yeasty flavours.

Removal of Sediment The bottle is gradually rotated (over six to eight weeks when done by hand) so that the sediment slides down to the neck, a procedure known as *remuage*. The neck is then frozen, the bottle stood upright and the crown cap removed. The frozen sediment is then expelled under pressure – a process known as disgorgement *(dégorgement)*.

Dosage & Corking *Dosage* is the term given to the replenishment of the small amount of wine lost during disgorgement. The liquid used to refill the bottle – the *liqueur d'expédition* – contains a mixture of reserve wine and sugar. The amount of sugar depends on the style required. A cork is then forced into the bottle at considerable pressure, and a wire basket is then fastened on top to reinforce it.

In Champagne there are strict laws on how much juice can be extracted from each batch of grapes

Regional Information at a Glance

Latitude 48–49.5°N. The location at the northern edge of the winemaking belt means ripening can only be achieved by stretching the vine's growth cycle to the limit.

Altitude 60–360m.

Topography A gently undulating, windswept plain intersected by rivers flowing east to west. Vineyards nestle on the hillsides and the gentler slopes of the river valleys, where there is protection from the westerly wind.

Soil Porous chalky subsoil that drains well and holds water for the vine. Chalk breaks through the thin surface soil in places, reflecting sunshine onto the vines.

Climate Champagne is a "cool climate" appellation, exposed to storms and wind from the English Channel.

Temperature July averages are 18.5°C in Reims and 19.5°C in Épernay

Rainfall Annual averages are 600mm in Reims and 670mm in Épernay

Viticultural Hazards pring frosts – in 2003, temperatures plunged below -6°C and more than half the harvest was lost.

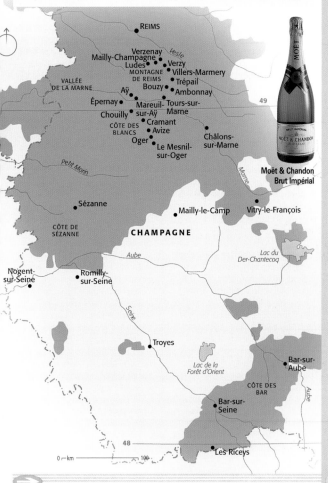

Moët & Chandon
Brut Impérial

Vineyards and château in Champagne

Major Champagne Producers

Champagne Bollinger
Based in Aÿ, the family-owned house of Bollinger has a 143-ha estate that supplies 70 per cent of its grapes. This underpins the high standard of its muscular, complex Pinot Noir-based wines, which age gracefully. Bollinger RD (recently disgorged) is vintage wine that is aged for longer on its lees, and only disgorged just prior to release to preserve freshness. Lovers of rich, mature wines are better off buying the considerably less expensive Grande Année and ageing it themselves. There is also a Vielles Vignes Françaises – Blanc de Noirs from three tiny parcels of pre-phylloxera vines that has much in common with single-vineyard Champagnes. ✆ 18 blvd du Maréchal de Lattre de Tassigny, Aÿ ● 03 26 53 33 66 ● www.champagne-bollinger.fr ★ Grand Année: white, rosé

Champagne Charles Heidsieck
Most Champagne houses like to be judged on the quality of their non-vintage Brut. On that basis alone, Heidsieck deserves its reputation for excellence. Its Mis en Cave non-vintage regularly stands out in tastings. Other wines also delight, notably the 100 per cent Chardonnay Blancs des Millénaires. It will be interesting to see if this quality continues following the death of inspired winemaker Daniel Thibault in 2002. ✆ 4 blvd Henry Vasnier, Reims ● 03 26 84 43 50 ● www.charlesheidsieck.com ★ Mis en Cave, Blancs des Millénaires

Champagne Lanson
Lanson's Black Label is the only popular non-vintage Champagne not to undergo malolactic fermentation (which makes the wines more approachable in their youth), and it can seem acidic as a result. However, a couple of years' bottle age shows just how well it is made. Vintage Lanson can be exceptional (as in 1995, 1989, 1988, and 1976), and the brand's two prestige cuveés – vintage Blanc de Blancs and Noble Cuvée – are wines of real elegance. ✆ 12 blvd Lundy, Reims ● 03 26 78 50 50 ● www.lanson.fr ★ Blanc de Blancs, Noble Cuvée

Champagne Perrier Jouët
Perrier Jouët's fortunes have changed under new owner Allied Domecq, as demonstrated by significant improvement in the non-vintage Grand Brut. Since winemaker Hervé Deschamps took over in 1993, the vintage wines have also blossomed. Cuvée de prestige Belle Époque, packaged in the famous Art Nouveau flower motif bottle and made in white and rosé styles, has barely flagged, apart from disappointments in 1989 and 1990. ✆ 26 ave de Champagne, Epernay ● 03 26 53 38 00 ● www.perrier-jouet.com ★ Belle Époque

Champagne Salon
Considered by many to be without equal, Salon comes only from grand cru Le Mesnil-sur-Oger in the Côte des Blancs, and is made

Cuvées de prestige are top-of-the-range wines (sometimes single vintage) using the region's finest grapes and matured for long periods solely from Chardonnay. A vintage wine, it is made only in remarkable harvests, with no more than 10,000 cases in any year, and it is typically aged for at least a decade before release. Even then it still tends to be piercingly fresh, not developing its full complexity for a couple of decades or more. 🕸 *Le Mesnil-sur-Oger • 03 26 57 51 65* ★ *Salon*

Champagne Taittinger

Taittinger is one of the bigger houses still in family ownership, with good vineyard holdings in the Côte des Blancs. These are put to excellent use in its Blanc de Blancs *cuvée de prestige*, Comtes de Champagne, which can develop richness and complexity with age. Sensibly, Taittinger is focusing on this wine, which also comes in a rosé style, and no longer makes its overpricedVintage Collection. 🕸 *9 place Saint-Nicaise, Reims • 03 26 85 45 35 • www.taittinger.fr* ★ *Cuvée Comtes de Champagne (white)*

Champagne Veuve Clicquot Ponsardin

The next largest producer of non-vintage Brut after Moët has suffered from its success. The increase in volume has meant sacrifices in quality and style, and wines have become younger and lighter. However, the muscular, Pinot Noir-based vintage wines, made in white and rosé versions that age particularly well, maintain their high quality. The *cuvée de prestige* La Grand Dame is also consistently good, but expensive. 🕸 *13 rue Albert Thomas, Reims • 03 26 89 53 90 • www.veuve-clicquot.fr* ★ *vintage wines, La Grand Dame*

Krug

Established in 1843, Krug is now in the hands of LVMH, which also owns Dom Pérignon and Ruinart. At Krug, even the non-vintage Grande Cuvée is matured for at least six years before release. Top wines are kept back much longer, but to appreciate a vintage Krug fully, it should be cellared for several years, even a decade, after its release. At a tasting in 2002 to celebrate Henri Krug's retirement, almost every released vintage that he was involved with (1962 to 1988) was opened, and the 1981 vintage was the youngest wine to be nearing its peak. 🕸 *5 rue Coquebert, Reims • 03 26 84 44 20 • www.krug.com* ★ *Grande Cuvée, vintage Krug*

Laurent-Perrier

Winemaker Alain Thierry is one of the best in Champagne, and he makes two of its greatest wines: Laurent-Perrier's *cuvée de prestige* Grande Siècle and Salon. The company is probably best known for its non-vintage rosé, but its light non-vintage Brut also merits attention. The Grande Siècle *cuvées*, particularly the rosé, are just what prestige Champagne should be. 🕸 *Ave de Champagne, Tours-sur-Marne • 03 26 58 91 22 • www.laurent-perrier.fr* ★ *Grande Siècle, NV Brut*

Champagne Styles

Sweetness depends on the amount of sugar added at *dosage*. It ranges from *ultra brut* (very dry) and *brut* (dry) to *demi-sec* (medium sweet) and *doux* (very sweet).
Non-vintage Champagne (NV) is made from a blend of grapes from different years and matured for at least 15 months on its lees.
Vintage Champagne must come from a single harvest and requires at least three years of maturation.
Blanc de blancs is made entirely from white grapes (almost always 100 per cent Chardonnay). This is the longest-lived of all Champagnes.
Blanc de noirs is made entirely from red grapes and tends to be fruitier than ordinary Champagne.

Louis Roederer

Louis Roederer wines are elegant, subtle, complex, and long-lived. A large holding of top quality *grand cru* vineyards forms the basis of this dazzling range. The delicious non-vintage Brut Premier puts most non-vintage Champagne to shame, while Roederer's top wine, Cristal, is one of Champagne's icons of excellence. The vintage Blanc de Blancs is a beautifully refined, less celebrated star, for those who do not have the cash for Cristal.
⊗ *21 blvd Lundy, Reims • 03 26 40 42 11 • www.champagne-roederer.com ★ NV Brut Premier, vintage Blanc des Blancs.*

Moët & Chandon

The best known and biggest selling non-vintage brand is Moët & Chandon's Brut Impérial. Given the volume produced (over 16 million bottles a year), the consistent quality of this wine is laudable. Moët's recently introduced non-vintage rosé is good enough to rival Laurent-Perrier's, and its vintage wines can be classy and develop well with age. Moët's Dom Pérignon continues to excel in the hands of winemaker Richard Geoffroy, although unfortunately most is drunk long before its peak, rarely reached before 15 years of maturing. ⊗ *18 ave de Champagne, Epernay • 03 26 51 20 20 • www.moet. com ★ Dom Pérignon, NV rosé*

Pol Roger

After a period of investment in its winery, Pol Roger is back on top form. Its fine, long-lived vintage wines are much sought after and attractively priced. They need time to reach their full potential, so anyone who has already drunk a 1988 vintage is missing a treat for the future. Prestige style, the vintage Sir Winston Churchill Cuvée, has few peers. The installation of Krug's former winemaker, Dominique Petit, is unlikely to set things back. ⊗ *1 rue Henri Lelarge, Epernay • 03 26 59 58 00 • www.polroger.co.uk ★ Sir Winston Churchill Cuvée, various vintage cuvées*

Ruinart

Ruinart, the oldest house in Champagne, founded in 1729, is the only producer in the LVMH camp to specialize in Chardonnay and *blanc de blancs* styles. With the launch of a non-vintage *blanc de blancs* and a top-of-the-range, multi-vintage blend named L'Exclusive, it now has three such wines. However, it is the vintage Dom Ruinart Blanc de Blancs, a blend of Côte des Blancs *grands crus* with Chardonnay from the best villages in the Montagne de Reims, that maintains this house's reputation. ⊗ *4 rue des Crayères, Reims • 03 26 77 51 51 • www.ruinart.com ★ vintage Dom Ruinart Blanc de Blancs*

Other Major Champagne Producers

Billecart-Salmon *40 rue Carnot, Mareuil-sur Äy • 03 26 52 60 22 • www.champagne.billecart.fr*

Champagne Alfred Gratien *30 rue Maurice-Cervaux, Épernay • 03 26 54 38 20 • www.alfredgratien.com*

Champagne Deutz *16 rue Jeanson, Äy • 03 26 56 94 00 • www.champagne-deutz.com*

Champagne Drappier *11 rue Goiot, Reims • 03 25 27 40 15 • www.champagne-drappier.com*

Champagne Henriot *3 place des Droits de l'Homme, Reims • 03 26 89 53 00 • www.champagne-henriot.fr*

Champagne Jacquart (co-operative) *16 Rue de Mars, Reims • 03 26 07 88 40 • www.jacquart-champagne.fr*

Champagne Philipponnat *13 rue du Pont, Mareuil-sur Äy • 03 26 56 93 00 • www.champagnephilipponnat.com*

Union Champagne (co-operative) *7 rue Pasteur, Avize • 03 26 57 94 22 • www.de-saint-gall.com*

The Wines of Alsace

Poised between French and German cultures, Alsace is quite unlike any other wine region in France. Its ribbon of vineyards running through the foothills of the rugged Vosges Mountains produces versatile, fruity, and full-bodied wines, which, unusually for France, take their names from the local grape varieties.

Key

 Alsace

A Disputed Region

Four centuries of territorial disputes between France and Germany – including German annexation after the Franco-Prussian War (1871) and France's recovery of the region after World War I (1918) – have left their mark on the identity of Alsace's wines. The vineyards face towards Germany, only 30km away, and, although Alsace has been firmly under French rule since 1945, German influences are in evidence throughout the region, from village names to grape varieties. However, the concentrated, powerful wines of Alsace are in a league of their own. With an effortless balance between fruit and acidity, Alsace wines are produced in both dry and sweet styles. Wood is rarely used in the vinification so the grape flavours are pure, and the varied microclimates, created by foothill topography, accentuate the wines' all-important acidity.

The majority of Alsace wine is white: Gewürztraminer, Riesling, Muscat Blanc à Petits Grains, and Pinot Gris are the signature grapes. Muscat and Pinot Gris are native to France, while the other two are rejected by AOC rules elsewhere in the country. Pinot Noir, the only red grape grown here, accounts for just nine per cent of total production.

Alsace's famed and beautiful Route du Vin runs through the heart of its two départements – Bas-Rhin and Haut-Rhin – which together have some 15,000ha of vineyards. The finest Alsace wines come from Haut-Rhin's central section, where the height of the Vosges Mountains protects the vines from rain and wind from the west.

limestone, sandstone, gravel, clay mixtures (Bas-Rhin) *Pinot Noir* *Riesling, Gewürztraminer, Pinot Gris, Muscat à Petits Grains, Sylvaner* *white*

VINCENT GASNIER'S TOP 10 Winemakers in Alsace

1. **Marcel Deiss** 15 route du Vin, Bergheim, 03 89 73 63 37
2. **Maison Trimbach** www.maison-trimbach.fr
3. **Dopff au Moulin** www.dopff-au-moulin.fr
4. **Marc Kreydenweiss** www.kreydenweiss.com
5. **Rolly Gassmann** 1 rue de l'Église, Rorschwihr, 03 89 73 63 28
6. **Zind Humbrecht** 4 route de Colmar, Turckheim, 03 89 27 02 05
7. **Weinbach** www.domaineweinbach.com
8. **Schlumberger** www.domaines-schlumberger.com
9. **Clos St-Landelin** www.mure.com
10. **Hugel & Fils** www.hugel.com

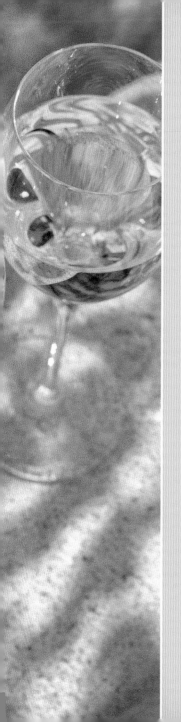

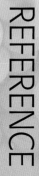

REFERENCE

Wine Styles

Obviously no two wines are ever exactly alike, but wine styles (excluding fortified wines such as port and sherry) can be broadly divided into the ten categories set out below. Examples from France are given for each style.

Sparkling

Sparkling wines run the gamut from light-as-air Italian prosecco and elegant, steely French Champagnes that mellow with age, to rich, heart-warming toasty bubblies from warmer New World vineyards and ripe-fruit red sparkling Shiraz from Australia. The classic blend for sparkling wine (Champagne in particular) is Chardonnay, Pinot Noir, and Pinot Meunier. This combination develops fruitiness with firmness and fragrance. Top sparkling wines also gain complexity from the second fermentation in bottle and contact with the finished fermentation yeasts. Good Champagne should have complex toast, nut, butter, and biscuit flavours, and the bubbles should give a tingling sensation to balance the flavour.
★ *Champagne, Crémant de Loire, Crémant de Die, Blanquette de Limoux*

Crisp, dry, light-bodied whites

Expect pale, white, even green-tinged colours in the glass, and green apple, fresh-mown grass, wet stones, and sometimes gooseberry on the nose. These wines will be light, with neutral aromas backed up by crisp acidity and tangy, refreshing fruit on the palate – with flavours of apples, pears, citrus fruits. Grapes to watch out for are Pinot Blanc, Sauvignon Blanc, Riesling, and lighter versions of Chardonnay. These wines are not widely found in the New World (except the coolest parts of New Zealand); classic examples from the Old World include Vinho Verde from Portugal and Chablis and Muscadet from France. Oak-ageing does a crisp, dry white no favours; it should be refreshing on the palate and is best drunk young.
★ *Chablis, Muscadet Sèvre et Maine*

Aromatic or flowery, dry to medium-sweet whites

Aromatic wines may have a strong colour, but it is on the nose that they really make their mark. Expect anything from honey, diesel, and hay (Riesling), to smoky citrus notes (Pinot Gris), peaches (Viognier), to pure grape flavours (Muscat) and even roses, lychees, and Turkish delight from the most aromatic grape of all, Gewürztraminer. Most of these aromas will be backed up on the palate with similar flavours, but wines can vary from light and delicate (Germany, Greece) to robustly perfumed and weighty (Alsace, Australia). The powerful aromatic character of these wines can integrate well with a touch of sugar, so some are made in an "off-dry" or medium-sweet style.

No sensible producer will smother the lively character with oak.
★ *Gewürztraminer (Alsace)*

Tangy or steely, medium-bodied whites

Less flamboyant on the nose, but more assertive on the palate than aromatic wines, tangy/steely styles are some of the best to pair with food. Expect creamier, smoother aromas and allow time for these to open out in the glass as the wine warms up, and as it ages. Firm-fruited flavours tend to mellow as the wine gets older. Tangy wines suggest hazelnuts (Chardonnay), damp stones (Chenin Blanc), and beeswax (Sémillon); steely ones lean towards flint and gooseberries (Sauvignon Blanc), and limes (Riesling). In general tangy wines respond better to oak-ageing than steely ones, but not for long: the strong vanilla flavours of oak can easily overpower them.
★ *Chablis premier and grand cru, white Burgundy, white Bordeaux, Sancerre, Pouilly-Fumé, Menetou-Salon, Riesling (Alsace)*

Full-bodied, rich flavoured whites

Full-on, bold, and golden in the glass, these wines look as luscious as they taste. Expect a waft of buttery, honeyed aromas, along with tropical fruit, peaches, nectarines, even pineapple. There will be a similar barrage of rich, mouth-filling flavour on the palate. Full-bodied whites often have higher alcohol, but the best of them still have a twang of acidity to keep them balanced. They all benefit from

additional vanilla oak characters, but should not be overwhelmed by them. Many gain complexity with age. Full-bodied whites hail mainly from warmer New World countries, but pockets of the Northern Rhône, Languedoc-Roussillon, and central Spain also produce powerful whites.
★ *Condrieu and white Rhône*

Rosé
Made from red grapes, but left only for a limited time with the colour-giving grape skins, rosé can vary from palest powderpuff pink (California Zinfandel), to deep opaque red (Australian Grenache), depending on how long the grapes macerate. Many have the weight of a white wine on the palate, but the aromas of red fruits and hedgerow berries nearly always give away their red grape origins. Lighter wines – generally from Old World countries (Loire Valley and Provence in France, Navarra in Spain) – will be delicate, thirst-quenching, and tangy with a hint of red fruits. Heavier ones – from the Rhône Valley and Australia – have richer, deeper, almost red wine flavours, with a touch of tannin.
★ *Tavel, Lirac, Anjou rosé*

Fresh, fruity, low tannin reds
This style is red wine at its simplest, freshest, and most juicy. These pinky reds are for drinking as young as possible, as they will greet you with pure, primary fruit aromas of raspberry, red apple, and cherry, backed up with cheery red-fruit characters which fill

the palate. There will be no chalky tannins getting in the way of their satiny smoothness, and any acidity will be soft and supple. Fresh, fruity reds are as likely to come from the Old World as the New, from grapes low in tannin, such as Gamay, Grenache, and Barbera. In hotter countries where grapes get riper in the sun, tannins are often overtaken by full fruity flavours, so a usually robust grape like Merlot can exchange its tannin for plummy fruit. These reds trade on their fruity freshness, so are best without ageing in oak.
★ *Beaujolais, Chinon, Saumur-Champigny*

Medium to full-bodied reds
This group includes the world's classic red wines, which first and foremost have a firm structure and plenty of backbone. In medium- to full-bodied Old World wines – such as Burgundy, Bordeaux and Barolo – aromas and flavours might not be very expressive at first, but with a year or two's age, the wines will open up to reveal wafts of bramble fruit, mulberry, plum, and violet. They develop in a similar way on the palate too: youthful hard tannins will soften, and as the wines mature, their range of fruit flavours will evolve to include cranberries, spice, truffles, and chocolate. Medium- and full-bodied reds call out for oak, which adds both structure and a touch of vanilla aroma. These wines match perfectly with red meat and game dishes.
★ *Burgundy, Bordeaux, Châteauneuf-du-Pape, Côtes du Rhône Villages*

Full, powerful, often spicy reds
These are the most mouth-filling wines of all. Grapes such as Cabernet Sauvignon (blackcurrant), Shiraz (spicy plum and liquorice), and Zinfandel (leather and strawberries) dominate this category. The wines are a rich, inky colour in the glass, show intense, sweet dark fruit on the nose, then dense, velvety-smooth fruit on the palate. These wines are mainly from grapes tough enough to survive in the hot vineyards of the New World or the Rhône Valley. Many will develop in the cellar but their overwhelming ripeness also makes them fruity enough to drink young. They all need oak to balance their powerful fruit flavours.
★ *Côte Rôtie, Hermitage*

Sweet/Dessert
Sweet wines vary from light, delicate, grapey versions from the Muscat grape to full-on Australian liqueur wines (again Muscats), which display all the golden sunshine of their origins. The former are apéritifs, the latter dessert wines, too concentrated for drinking with a meal. In between are a host of sweet wines with rich, honeyed aromas and buttery-smooth flavours, the finest of all being Sauternes. All sweet wines should have a crisp acidity to balance the sweetness of their fruit or they become lifeless. Wines from the Riesling grape, especially from Alsace are some of the zestiest; but Tokaji from Hungary has the tangiest, most lingering sweetness of all.
★ *Alsace vendange tardive, Sauternes, Barsac, Monbazillac, Vouvray*

Tasting Wine

Wine can simply be consumed like any other beverage. Tasting wine, however, entails a more thoughtful, methodical approach. The following notes are designed to help you to maximize the pleasure you derive from every glass.

Practicalities

It is best to taste wine in a naturally lit, odourless room to allow its true colour to be examined and to avoid other aromas interfering with the sense of smell. Avoid perfume, mints, and smoke. The most important factor when tasting is the shape and size of glass, as this can have a major impact on the taste of a wine *(See p146)*.

Look

Looking at a wine can provide valuable clues to its character. Note the colour and check that the wine is clear – cloudiness can indicate a fault. For reds, tilt the glass away from you against a white background and inspect the rim of the liquid to see the true colour. As a red wine ages, it changes from bright purple to tawny and then to brown. So if a red wine looks brown, it may be past its best (although brown would be normal in wines such as sherry and tawny port). A deep golden colour in a white wine may indicate the wine has been aged in oak, but it can also indicate a sweet wine style or particularly ripe fruit.

Smell

Smelling wine will vastly improve your enjoyment and knowledge. Firstly, gently sniff the wine. Make a note of any first impressions, as they are often the most revealing.

Holding the glass by its stem, swirl the wine in order to help release its aromas. Then take another sniff. Note the fruit aromas you detect now. Are they intense or relatively subdued? Is there a range of suggested "flavours"? If so, this might indicate complexity, a sign of quality. Does it smell of the fruity flavours often found in a young wine, or does it boast more mature, developed aromas such as mushrooms, leather, and diesel? Is any one smell dominant, and do you like it? *See pp140–141 for help in identifying some of the aromas you may detect.*

Taste

This stage often merely confirms the impression received on the nose. Take a small sip and allow the wine to linger on your tongue and mouth. You can enhance the flavours by pursing your lips and sucking a small amount of air into your mouth. This takes practice, but it is something professional tasters encourage as the presence of oxygen amplifies the flavours experienced. If you are tasting a lot of wines in one session, it is normally sensible to spit out each wine after noting the flavours and neutralize the palate by eating a cracker or taking a sip of water. Here are some further guidelines:

• Note the sweetness of the wine, detected on the tip of the tongue. Is it dry, medium, or sweet?

• Consider the acidity – the element of a wine that keeps it fresh – detected on the sides of the tongue. Is it in balance with the rest of the flavours?

• How heavy does the wine feel in your mouth? Do you think it is light-, medium- or full-bodied?

• Assess the wine's fruit qualities. Are they pure and fruity (as in a young wine), or mature and complex (as in an older one)?

• Can you recognize any individual flavours?

• With red wines, think about tannins – the drying, mouth-puckering elements picked up by your gums. Are they harsh and bitter, or in balance with the wine?

Finish

Consider how long the flavours last in your mouth after you spit or swallow. This is known as the "finish" and, in general, the longer it lasts, the better the wine.

Describing a Wine

It is virtually impossible to express in words the complexities and subtleties of even the most basic of wines. When it comes to identifying aromas and flavours, wine tasters borrow their vocabulary from all kinds of areas, including fruits, flowers, spices, nuts, and types of wood. Some of the flavour compounds actually exist in certain wines. For example, vanilla aromas come from vanillin, which occurs naturally in new oak barrels. However, others are mere impressions that wines create in the mind of the taster. Everyone's sense of smell and taste is, of course, different, as we all have our own memory bank of flavours.

For more details on French grape varieties **See p13**

Descriptive Terms

There are a large number of commonly used words and phrases for discussing the style and character of a wine. Definitions are not water-tight and there is often a large margin of overlap between the various terms.

age-worthy Applied to wines that will benefit from further maturation in the bottle. Typical examples of age-worthy wines are young with either powerful tannins, good acidity, or some sweetness.

aromatic A wine with lots of perfumed, fruity aromas, which normally leap out of the glass. Aromatic grape varieties include Sauvignon Blanc, Riesling, Gewürztraminer, and Muscat.

austere A wine that lacks fruity flavours and displays harsh, bitter tannins and/or high acidity.

acidic All wines need acidity to keep them balanced, but too much is a fault. Acidity is detected on the sides of the tongue.

balanced A wine with all its components (mainly acidity, alcohol, fruit, tannins, sugar, and extract) in harmony, with no one element prominent.

big A full-bodied wine that leaves a major impression on the senses, typically containing high levels of fruit, tannins, and/or alcohol. Also used to mean plenty of flavour.

bitter Normally a negative term used to describe a wine with an excess of harsh tannins, which leaves a bitter taste in the mouth, detected at the back of the tongue. In some reds, however, a certain amount of bitterness is a desirable characteristic.

blockbuster Used to describe exceptionally "big" wines. Think large

amounts of fruit, alcohol, tannins, or oaky flavours.

body The weight or feel of wine in the mouth, determined by its alcohol and extract. To work out whether a wine is light-, medium- or full-bodied, it may be useful to compare it to the feel of water.

clean Lacking faults in terms of aroma and flavour.

complex A wine with many layers of aroma and flavour – many different fruits, plus characteristics such as spice and vanilla. Complexity is one of the elements that separates an average wine from a good or great one. The most complex wines have typically gone through a period of ageing, allowing more flavours to develop.

concentrated An intense taste, normally found in wines with high levels of tannin, sugar, and flavouring and colouring compounds.

crisp Noticeable acidity but in a positive, refreshing way. Usually used for white wines with clean, fresh flavours.

dry No obvious sugar or sweetness in the wine. Note that very ripe, fruity flavours and new oak flavours can sometimes give the impression of sweetness, although the wine itself can still be dry. "Dried-out" is a term given to red wines which have spent too long in barrel or bottle and have lost their fruit flavour.

easy-drinking A relatively simple wine that can be enjoyed without much thought. It will be fruity and, if red, low in tannin.

elegant A subjective term, used to describe a good quality, subtle, balanced wine which is not too fruity, and is extremely pleasant to drink.

extract All the solid matter in a wine such as

tannins, sugars, and colouring and flavouring compounds. Extract is what gives a wine its body.

finesse Quality of a wine that displays elegance.

flabby A negative term used for a wine which has low acidity and is therefore unbalanced. It can make for a slightly cloying taste.

fleshy A wine which feels almost solid in texture when in the mouth, thanks to high levels of fruit and extract.

fresh Like crisp, noticeably acidic in an attractive, refreshing way. Normally used for young white wines.

fruity A wine with plenty of attractive fruit favours.

harsh Rough around the edges, lacking in subtlety.

heavy Normally refers to a full-bodied, tannic red wine, and means it is tough to drink or heavy going. It may indicate that the wine needs to spend further time in bottle.

mature Ready to drink. Generally used for quality wines that require time in bottle. Over-mature is a euphemism for past its best.

oaky Normally a negative term to describe when oak flavours dominate other flavours in a wine. If the wine is young and good quality, it may lose some of its oakiness with a few years in bottle. Oak flavours can be desirable but only if they are balanced by fruit.

powerful A "big" wine with high levels of extract and/or alcohol. Can be used in a positive or negative sense.

racy Word similar in meaning to crisp and fresh, used to describe wines with noticeable levels of refreshing acidity. It is especially associated with Riesling.

rich Like concentrated, implying deep, intense flavours in the mouth. Can also be used to mean slightly sweet.

ripe Wine made from ripe grapes and showing flavours of richer, warmer-climate fruits, such as pineapples (rather than apples). Ripe wine might also suggest a certain sweetness, even though it may not contain sugar.

simple Lacking complexity, with one-dimensional flavours. This is a fault in expensive wine, but it may not be a problem for everyday drinking wine.

soft A red wine with gentle tannins. Also known as smooth.

structured Normally refers to the tannins in a red wine, which support the other elements. In a "well-structured" wine the tannins are noticeable but still balanced. Sometimes used for acidity in white wines, for example a wine can be described as having a "good acidic structure".

subtle Normally linked to finesse, it means a wine contains a number of different nuances and tastes. It can also be a euphemism for a wine lacking in fruity flavours.

sweet A wine with noticeable levels of sugar, detected by the tip of the tongue. The phrase "sweet fruit flavours" may be used to describe an extremely ripe style of wine.

tannic An excess of tannins, the drying compounds that come from the skins, pips, and stalks of grapes. Some tannic wines simply require further maturation in bottle. Tannins are not necessarily a bad thing, they just need to be balanced by fruity flavours.

up-front Used to describe an easy-drinking style of wine with straightforward, fruity flavours.

warm A wine with an excess of alcohol leaves a "warm" finish. Can be used to describe full-bodied, spicy red wines.

Aromas and Flavours

There are obviously thousands of different identifiable aromas and flavours in wine, but here is a list of some of those most commonly detected. Certain flavours (such as blackcurrant) speak for themselves, whereas others, such as "mineral" or "vegetal", require a little explanation. Entries include examples of grape varieties or wines where the flavour is usually encountered.

apple Often found in cooler-climate, dry white wines, such as Chablis, Muscadet, and Vouvray.

apricot Common in riper styles of white wine such as Viognier and oak-fermented Chardonnay.

blackcurrant Widely associated with Cabernet Sauvignon and some other red grape varieties such as Merlot, Syrah/Shiraz, and Cabernet Franc. Occasionally a certain underripe blackcurrant flavour can be detected in Sauvignon Blanc.

buttery A creamy texture reminiscent of butter (rather than a specific flavour) is commonly found in oak-fermented Chardonnay and other white wines. This is caused by malolactic fermentation in the barrel, particularly where lees stirring is used.

cherry Found in a wide range of red wines, especially in cool-climate Pinot Noir.

citrus A character widely found in white wines, particularly fresh, aromatic styles. Can be further narrowed down to lemon, lime, orange etc.

coconut A flavour commonly associated with both whites and reds that have been fermented or matured in new American oak barrels. In excess it can indicate a fault.

creamy Used to indicate a smooth, quite full-bodied texture in a wine, or a smell of cream.

diesel Widely found in mature bottles of Riesling.

earthy A soil-like aroma commonly identified in older bottles of red Bordeaux.

farmyard A slightly dirty, earthy, manure-type aroma. In a young wine it may indicate poor (unclean) winemaking practices. In an older bottle of red Burgundy it can be a desirable, developed character.

floral A number of cool-climate whites display aromas vaguely reminiscent of flowers. Some are easy to identify, such as elderflower (aromatic whites), violets (mature Bordeaux), and roses (Gewürztraminer).

game/gaminess A decaying, fleshy aroma commonly associated with older bottles of Pinot Noir (red Burgundy), Syrah (Northern Rhône), and other mature red wines.

gooseberry The classic aroma and flavour of Sauvignon Blanc. Also found in other aromatic, zesty white wines.

grapey A term meaning smelling of grapes a vaguely "sweet" fruity aroma. The only variety for which this is true is Muscat (and all its various names and clones).

grass Widely found in fresh, aromatic wines from cooler climates from grapes such as Sauvignon Blanc, Sémillon, and Chenin Blanc.

honey Normally found in sweeter styles of wine – particularly Sauternes, Tokay Pinot Gris (Tokay d'Alsace), and sweet wines from the Loire Valley – in which the grapes have been affected by the disease botrytis.

jammy A slightly derogatory term for a red wine bursting with up-front flavours of blackcurrant, raspberry, and other fruits, but lacking in structure. It normally implies the wine lacks finesse.

lemon Widely found in white wines, particularly those from cooler climates.

liquorice Commonly associated with full-bodied reds made from Syrah.

lychee An aroma widely found in wines made from Gewürztraminer.

mineral It is difficult to taste mineral but the term is usually used to describe a sharp, earthy character in cool-climate wines such as Chablis and Sauvignon Blanc from Sancerre and Pouilly Fumé.

mint Particularly associated with Cabernet Sauvignon grown in warm-climate countries.

mushroom An aroma displayed by Pinot Noir as it matures.

pepper (black) Commonly associated with the red wines of southern France (especially from the Rhône Valley and the Grenache grape variety).

plum Apparent in many red wines but particularly those made from Merlot.

rose Found in Gewürztraminer and wines made from the Nebbiolo grape variety.

rubber Can indicate a wine fault caused by excessive sulphur, or is widely (and positively) associated with the Syrah grape variety.

spice Found in wines

fermented and matured in new oak barrels. Also apparent in certain red grape varieties, such as Grenache (which often has a peppery flavour) and other wines from southern France.

summer fruits Aromas such as strawberry, raspberry, and cherry. Especially associated with young Pinot Noir.

tangy Similar to zesty, but perhaps with more orange fruits. Mostly applies to whites but can also be used to describe reds such as fruity, crisp Cabernet Franc from the Loire.

tobacco A mature, developed aroma found in older bottles of Cabernet Sauvignon, particularly red Bordeaux.

toast The word "toasty" is most frequently used to describe the aroma imparted by oak barrels, but "toastiness" is also a quality of mature

Champagne, especially *blanc de blancs*.

tropical fruits Ripe flavours such as banana, pineapple, and mango, which are normally associated with New World Chardonnay.

vanilla Derived directly from new oak barrels. The wood contains vanillin, the substance that gives vanilla pods their aroma.

vegetal Rotting vegetable-type aromas found in older bottles of red and white wines, especially Burgundy (of both colours). It might sound unpleasant, but it is a desirable attribute in these styles of wine.

yeast Bread-type aroma widely associated with Champagne (and the secondary fermentation process used to create it).

zesty Aromas of lemon, lime, and, sometimes, orange. Normally found in crisp, refreshing dry white wines.

Common Faults

Wine today is much more reliable than ever before. With the exception of a corked bottle, seriously flawed wine is rare. There are, however, a number of problems you may encounter, which would warrant returning a bottle of wine to the place of purchase.

corked This is the most common wine fault, found in 2 to 5 per cent of all wines sold. It is caused by a mould found in some natural corks that can taint the wine, and has nothing to do with pieces of cork floating in your glass. Corked wine smells musty and lacks fruit flavours, but this may not become obvious until it has spent a few minutes in the glass. Plastic corks or screwcaps eliminate this problem.

oxidized Over-exposure to oxygen harms wine, eventually turning it into vinegar. A winemay become oxidized if its seal is insufficiently airtight, if left too long in bottle before opening, or if left too longonce opened.

sulphur All wines are bottled with a dose of sulphur, which acts as a preservative. However, if too much sulphur is added, the wine acquires an astringent, rubbery smell. In large quantities, it can be dangerous for asthmatics.

poor winemaking If you taste a wine with excess acidity, tannins, or oak, or with an absence of fruity flavours, it may simply be the result of poor winemaking.

Wine and Food Matching

Wine and food have complemented each other for thousands of years. Wine comes into its own at the dinner table thanks to its moderate alcohol, refreshing acidity, and sheer range of flavours. It is worth knowing some successful pairings of food and wine that have stood the test of time.

Guidelines

Whether selecting a bottle to accompany a take-away, or choosing different wines for each course at a dinner party, there are a number of basic guidelines:

• Decide on the dominant taste and choose a wine to accompany it.

• Select a wine to match the weight and power of your food. Full-flavoured foods require full-flavoured, full-bodied wines. Delicate dishes are overpowered by heavily oaked or tannic styles, so they require light wines. Full-bodied whites have similar power and weight to lighter reds, so work equally well with dishes such as grilled tuna or roast turkey.

• Sweet food should be matched by a similarly sweet wine. Many Thai dishes, for example, contain a lot of sugar, which is why off-dry styles such as Gewürztraminer from Alsace work so well.

• Tannins in a red wine taste softer when drunk with red meat. This is why classic combinations like beef with red Bordeaux are so effective.

• The more complicated the flavours in a dish, the more difficult it is to find a wine to pair with it, though some wines do work well with a range of flavours *(See In Restaurants p144)*.

• If serving top-quality wine, simply prepared dishes using the finest ingredients allow the wine to take centre stage.

• Try to match regional dishes with the same region's wines.

Apéritifs

An apéritif should simply whet your appetite, leaving you ready to enjoy the food and wine to come, so never choose anything too heavy or overbearing.

• Dry, light, and refreshing white wine works well. Avoid oaked wine. Think unoaked Sémillon or Pinot Blanc from Alsace.

• Champagne and sparkling wines are ideal, particularly for special occasions. Their dryness and relative acidity stimulates the tastebuds.

• Do not serve the best wine of the evening as an apéritif. A well-made, basic bottle will allow true appreciation of the subtleties of the better wines to follow.

With Starters

Bear in mind the best order for serving wine when choosing your starter – white before red, dry before sweet, light- before fuller-bodied, and in ascending order of quality. If the choice of menu requires a full-bodied red for the starter, avoid serving a dish that needs a light wine for the main.

Asparagus: Sauvignon Blanc. If served in a creamy sauce, a fuller-bodied wine such as Chablis.

Foie gras: Sauternes, although serving a sweet wine this early in the meal could present problems later. Champagne and Gewürztraminer also work.

Gazpacho: Relatively neutral, dry whites.

Pâtés and terrines: A wine that works with the main ingredient in its cooked form (see fish and meat sections).

Salad (no dressing): Sauvignon Blanc, Riesling, and unoaked Chardonnay are good options.

Salad (with creamy dressing): Chablis or Pinot Blanc.

Salad (with vinaigrette): A wine with high acidity like Sauvignon Blanc, or dry Riesling.

Soup (chicken): Medium-bodied Chardonnay or Pinot Blanc.

Soup (chunky, meaty): Southern French reds (Côtes du Rhône or Vin de Pays d'Oc, for example).

Soup (creamy and fishy): Fuller-flavoured Chardonnay or wines like Muscadet or white Bordeaux. Sparkling wines can also work well, as can light rosés.

With Fish & Seafood

The dominant flavour in seafood dishes will often be the sauce. Creamy dishes demand a full-bodied white, whereas tomato-based ones require a medium-bodied red. Also consider the intensity of the cooking method, and the quality of the ingredients.

Bouillabaisse: Inexpensive whites, reds, and rosés from the South of France.

Chowder (creamy): Basic Chardonnay.

Chowder (tomato-based): Medium-bodied reds.

Cod (battered): Crisp, dry whites, such as Sauvignon Blanc or Chenin Blanc.

Cod and haddock (fresh): Unoaked Chardonnay or dry white Bordeaux.

Reference – Wine and Food Matching

Crab: Sauvignon Blanc or dry Riesling.
Herring: Muscadet.
Lobster: Good white Burgundy.
Mackerel and sardines (fresh): Sauvignon Blanc, Muscadet, or light rosés.
Mackerel (smoked): Oily white like Alsace Pinot Gris.
Mussels/Oysters: Muscadet or Sauvignon Blanc.
Salmon (barbecued): Lighter reds such as Pinot Noir or Beaujolais.
Salmon (grilled): Unoaked Chardonnay or Alsace Pinot Blanc. White Rhône, white Bordeaux, and dry Riesling are also decent matches.
Salmon (poached): A delicate Chablis or dry white Bordeaux.
Salmon (smoked): Chablis, Sauvignon Blanc or dry Riesling. Champagne and other sparkling wines also work well.
Sea bass (with butter sauce): White Burgundy.
Sea bass (with tomato sauce): Medium-bodied reds from southern France (such as Côtes du Rhône).
Trout (fresh): Pinot Blanc, Chablis, or unoaked Chardonnay.
Trout (smoked): A good white Burgundy.
Tuna (fresh): Fuller-bodied, dry white such as Sémillon or light to medium red like Pinot Noir or Beaujolais.
Turbot: Good quality white Burgundy, or top, dry white Bordeaux.

With White Meats

In general, white meat has a relatively neutral flavour. Take note of the recipe used when selecting a wine to show it off.
Chicken (barbecued): Chardonnay, Sauvignon Blanc, or light red wines such as Beaujolais.
Chicken (creamy sauce): White Bordeaux, Alsace Riesling, or Chenin Blanc from Anjou-Saumur or Touraine on the Loire.
Chicken (roast): Chardonnay, Pinot Noir, or soft Merlot.
Coq au vin: Red Burgundy, but inexpensive Côtes du Rhône can also be served.
Pork (roast): A range of wines from white Burgundy and Sauvignon Blanc through to lighter reds like basic Merlot, Pinot Noir, or Beaujolais.
Pork (spare ribs): A fruity Syrah from the Rhône or the South of France.
Pork sausages: Reds from southern France.
Turkey (plain roast): Oaked Chardonnay or red wine such as a soft Merlot or Pinot Noir.
Turkey (with cranberry sauce/stuffing): Red wine such as Burgundy, Merlot-based Bordeaux, Northern Rhône Syrah.
Veal: Dry whites such as unoaked Chardonnay or a Northern Rhône wine, or soft fruity reds like Merlot.

With Red Meats, Barbecues & Game

These meats call for fuller-bodied styles of wine. Beef and lamb in particular tend to be complemented by tannic red wines. However, the sauces served also affect the choice.
Barbecues: Powerful reds, such as Syrah or Merlot.
Beef (hamburgers, steak au poivre, or in pastry): Syrah from the Rhône or South of France.
Beef (roast beef or steak): Full-bodied reds from Bordeaux and the Rhône.
Beef (with wine sauce): Red Burgundy.
Duck (roast): Red Burgundy.
Duck (with apple/orange sauce): Alsace Riesling.
Game: Red Bordeaux or Burgundy.
Lamb (casseroles and stews): Spicy reds such as Vin de Pays d'Oc, Coteaux du Languedoc, or Côtes du Rhône.
Lamb (chops): Good quality red Bordeaux.
Lamb (roast): Top quality Bordeaux or Burgundy.

With Vegetarian Dishes

Vegetarians and vegans may find some wines unsuitable due to animal products used in them. Consult the back label or ask the retailer to pinpoint vegetarian- or vegan-friendly wine. It can be difficult to pair vegetarian food with top white Burgundy or full-bodied reds, but mushroom and pumpkin risotto stand up to the challenge.
Lentil- and vegetable-based casseroles: Reds from the South of France.
Mushroom risotto: Good red Burgundy.
Pasta (creamy sauce): Unoaked Chardonnay, Pinot Blanc, or Sémillon.
Pasta (tomato-based sauce): Light red such as Chinon or Saumur.
Pumpkin or butternut squash risotto: Good quality white Burgundy.
Quiches and omelettes: Unoaked Chardonnay, Pinot Blanc, or light red like Beaujolais.
Quorn and tofu: Choose a wine according to the flavour of the ingredients with which they are cooked, as they tend to take on the same flavour.
Vegetarian chilli (with Quorn mince): Hearty reds from the South of France, or a fruity Merlot.
Vegetarian lasagne (with tofu): Full-bodied whites such as Chardonnay or Pinot Gris.
Vegetable tarts, pies and pasties: Spicy reds from southern France.
Veggie burgers and nut roast: Shiraz or red Bordeaux as these dishes can taste quite "meaty".

Vegetarians and vegans should note that gelatin, isinglass (made from fish), and egg whites are sometimes used to fine (clarify) wines

With Ethnic Dishes

Chinese: Riesling, Gewürztraminer, Pinot Gris, or Sauvignon Blanc.
Indian: With mild dishes an inexpensive Chardonnay. With medium-hot dishes, a soft, fruity red such as Merlot. With really hot and spicy dishes, avoid wine and choose lager, water, or lassi instead. **Japanese (sushi):** A "rice wine" such as saké is traditional.
Japanese (teriyaki sauces): Fruity red such as Merlot or Cabernet Franc.
Thai (curry): Inexpensive Sauvignon Blanc.
Thai (general): Off-dry white such as Alsace Gewürztraminer.

With Desserts

Always try to select a wine that is sweeter than your dessert. You can also choose a wine with a slightly higher alcohol content here as it is the end of the meal. Intensely flavoured desserts are well complemented by powerful, fortified styles.
Chocolate cake: Select your wine depending on the richness of the chocolate. The orange flavours in certain Muscats can work sensationally.
Crème brûlée: Sauternes is classic but most sweet wines work successfully.
Fruit: A wide variety, such as sweeter styles of Riesling, Sémillon, or Chenin Blanc.
Fruit tarts and pies: Choose a wine based on the dominant flavour – normally the fruit itself.
Ice cream: Powerful sweet *vin doux naturel*.

With Cheeses

Cheese and wine can be a wonderful combination, but pairing them is not as easy as many people think. The diverse flavours and textures of different cheeses mean that anything from a sweet white to a fortified red can be served successfully.
Blue cheeses: A sweet wine is generally required. Roquefort and Sauternes is a classic combination.
Brie: Beaujolais, or other light and fruity reds.
Camembert: Beaujolais or other light and fruity reds, but can also be paired with whites such as Chablis.
Goat's cheese: Sauvignon Blanc, particularly from the Loire Valley.
Gruyère and Emmenthal: Wines such as Shiraz, Northern Rhône reds, or Merlot. However, Riesling can work well, too.
Mature Cheddar: Good red Bordeaux, Châteauneuf-du-Pape, or tawny port.
Mozzarella: Unoaked Chardonnay.
Sheep's cheese: Sweeter styles of white wine like Riesling and Muscat, as well as spicy reds from southern France.
Traditional English hard cheeses: Cool-climate, dry whites such as Sauvignon Blanc or Chenin Blanc.

Social Occasions

With food: The general rules of wine and food matching still apply. It is often wise to select generally food-friendly wines (*see In Restaurants below*), as guests are then able to enjoy one wine with all the canapés and different courses served.
Without food: In general, wines to be enjoyed on their own should be light and unpretentious. For parties and social events where no food is on offer, steer clear of anything too full-bodied and avoid high acidity or powerful tannins. Also take the time of year and weather into account.
In summer: Choose crisp, refreshing wines like Riesling, Chenin Blanc, and other cool-climate, relatively low-alcohol whites. You could also go for light, fruity reds suitable for a brief chilling. Beaujolais, basic Merlot, and Pinot Noir are good choices.
In winter: A medium-bodied wine, whether red or white, focusing on bright, fruity flavours and avoiding lots of oak. Good bets are Sémillon, unoaked Chardonnay, and Pinot Blanc, as well as whites from the Southern Rhône. Merlot-based reds are also highly enjoyable at this time of year.
At celebrations: Champagne and sparkling wines are the classic choices. Champagne tends to be more expensive, so is generally only an option for those with a bigger budget. Other sparkling wines can work very well, however, and are normally a better choice to use in cocktails such as buck's fizz.

In Restaurants

Many top restaurants have a sommelier to offer diners advice on wine. If no sommelier is on hand, there are a few types of wine that are good with most foods. If you are all ordering different dishes, half bottles can help everyone get something to complement their particular meal.

• Opt for medium-bodied styles, avoiding extremes. For whites, unoaked Chardonnay, Sémillon, or Sauvignon Blanc are the most versatile. For reds, Pinot Noir, inexpensive Merlot, or a fruity Cabernet-Merlot blend are excellent choices.

• If the restaurant focuses on a particular nationality or style of cooking, you should naturally try and choose wines of the same nationality.

Buying Wine

There has never been so much choice when it comes to buying wine: supermarkets for price and convenience; specialized wine merchants for expert advice; and on-line merchants to shop around. Buying at auction can fulfil a sense of adventure, as well as make a potential investment.

Supermarkets

Supermarkets are a reliable, if not especially adventurous, source of wine. All the major chains in Britain now have good ranges, although they tend not to stock obscure styles or wine from small producers. What they lack in breadth they make up for in special offers and value for money. Their own brand ranges can be particularly good value. Two of the best supermarkets for wine are Booths in the north, and Waitrose in the centre and south. Both sell quality wines and champion smaller producers.

Wine Merchants

These range from large off-licence chains such as Threshers, Victoria Wine, and Haddows (all owned by the same company: www.threshergroup.com), through to national wine specialists such as Oddbins (www.oddbins.com), and more local outfits, such as London-based Berry Brothers & Rudd (www.bbr.com) and Philglas & Spiggot (www.philglas-spiggot.com).

Off-licences have been improving, but their main advantage is still one of convenience. Specialist wine merchants remain the destination of choice for wine lovers. They have much to offer in terms of advice, range, and wines from small, high-quality producers. Owners and staff have often tasted most of the wines and are happy to share their knowledge. Take time to discuss your requirements and preferences: price, styles of wines you enjoy, food with which you plan to drink the wine.

Mail Order

A considerable volume of wine is bought by mail order from companies or clubs, such as The Sunday Times Wine Club (www.sundaytimeswineclub.co.uk) and The Wine Society (www.thewinesociety.com). These offer discounts and exclusive wines sourced directly from producers, as well as regular mailings and tasting events. The quality of the wines, however, can be variable. Many specialist wine merchants (see below) also offer a mail order service.

Auctions & Exchanges

It is not without risk, but buying at an auction or internet exchange can be an excellent way of acquiring cases of wine, particularly older, rarer vintages. Major auction houses such as Christie's (www.christies.com) and Sotheby's (www.sothebys.com) hold regular wine sales, as do smaller, local houses. Be aware of commission charges (10 to 15 per cent on top of the hammer price plus VAT) and learn as much as possible about the condition and provenance of lots before bidding.

Companies like Uvine (www.uvine.com) conduct their business over the internet. Sellers place an offer price for a wine on the site, and if a buyer accepts the price, the wine is traded. Uvine inspects the condition of the wine, and charges an additional fee of 10 per cent plus delivery and VAT.

Direct from Producers

Wine almost always tastes better at its source, and gives you a chance to meet the people who created it. It is customary to buy at least a couple of bottles when you have enjoyed the hospitality of an estate. However, there will not necessarily be any great savings on the standard retail price.

On the Web

Most supermarkets, wine merchants, and mail order companies also sell on the internet. In addition, there are a number of web-only companies. Virgin Wines (www.virginwines.com) is one of the most successful. Everywine (www.everywine.co.uk) also has an extensive selection of wines, but the sheer choice can be bewildering and many are only available by the case.

Other Good UK Wine Merchants

Adnams
www.adnamswines.co.uk

Corney & Barrow www.corneyandbarrow.com

Justerini & Brooks www.justeriniandbrooks.com

Lay & Wheeler
www.laywheeler.com

Majestic
www.majestic.co.uk

Tanners
www.tanners-wines.co.uk

Storing and Serving Wine

Over the years wine has become associated with a number of procedures, such as cellaring, breathing, and decanting. While it is not essential to understand the scientific principles involved to enjoy wine, these practices can maximize the pleasure gained from both buying and drinking it.

Storing Wine

The majority of wines sold today are designed to be enjoyed young. Almost all mid-priced bottles will survive in a rack for around 12 months, but are likely to deteriorate if left for longer. Many finer wines, however, are worth cellaring as they will improve with age. If in any doubt, it is always better to drink a wine too young rather than too old.

Wine is best stored on its side, as constant contact between cork and liquid prevents the cork from drying out. Sparkling wines and wines with a screwcap can be stored upright because this problem does not arise. If you want to cellar wine but lack the ideal conditions, there are alternatives: buying a wine fridge or cabinet which can hold bottles in perfect storage conditions; or paying for dedicated storage with a professional firm. Contact your local wine merchant for advice.

Cellars

A cellar can range from a humble, under-stair cupboard to a vast underground labyrinth, as long as conditions are right for maturation. Key considerations when choosing the perfect "cellar" are as follows:

• A constant temperature between 10 and 15°C is preferable. Slightly higher than this is not a major concern: the wine will mature more quickly, but slightly less favourably. It is temperature variation that causes most harm.

• Wine dislikes light, which is why many bottles are made of coloured glass. Dark rooms or sealed boxes are best.

• A lack of moisture can cause corks to dry out, contract, and let air into the bottle, oxidizing the wine and eventually turning it into vinegar. Slightly damp cellars, on the other hand, will not harm the wine.

• Excess movement or vibration can damage wine so avoid storage next to fridges and washing machines, and also avoid handling or unnecessary transport.

Effects of Ageing

As wines sit in the bottle, a series of chemical reactions changes relatively simple fruity flavours to more developed, complex tastes. In reds, the colour becomes lighter, the tannins get softer, and the wine takes on aromas such as cedar, leather, or mushrooms. Whites, on the other hand, deepen in colour, and become less sweet and more intense.

Typical aromas of a mature white wine include nuts, wax, and even diesel. The effects of oak barrels – hints of vanilla, coconut, and spice – lessen in all wines as they mature.

Serving temperature

The correct temperature is extremely important to the taste of wine. White wines are often served too cold, and reds too warm. Some guidelines to follow:

• Sparkling wines: Cool temperatures of around 8°C.

• Light, aromatic whites: Quite cold – around 10°C or a few hours in the fridge. Chilling emphasizes the crisp, fresh taste and does not dull the aromas.

• White Burgundy and other Chardonnays: These are less aromatic, so serve around 12°C.

• Light- and medium-bodied reds: Chill slightly to around 12 or 13°C (half an hour in the fridge), particularly in summer.

• Full-bodied reds: Low temperatures emphasize the tannins in the wine, so serve these reasonably warm, around 15°C.

Serving Order

There are a number of generally accepted rules for the order in which wines should be served:

• White before red – although a light-bodied red can be enjoyed before a full-bodied white.

• Dry before sweet whites – this avoids making the wine taste excessively acidic.

• Light reds before heavy reds – lighter wines tend to taste thin after a heavier example.

• Lower quality wines before finer ones. There is no clear consensus on whether young or old wines should be consumed first. Much depends on the individual wines in question.

Decanting

Certain high quality wines (mostly reds), such as a 2000 Bordeaux, opened before their peak, can benefit greatly from exposure to oxygen in the air – or breathing – before drinking. Simply pulling the cork on a bottle and allowing it to stand open is unlikely to make much difference. Using a decanter, however, will. The actual shape of the vessel used makes little difference, as long as it is made of glass and open-topped.

Another reason to use a decanter is to separate a wine from its sediment or deposit, especially if it is unfiltered. Wines that "throw" a sediment include vintage port, crusted port, and older vintages of full-bodied reds.

To decant a wine, stand the bottle upright for at least 24 hours to allow the sediment to fall to the bottom. Then, pull the cork and, with a source of light, either a lighted candle or a naked light bulb, behind the neck to allow you to see the contents, slowly pour the wine into the decanter. Stop when you see the sediment reach the neck of the bottle. Do not leave wine in a decanter for long, as prolonged exposure to oxygen will ruin it.

Opening Fizz

The correct procedure for opening a sparkling wine or champagne is as follows:
• Hold the bottle at an angle of approximately 55 degrees to the horizontal.
• Point the neck of the bottle away from other people and away from breakables.
• Carefully remove the foil and wire muzzle.
• Holding the bottle in one hand and the cork in the other, gently twist the bottle (not the cork) until the cork eases with a satisfying pop.

Glasses

Using the correct wine glasses can influence the taste of a wine. Although you can buy individual glass designs for different wines, a good all-purpose wine glass will normally suffice. This should have a stem so that you do not have to handle the bowl; and the bowl should be large enough to hold a decent measure, yet still allow room for the wine to be swirled. The bowl should be narrower at the rim than at the base, directing the aromas towards your nose. Finally, clear glass – not cut, coloured, or patterned – allows the colour of the wine to show through. The only major styles that require a different shape of glass are Champagne and sparkling wines. Their tall, straight, thin glasses are specifically designed to show off and retain the bubbles.

How Much per Person?

Serving quantities depend on the occasion and, of course, the drinking capacities of your guests. At dinner parties estimate between half a bottle and a whole bottle of wine per person per evening. When ordering large amounts of wine for an event, remember that many retailers operate a sale or return policy, which allows customers to return unopened bottles. In this case, err on the generous side when ordering.

Leftover Wine

Leftover wine should be poured into the smallest appropriate bottle size, sealed with the original cork if possible, and kept in the fridge. It should be finished off within 24 to 48 hours, as deterioration will quickly set in.

Red and White Wines to Keep

Keeping times depend on the quality of the producer, vineyard site, and vintage. Below are some broad storage recommendations. Bear in mind that only the finest wines can age for longer periods:

Whites

Chardonnay: 2 to 5 years for top quality wine from outside Burgundy.

Riesling: 2 years for cheaper wines; 5 to 20 years for the best ; sweeter styles keep longer than drier.

Sweet wine: 5 to 20 years for the best examples from Sauternes.

White Burgundy: 1 to 10 years for Chablis; 2 to 8 years for other good white Burgundies.

White Rhône: 3 to 10 years for wines made from Marsanne and Roussanne.

Reds

Cabernet Sauvignon-based wines: 3 to 10 years.

Merlot: 3 to 15 years for good quality St-Émilion or Pomerol; less time if from elsewhere.

Red Bordeaux: 5 to 20 years.

Red Burgundy: 2 to 10 years.

Rhône: 5 to 15 years for the best vintages; wine from Southern Rhône needs less time than the Northern Rhône.

Glossary

Like any other specialist subject, wine has its own unique vocabulary, which includes a large number of French words and phrases. This glossary contains the most common terms used in this book.

A

acid/acidity All wines contain various acids, including tartaric, malic, and citric. Acidity is an essential element in wine, helping to maintain freshness and balance – too much and it can taste unduly sharp, too little and a "flabby", cloying wine will result.

acidification The addition of chemical acids to the must during winemaking to compensate for a lack of natural acidity in the grapes.

ageing Most wines are designed to be enjoyed as soon as they are released. However, a proportion will improve in bottle if stored in a cool, dark place. Full-bodied reds, sweet whites, and fortified wines can all benefit from ageing.

American oak Wood originating from forests of the eastern USA, used to make oak barrels. Popular in North and South America, Spain, and Australia, American oak barrels tend to impart a more powerful vanilla flavour than their European counterparts.

appellation A legally defined area where grapes are grown and wine is produced, sometimes used as a shortened version of AOC or AC.

Appellation d'Origine Contrôlée or **AOC** (French) Also known as Appellation Contrôlée (AC). The highest quality classification for wines produced in France. It guarantees that a bottle has been made in a specific region, according to local regulations. Not all AOC or AC wines are good quality, but on average they should be better (though not necessarily better value) than wines with a lower classification such as *vin de pays* or *vin de table*.

B

barrel Barrels or casks can be used at several stages of winemaking. Better quality whites may be fermented in barrel to produce subtle and complex wood flavours. Maturation in barrel helps to soften the wine and, if the oak is new, pick up aromas such as cedar or vanilla. "Barrel select" may imply quality, but has no legal definition. See also **American oak** and **French oak**.

barrel-aged The process of maturing wine in oak barrels, softening its taste and possibly adding oak flavours.

barrel-fermented This indicates a wine has been fermented in an oak barrel. Normally applicable to white wines, the process helps to integrate oak flavours.

barrique (French) A small oak cask or barrel that holds 225 litres of wine. Now often used for any small oak barrel.

base wine The still wine used to create champagne and other sparkling wine.

bin Originally a collection or stack of wine bottles. It is commonly found on wine labels, to signify different brands of wine.

biodynamism An extreme form of organic viticulture which emphasizes the health of the soil. Some of its methods may sound bizarre, but a number of world-class wines are produced using this approach.

blanc de blancs (French) White wine made entirely from white grapes. The term is commonly used for Champagne and other sparkling wines.

blanc de noirs (French) White wine made entirely from red grapes, usually applied to Champagne and other sparkling wines.

blend A mixture of wines of different grape varieties, styles, origin, or age, contrived to improve the balance of the wine or maintain a constant style.

blush A term used in the USA for a pale pink wine.

bodega (Spain) Winery or cellar.

Bordeaux A wine from the Bordeaux region of France made using the grape varieties and/or techniques common in this area. Bordeaux is a famously full-bodied red wine made from a blend of Cabernet Sauvignon, Merlot, Cabernet Franc, Malbec, and Petit Verdot which is often matured in oak barrels. It can age for decades.

botrytis A vine disease, also known as noble rot, responsible for some of the world's greatest dessert wines. In the correct conditions, the fungus *(Botrytis cinerea)* produces shrivelled, sugar-rich grapes which can be fermented into a naturally sweet and intensely flavoured wine.

bottle fermentation The technique which gives champagne its "fizz". After a normal fermentation, still wine is placed into a bottle with sugar and yeast. A secondary fermentation begins, producing carbon dioxide gas inside the bottle and creating a sparkling wine. The term is normally used by sparkling wine producers outside the Champagne region.

Bourgogne The French word for Burgundy.

brut Means dry. Normally found on Champagne and other sparkling wines.

Burgundy A wine from the Burgundy region of France, made using the grape varieties and/or techniques common in this region. Burgundy is world famous for its dry whites made from Chardonnay and medium-bodied reds from Pinot Noir.

C

canopy All parts of the vine that are visible above ground including the trunk, leaves, shoots, stems, and grapes.

canopy management The practice of manipulating the vine and its canopy to ensure the grapes and leaves are correctly exposed to the sun. It also aims to ensure a good circulation of air through the vine, helping to prevent fungal diseases. Canopy management includes training and pruning.

cantina (Italian) Winery.

carbonic maceration Winemaking technique associated with Beaujolais in France. The grapes are fermented as whole berries, producing a deep coloured, fruity wine, light in tannin.

chaptalization The practice of increasing alcohol levels through the addition of sugar during winemaking. Common in cooler wine regions where the climate may struggle to produce sufficient natural sugar in the grapes.

château (French) Used to denote a French winegrowing or wine-producing estate. The term is widely used in Bordeaux.

clairet (French) A dark pink style of wine between a rosé and a light red.

claret A uniquely English term for red bordeaux.

clone A group of vines all descended from a single parent vine using cuttings or buds. They are genetically identical to the parent plant and are usually selected for characteristics such as fine flavour or good colour.

cold fermentation A slow fermentation at low temperatures to extract freshness and fruit flavour from the grapes.

co-operative Organization collectively owned by its members. Typically wine co-operatives consist of a number of growers who join together for winemaking and marketing purposes. Quality can vary from good to extremely poor.

corked Wine which has been affected by a mouldy, musty taint from a defective natural cork. The wine may be stripped of its normal fruit flavours and can have a slightly bitter taste. It is believed that around six per cent of wines using natural corks are corked, and many producers and retailers have changed over to screwcaps and synthetic stoppers.

côte(s)/coteaux (French) Hill or hillside.

crémant (French) Indicates a sparkling wine produced outside the Champagne region, but using the same methods as Champagne.

cru (French) Literally "growth" or "vineyard". Hence *cru classé* means classified vineyard. *Cru bourgeois* is a classification for estates in Bordeaux's Médoc appellation. *See also* **premier cru** and **grand cru**.

cuvée (French) Normally used to mean blend. Wine labels that say *cuvée de prestige* or *tête de cuvée* are no guarantee of exceptional quality. In Champagne, *cuvée* denotes the first and finest juice to come from the press.

cuvée de prestige (French) Term normally associated with Champagne referring to a top quality, luxury wine from the best vineyards and matured for many years before release. Examples include Dom Pérignon from Moët & Chandon and La Grande Dame from Veuve Clicquot Ponsardin.

D

decanting The process of pouring wine from its original bottle into another vessel or decanter. The technique is normally used for old or unfiltered wines to separate the liquid from the sediment deposited in the

Key Climatic Terms

continental climate A climate characterized by extreme temperature variations across the year. Usually found in regions well away from the influence of water (sea or lakes). Cold winters and hot summers are the norm.

degree days A unit devised to measure the suitability of climates for viticulture.

macroclimate The overall climate within a region.

maritime climate A climate which is influenced by a large body of water, typically a sea or lake. Temperatures will tend to remain relatively stable across the year with mild winters and warm summers.

marginal climate A climate that is barely sufficient to permit viticulture. Normally applied to weather that is too cold rather than too warm. Expect regions with a marginal climate to have wide variations in quality between vintages.

mesoclimate The climate in a small district or even an individual vineyard.

microclimate A specific climate within a very small area.

moderate climate A climate with only minimal temperature variation over the course of the year. Most commonly found near to a large body of water. *See* maritime climate.

bottle. It can also be used for younger wines, to allow them to be exposed to air, or "breathe".

dessert/sweet wine Wine containing large amounts of sugar. It tastes sweet and is traditionally used to accompany dessert.

disgorgement The process by which sediment is removed from a Champagne bottle following the second fermentation.

domaine (French) Estate.

dosage (French) The replenishment of the small amount of wine lost during disgorgement in the process of making Champagne. Sugar is also normally added at this stage.

doux (French) Sweet.

dry-farmed Vines grown without the use of irrigation, thus relying entirely on natural rainfall.

E

en primeur Wine sold by a producer before it has been bottled. Typically customers pay for the wine six months after the harvest, then wait a further 18 months to receive it. This is the best way to secure a wine limited in quantity, but is no guarantee of a cheaper price.

estate bottled/grown Today, most quality producers bottle on site. It is no guarantee of quality, but is generally a good indicator. In the USA, estate bottled wine must also come from the producer's own vineyards or those on a long-term lease. The equivalent in France is *mise en bouteille à la propriété/ au domaine/au château*.

F

fermentation The process that turns the juice of crushed, pressed, or whole grapes into wine. The natural sugars within the berries are converted into alcohol and carbon dioxide using yeast. Fermentation generally takes place in stainless steel, lined concrete, or large wooden vats, or in oak barrels. *See also* **malolactic fermentation**.

filtration A technique which removes the tiny solid particles from a wine before bottling, leaving it clear and bright. Some producers believe that filtration can strip a wine of its flavour and will avoid the technique – often including words such as unfiltered or *non-filtré* on their label. Wines which have not been filtered will generally require decanting.

fining A process used to remove suspended deposits in wine. When a fining agent such as egg white or bentonite clay is added, it binds with the deposits and causes them to fall to the bottom of the cask.

first growth *See* **premier cru**.

flying winemaker An individual who produces wine in a number of locations around the world. The term was originally coined when highly trained New World winemakers were brought in to revitalize old fashioned, traditional estates in Europe.

fortified A wine bolstered by the addition of a spirit – usually grape spirit – such as port, sherry, or madeira.

French oak A type of wood originating from forests in France such as Allier and Vosges. French oak is widely considered to make the finest barrels for fermenting and maturing wine.

fruit set When the fertilized vine flowers become grape berries – not all flowers will actually turn into berries.

fungal diseases A collective term for a number of diseases such as powdery mildew, downy mildew, and black rot. The fungi attack grapes or foliage and, without preventative measures, can cause considerable damage. The benevolent disease *Botrytis cinerea* is also included in this category.

futures The American term for *en primeur*.

G

garage wine A relatively recent term given to the tiny quantities of top quality (and often very expensive) wine made by small-scale producers. Equipment and facilities are generally basic and production may even take place in a garage, hence the name.

grand cru (French) Meaning literally "great vineyard." In Burgundy the term *grand cru* is applied to the finest vineyards in the region. In the St-Émilion area of Bordeaux, the best châteaux are classified as *grand cru classé*, with the top tier known as *premier grand cru classé*. *See also* **premier cru**.

grand vin (French) Often seen on French AOC labels, this literally means "great wine" and is often used to indicate that this is the top wine of a particular estate.

green harvesting The practice of removing and discarding grapes in the build-up to the (conventional) harvest. The idea is to allow the vine to concentrate its energies on ripening the grapes that remain.

H

hybrid A plant created from parents which belong to different species of vine. An example is the Baco Noir grape variety, made by crossing Folle Blanche of the *Vitis vinifera* species with a variety of *Vitis riparia*, a native American species of vine. In the EU, quality wine can only be made entirely from *Vitis vinifera* plants.

IJ

jeroboam A large bottle size, most commonly used for Champagne, containing three litres or four conventional (75cl) bottles.

KL

late harvest *See* *vendange tardive*.

lees Known as *lie* in France, lees are the remains of yeast, grape seeds and other sediment that settle in a wine after fermentation. Extended contact with the lees plays an important role in wines such as Muscadet and Champagne, which are said to be made *sur lie* (on the lees). Lees stirring (*bâtonnage* in French) in cask helps to accentuate this process.

limited release A term used by marketing people on wine labels. It may indicate additional quality, but there is no guarantee.

long-lived This term describes a wine able to develop and improve in bottle over years or decades. Only a small proportion of wines are capable of this. *See also* **ageing**.

M

maceration The practice of soaking grape skins in their juice or must. This gives red wines their colour, tannins, and flavours.

madeira A fortified wine produced on the Portuguese island of Madeira.

maderized A wine which has been exposed to oxygen and/or heated to make it taste like madeira. The term is also used occasionally to describe a wine which has been oxidized.

magnum A 1.5 litre bottle (equivalent to two conventional bottles). Wine in a magnum tends to mature more slowly and elegantly than in 75cl bottles and this is believed to be the ideal size for Champagne.

malolactic fermentation A process which converts tart malic acids (as found in apples) into softer lactic acids (as found in milk). It occurs shortly after the first (conventional) fermentation. Most red wines undergo malolactic fermentation; in whites the decision largely depends on the style of wine the producer is trying to achieve.

Master of Wine or **MW** An extremely demanding wine qualification developed by the Institute of Masters of Wine in London. It covers winemaking, distribution, tasting, and commercial aspects of the industry. There are currently fewer than 250 MWs worldwide.

maturation The process of ageing or maturing a wine in cask or bottle, normally at the winery. Once the wine is released it may be matured further by the purchaser, but this is more commonly referred to as cellaring or laying down.

Meritage A wine made from the same blend of grape varieties as Bordeaux (Cabernet Sauvignon, Merlot, Cabernet Franc, Malbec, and Petit Verdot for reds; Sauvignon Blanc and Sémillon for whites) but from an alternative origin, usually California or South Africa.

méthode champenoise/ classique (French) Alternative terms for *méthode traditionelle*.

méthode traditionnelle (French) Sparkling wine made using the same techniques as Champagne. In particular it indicates the wine has undergone a secondary fermentation in bottle.

moelleux (French) Medium-sweet.

monopoly or **monopole** (French) A term used for a vineyard completely owned by one individual or organization.

must The mass of grape juice, skins, seeds, stems, and other matter before fermentation begins.

mutage A French word to describe the process of halting the fermentation of a wine before it has naturally finished, normally through the addition of a spirit. The technique is used to create port or *vin doux naturel*.

N

négociant (French) Literally merchant; a person or organization that buys grapes, must, or wine from growers to bottle under its own label. Particularly important in areas with large numbers of small vineyard holdings such as Burgundy. The quality of *négociant* wines can range from poor to excellent.

noble rot *See* **botrytis**

non-vintage (NV) Blend of wines from different years. Although the term "vintage" is often used to imply high quality, there is nothing inherently wrong with non-vintage wine – indeed most Champagnes are non-vintage.

O

oak The wood favoured by winemakers to ferment and mature wines. Many cheaper wines receive their oaky taste from oak chips or oak staves submerged in the tanks. *See also* **American oak**, **French oak**.

oaked A wine made in a deliberately creamy, oaky style through the use of oak barrels, oak chips, or oak staves. *See also* **unoaked**.

oenology (or enology) The study of wine. The term is principally associated with winemaking.

old vines *See* *vieilles vignes*.

organic It is very difficult to produce a completely organic wine as certain chemicals are virtually essential during winemaking. Many wines advertised as such are simply grown without the use of chemical fertilizers, fungicides, and pesticides.

PQ

pétillant (French) With a slight sparkle.

Pierce's disease A potentially devastating bacterial disease for which there is no known cure. The disease is spread by small insects, known as sharpshooters, and attacks the leaves of the vine. It is most common in the southern part of the USA and South America.

phylloxera A vine disease which devastated the vineyards of Europe at the end of the 19th century. Phylloxera is a small insect or aphid that feeds on the roots of grapevines and ultimately kills the plant. Even today there is no cure for the pest – instead almost all European vines are grafted onto rootstocks from American species, which are phylloxera-resistant.

port A sweet, fortified wine produced in the Douro Valley in northern Portugal.

premier cru (French) First growth or first vineyard. In the Médoc region of Bordeaux, the finest châteaux are classified as *premier cru*. In St-Émilion just across the river, the top producers are known as *premier grand cru classé*. Confusingly in Burgundy *premier cru* vineyards lie just below *grand cru* in the classification hierarchy.

quinta (Portugal) Estate.

R

racking The process of separating a wine from its sediment in the winery. The sediment is normally allowed or encouraged to fall to the bottom of the barrel. The liquid is then drained or pumped into a clean vessel.

raisining The practice of drying grapes either on the vine or after picking. Raisined grapes are normally concentrated with sugar, making excellent sweet wines.

reserve A term seen regularly on wine labels to denote a special bottling or release. Unless the wine comes from a reputable producer, however, it is no guarantee of special quality.

residual sugar Sugar that remains in a wine after fermentation. High levels of residual sugar make a wine taste sweet.

riserva (Italian) A wine which is given extended ageing before it is released and has a higher alcoholic strength.

rootstock The root system of a vine. Today almost all vines consist of an American rootstock grafted onto a fruiting European variety to protect against phylloxera.

rosé (French) Wine with a pink colour, a halfway house between a red and a white wine. The only region allowed to produce rosés by mixing red and white wines is Champagne; the vast majority of other rosés are made using red grapes and a short period of maceration.

ruby port The youngest and fruitiest style of port.

S

sec (French) Dry.

sediment Solid matter found in wine. This may come from yeasts, fragments of grape skin and pulp during winemaking, or it may form naturally in the wine. Certain wines "throw" a sediment when matured in bottle for a long period. Such wines will need decanting.

Sélection de Grains Nobles (French) Classification in Alsace for wines made from extremely ripe grapes, which will normally have been affected by noble rot. SGN wines are only made in exceptional vintages and will be sweet.

sherry A fortified wine from the Jerez region of Spain.

single vineyard Wine made using grapes from just one vineyard.

stabilization The processes in the winery designed to ensure a wine undergoes no further fermentation or reaction once it is bottled. These include fining and filtration.

structure A tasting term used primarily for red wines to describe the weight of fruit and tannins on the palate. Full-bodied wines such as high quality red Bordeaux should have a "good structure".

superiore (Italian) Usually applied to DOCG wines with a higher alcoholic strength, not an indicator of quality.

sur lie (French) See lees.

T

table wine In theory, the lowest wine classification in the European Union. In general, these wines are cheap and not so cheerful. However, some of Europe's finest wines are labelled "table wine". Price is a good guide to quality here – finer wines in this category tend to cost significantly more than basic table wine.

tannins The astringent, mouth-drying compounds found when a teabag is soaked in water too long. Tannins in grapes are found in the skins, seeds, and stalks, and are particularly important in the composition of a red wine. They provide the wine with its structure and weight and also act as a preservative, helping it to mature in bottle. A wine with excessive tannins is described as "tannic".

tawny port A style of port characterized by its distinctive tawny colour. Better examples achieve their appearance and soft, mellow taste through extended maturation in cask.

terroir French word used to describe the overall growing environment of a vineyard, covering its climate, soil, slope, and exposure, among other factors. Advocates of *terroir* believe that a wine

should not simply taste of fermented grape juice, but rather it should express a sense of the place where the grapes are grown.
traditional method *See* *méthode traditionnelle*.

U

unfiltered/*non-filtré* *See* **filtration**.
unoaked A wine deliberately made without oak barrels to emphasize its fresh fruit flavours.

V

varietal A wine that has been labelled on the basis of its principal grape variety rather than its region of origin. It is also sometimes used as another word for "grape variety".
vendange tardive (French) A French term meaning late harvest. Grapes which have been harvested later tend to be riper and more concentrated, producing sweeter styles of wine. In Alsace the term carries a precise legal definition; elsewhere it can be used simply at the discretion of the producer.
véraison (French) The period in which grapes ripen, gaining in sugar (and also in colour, if black), but not increasing very much in size.
vieilles vignes (French) "Old vines". As a vine gets older it tends to produce fewer, but better quality grapes. It is no guarantee of a superior wine, as there is no legal definition of what constitutes "old".

vigneron (French) Winegrower.
vignoble (French) Vineyard.
vin de pays (French) Often excellent value, "country wines" sit between table wines and *appellation contrôlée* wines in the classification hierarchy.
vin de table (French) *See* **table wine**.
vin doux naturel (French) A sweet wine produced by adding spirit to fermenting must before all the sugar has been converted to alcohol. *See also* **mutage**.
vin gris (French) A pale, delicate rosé.
vin nouveau (French) *See* **vin primeur**.
vin primeur (French) Young wine made to be drunk in the same year that it is produced, the best-known example being Beaujolais Nouveau.
vine density The number of vines planted in a specified area in a vineyard. High density planting (around 8,000 vines per hectare) is practised in many European vineyards, as the competition between plants is believed to help lower yields and produce better quality grapes.
vine pull The removal of vines. In parts of Europe where overproduction is a problem, governments pay growers to pull up their vines in vine pull schemes.
vinification Essentially, "winemaking", the process that converts grape juice into finished wine.
vintage Can be used to mean either "harvest" or the year in which the grapes were grown to produce a

wine. A vintage wine must come from a single year. Vintage Champagne is only produced in exceptional years and must be matured for at least three years on its lees. *See also* **non-vintage**.
vintage port The very best port made from a single fine harvest and aged in wood for around two years. It is "declared" or released by producers only in the best vintages, on average three times a decade.
viticulture Vine growing – the science, techniques, and skills required to produce commercial-quality grapes.
Vitis vinifera The species of vine responsible for the majority of the world's wine.

WXYZ

wooded/unwooded *See* **oaked** and **unoaked**.
yeast A single-cell fungus that converts sugar into alcohol during fermentation. In many regions yeasts occur naturally on the skins of grapes and in the air. Many local winemakers prefer these "wild" strains, although cultured yeasts are often more reliable.
yield The total amount of wine produced by a vine or vineyard in a particular vintage. In general, lower yields produce better quality grapes and in European appellations maximum yields are prescribed by law. These range from around 38 hectolitres per hectare for *grand cru* red Burgundy to more than 100 hectolitres per hectare for less illustrious classifications.

Index